Opal & Gemstone Jewelry

Cutting • Designing • Setting

A Step-by-Step
Lapidary Instructional Guide

Created by
Noted Author of
"Opal Cutting Made Easy"

Paul B. Downing, *Ph.D.*

Majestic Press, Inc.
Estes Park, Colorado

CREATED FOR: Lapidary enthusiasts everywhere; young, old, beginning or experienced. I hope that my love of gemstones; digging for them, cutting & designing settings for them, and…most of all…appreciating the beauty in each and every stone whether precious, semi-precious or simply a rock, rubs off!

DISCLAIMER: Although every precaution has been taken in the preparation of this book, the publisher and author assume no responsibility for errors or omissions. Neither is any liability assumed for damages resulting from the use of the information contained herein. As with any equipment, carefully follow all manufacturer's instructions and use protective eye wear.

TRADEMARKS: Trademarked names appear throughout this book. Symbols have been provided for those names we have been able to determine that are either trademarked or registered. These names are used for editorial purposes and to the benefit of the trademark owner with no intention of infringing upon that trademark.

OPAL & GEMSTONE JEWELRY:
CUTTING * DESIGNING * SETTING

ORDERS: Majestic Press, Inc., P. O. Box 1348, Estes Park, CO 80517
http://www.majesticpress.com * Email: majesticpress@aol.com

ALL PHOTOS by Bobbi & Paul Downing
DIAGRAMS by Finlay Graphics and Perpetual Creations.
COVER DESIGN by Sykes Design Graphics

ISBN-10: 0-9817336-0-3
ISBN-13: 978-0-9817336-0-9

Dedication

To Burnell Franke

Burnie was my mentor and friend as I started exploring the lapidary field many years ago in Madison, Wisconsin. He taught me to love all gemstones, to cut them properly and to enjoy their beauty. I am forever in his debt.

Preface

My first cutting book, *Opal Cutting Made Easy,* came about on the long drive back from the West Palm Beach show in 1983. People kept asking me how to cut the rough opal I was selling. The book was created to serve this need. During this overnight trip on practically vacant Interstate 95, "Opal Lover" and "Harry Leadthumb" were born. *Opal Cutting Made Easy* was intended for cutters who knew how to cab but wanted to cut opal. Opal is different from other gems that are cut cabochon style so, as this book pointed out, a somewhat different approach was needed. Still, *Opal Cutting Made Easy* became the text for many general agate-based cabochon cutting classes all over the country. Instructors have told me they liked the simple step-by-step approach I offered.

Over the years after *Opal Cutting Made Easy* was published and subsequently revised, I began getting new questions. Clearly there were advanced cutting techniques that I had not covered in *Opal Cutting Made Easy*. Perhaps more important, people all over the world who had learned to cut opals using my book were faced with the problem of setting their beautiful stones into jewelry. I experienced the same difficulty and had taught myself how to create settings using the lost wax method. These needs, and my self-taught techniques, gave rise to my book *Opal Advanced Cutting & Setting*.

Opal & Gemstone Jewelry

With these two books I felt I was done. I had covered the field. But the world does not stand still. These books were reprinted time after time, but now I am faced with a dilemma...BOTH books are out-of-print. Should we reprint them as is? Revise and update them? Or... retire into the sunset. I chose none of these options. Instead I decided to write a new book that covers general cabbing and setting...as well as opal cutting. This new book takes a rank beginner through the process of cutting and setting an agate or other stone into a cabochon style piece of jewelry. No, opal is not neglected! All of *Opal Cutting Made Easy* and *Opal Advanced Cutting & Setting* is incorporated into this book in an expanded and updated form.

You might wonder what an opal guy is doing writing an agate book. Well, I was a rockhound; collecting, cutting and setting Lake Superior agate and jade... as well as opal...for over 20 years before I started my opal business. My friend, Burnie Franke, taught me to cut when I was in college. I even ran his rock shop one summer. I have been a member of several lapidary clubs and even president on occasion. I am not just "an opal guy." I love all gems. Okay — I admit I love opal most!

So, here we have a new book that teaches a beginning lapidary cutter how to cut and set agate, chrysoprase, jade and other stones while still providing detailed instruction on cutting my favorite of all stones...the opal.

Experienced lapidaries will find plenty of information to expand their knowledge of cutting and setting opal and other gems. It's like sitting next to me as I cut and set stone after stone.

I hope each of you find it useful.

Paul B. Downing, Ph.D.
Estes Park, Colorado
January 2009

Table of Contents

Opal & Gemstone Jewelry

Table of Contents

Table of Contents

Section One

Cutting a Cabochon

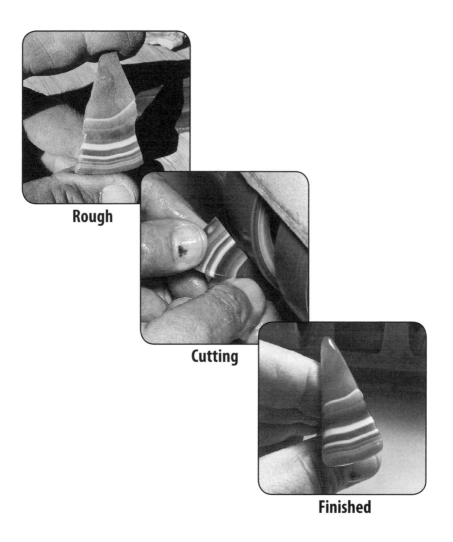

Rough

Cutting

Finished

Opal & Gemstone Jewelry

Chapter 1

Introduction: The Basics of Cabochon Cutting

Transforming a chunk of rock into a beautiful gem is a very rewarding experience. Enjoying that gem's beauty over the years as you, or someone special to you, wears it will fill you with pride in your work of art. Acquiring the skills you need to accomplish this transformation will take some time and study. The task may seem daunting at first, but believe me it is simpler than you think.

There are three general forms a gem can have when cut for use as jewelry. The *faceted* form...familiar to all from its prominence in diamonds...places small, flat surfaces (called facets) in a geometric pattern all over the surface of the stone. It is typically used for transparent gems. The *cabochon* form (cab for short) creates a smooth, rounded surface. It is the form typically used for opal, jade, agate and other opaque and translucent gems. The third form is *carving* where a stone is fashioned into an object such as a rose or a freeform shape. In this book I will concentrate on the cabochon form.

The term "cutting a cab" is somewhat misleading. Cutting is really a process of wearing away the parts of the stone you don't want, to generate the look you seek. This is done using wheels or flat laps that are impregnated with a harder rock; usually diamond. Placing the stone against the wheel wears the stone away to produce the shape you desire. Then it is further worn using smaller and smaller pieces of diamond (called *grits*) until the surface becomes so smooth it shines.

As with any new endeavor, the cutting process can be made simple by breaking it down into a few easily followed steps. Follow these simple steps and you will be successful. Skip or skimp on one or more and success will elude you. My purpose here is not to tell you how to accomplish cutting a cab. That is done in Chapter 3. Here I will give you a general idea of the process so you know what to expect. The simple steps I suggest are:

PLAN

Examine your rock carefully, planning how to get the most beauty from it before attempting to cut it.

SHAPE

Carefully remove unwanted material until your rock starts to take on the shape of the finished gem. Shape has

Outline

two aspects; the outline and the dome. Dome represents the rounded profile of the stone.

Dome

SAND AND POLISH

Once the desired shape is obtained, your gem must be sanded and polished using wheels with successively finer and finer diamond grit. Essentially, you are removing the large scratches left by the shaping process. Then, progressing through the wheels, the scratches from the previous wheel are removed. Finally the scratches are so fine you cannot see them. The result is a fine, lustrous, polished gem.

CABOCHON CUTTING RULES

Basically that's it. But before we head off to cut our first stone, let me offer you my two simple rules of cab cutting. These rules were developed in *Opal Cutting Made Easy* but they are applicable to all gems…not just opal.

Introduction: The Basics of Cabochon Cutting

Go Slow. The first rule is to go slow. It took nature thousands of years to produce the rock you are working on. Don't grind away that beauty. Examine the stone, looking for clues as to how it wants to be cut. Each stone has a unique form which will best display its beauty. Your job is to examine and consider carefully. Do not start with the attitude that you are going to cut "X" no matter what. Ask the stone if it wants to be "X." Perhaps it will be better off being "Y." By slowly examining and considering all options, you will discover what is best for the stone.

First Rule of Cabochon Cutting: Go Slow!

Go Slower. The second rule is to go even slower. No matter how carefully you plan your approach, as you work into the stone it will reveal things you did not…or could not…see before you started. Stop the cutting process frequently to examine your stone. Look for new clues and change your plans accordingly.

Second Rule of Cabochon Cutting: Go Slower!

Suppose you are working on a Laguna agate. It has a rich red center surrounded by bands of different colors. Now suppose that as you grind into that agate the red center starts to reveal the shape of a heart. Wouldn't it be neat to adjust your cutting plans to take full advantage of this unique pattern? Rushing through the process without examining the stone could cause you to miss this wonderful opportunity.

Well, that's the basics. But before we turn our attention to how to accomplish these simple steps, we need to consider the equipment you will use.

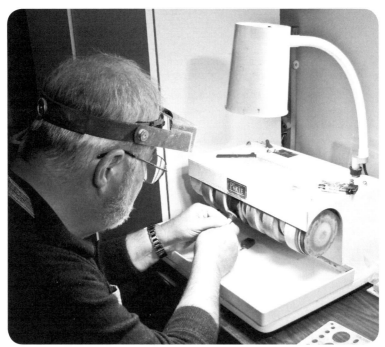

Paul Working on Stones for the Book.

Chapter 2

Equipment

WHAT WILL YOU NEED?

The process of wearing away the unwanted parts of a stone to make it into a cab can be accomplished by a number of means. Ancient people did it by hand, rubbing the stone against a rock. Slow and crude, but still effective. Over the years wheels became used to carry the grit to the gem. First, the wheels were powered by foot or hand. Later they were powered by a water wheel. As electric motors became available, they became the source of power.

The ancients used loose grit to do the cutting. Eventually this grit was impregnated into a wheel. The grit was initially some form of sand. Later carefully graded grits of various sizes where developed. The most prominent cutting medium in the 1950s and 1960s was silicon carbide. Essentially sandpaper shaped into a belt or disc, it was cheap and effective. With modern electric powered wheels, it could cut and polish a stone in hours that previously took many days.

Today silicon carbide has been replaced with diamond. Diamond is cleaner, faster, and lasts much longer. It also avoids most of the contamination problems encountered with silicon carbide. In short, I highly recommend working with diamond impregnated wheels if at all possible.

Below I discuss the two types of power equipment you will need to cab a gemstone.

SAW

A gem saw consists of a steel disc (blade) attached to a shaft (arbor) that is turned by an electric motor. The edge of the blade is impregnated with diamond. A table is attached to the arbor to form a holding platform for the stone being cut and a reservoir of liquid (water or oil) is used to provide lubrication and to remove waste from the cut. Diamond saws come in a range of sizes from huge…to cut large boulders…to quite small. You will not use a large saw (called a *slabbing saw*) in the beginning; simply a *trim saw*.

A trim saw is used to remove extra material from a rock to get it ready to shape. Because it uses a blade, it can separate that rock into two parts. This allows you to make more than one gem from your stone. Using a trim saw is a quicker way to generate the initial shape of your stone instead of grinding away all unwanted material. While not absolutely necessary, a trim saw will make your cutting life much easier.

Trim saws come in various sizes, designated by the blade diameter… usually 4" to 10". The smaller saws have the advantage of mobility and are less expensive. The larger trim saws allow you to work with bigger pieces of rock. A 4" or 6" trim saw is adequate for most applications.

There are many fine companies that produce quality trim saws. Unfortunately there are a few that produce junk that I would not recommend. Below I list two saws that I know work well. They are by no means the only ones, so if you find a saw to your liking, go for it. Just ask around to find out about how the saw performs before you commit.

Ameritool 4" Trim Saw. This surprisingly affordable little saw has a plastic housing, variable speed motor and an open table to make it easier to work with larger slabs or pieces of rough. It can be fitted with a thin blade for use with opal and other more valuable rough (see Source Directory).

Ameritool 4" Trim Saw

Diamond Pacific TC-6

Equipment

Diamond Pacific Model TC-6 - 6" Trim Saw. This saw offers rugged construction, an open table, and larger 6" blade so it is well suited to larger and tougher material. Diamond Pacific offers several other trim or trim/slab saws, including the unique Wizard Trim Saw (see SOURCE DIRECTORY).

CABBING MACHINE

A cabbing machine consists of a motor-driven arbor or shaft with a series of discs or wheels containing various grits. This cabbing system is used to grind the stone into its basic shape, then sand and polish it.

As with trim saws, there are several manufacturers that produce excellent equipment and a couple that don't. To some extent the rating of machines is a personal preference and may come down to what you learn on and are comfortable with. Some units require changing wheels to go from step to step, while others have all the wheels in place so you just move your stone from one to the next. Clearly the multi–wheel machines are more convenient, but the changeable machines are usually less expensive.

The two systems listed below are the two I have used over the years. You may find another more to your liking. Or here is an alternative idea. Look into a used system. Check with your local rock shop or rock club; even possibly in the paper or on the Internet.

Ameritool Universal Heavy Duty Grinding & Polishing Machine. This neat little machine has an arbor which accommodates a diamond grinding disc or any of three sanding and polishing discs impregnated with diamond plus a felt polishing disc. Additional sanding discs with different grits are available should you need them. The system is easy to use. Switching from one disc to

Ameritool Flatlap

9

another is simply a matter of unscrewing, by hand, a nut that holds the disc in place, replacing the disc and screwing the nut back on. There is no cleanup needed between steps. Coolant water is dripped onto the disc from a reservoir cup and waste water is collected in another cup. I prefer using a sponge pad beneath the sanding and polishing discs to provide a bit of flexibility. This reduces the problem of uneven spots or ridges on your stone.

I have used this machine for many years. It is reliable, clean and amazingly effective. If you are just starting out, this machine could fit the bill. Working on a flat surface is a bit different from working with wheels, but once you get used to it, it is surprisingly effective.

Diamond Pacific Pixie. This cabbing machine has a shaft that accommodate six wheels that are 4" in diameter. There is also a disc that screws into the right edge of the shaft to use for polishing. The Pixie comes equipped with a coarse (80 grit) and a medium (220 grit) grinding wheel. There are four Nova diamond impregnated wheels of

Diamond Pacific Pixie

280, 600, 1200 and 3000 grit to get you from sanding to pre-polish. The higher the grit number the finer the grit, so a 280 wheel does coarse sanding while a 3000 wheel will almost polish your stone. Polishing is done with a disc on the end impregnated with 14,000 diamond. In my experience this polishing can be improved by putting a Crystalite® Polypad on the canvas disc supplied and using 50,000 diamond rather than the 14,000 supplied. Coolant is sprayed up onto the wheels from a tray of water that also collects the waste washed down from the stone, yet this system somehow never contaminates grit from one wheel to the next.

Equipment

The Pixie is my full-time cabbing machine of choice. It is tough, reliable and easy to maintain. The Nova wheels are a marvel of modern technology. The soft rubber flexes with the stone to produce a smooth curve to a cab's surface. These wheels work quickly and effectively. And they last a long time. The only disadvantage of the Pixie is the relatively small space between wheels. This makes it difficult to do shapes like crosses, but otherwise this machine will do anything from tiny to huge cabs. It works wonderfully for opal. It does not offer a flat surface for doing opal doublets, but this can be solved by simply spinning a 4" Lapcraft® Diamond Disc on in place of the polishing disc.

For convenience in future discussions, I will use general terms for grit size rather than the size itself since different manufacturers use somewhat different grits. These general terms are listed below:

	Silicon Carbide Grit	Diamond Grit
Coarse Grinding	100	100
Fine Grinding	220	220
Rough Sanding	220 (worn)	220 or 280
Medium Sanding	320	600
Fine Sanding	600	1,200
Pre-polish	600 (very worn)	14,000
Polish	Tin Oxide Linde A Cerium Oxide	50,000

SUPPLIES

Other than the cabbing machine and saw, you will need relatively few supplies. It is easier to work a stone if it has a handle. The handle… called a dop stick…consists of a wooden dowel with green dop wax on one end. The wax has shellac in it which causes it to stick to the stone. It is heated with an alcohol lamp to mold it to the back of the stone.

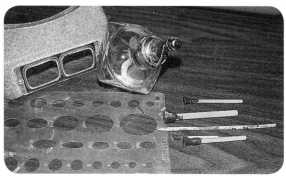

Cab Cutting Tools

For me, an OptiVISOR® is indispensable. This is a piece of head gear fitted with two magnifying lenses. It facilitates close inspection of your stone as you work it and the visor does not interfere with eyeglasses. See the photo of me on Page 6.

An apron is helpful, though not necessary. Substitute an old shirt and blue jeans that can get dirty if you wish.

SOMETIMES BORROWED

A cabbing machine and a saw can add up to a significant investment. If you are just starting out, it may be better to borrow someone's equipment. Check with your local lapidary club or rock shop. They often have equipment that you can learn on. They may even offer lessons. Failing this, ask around to find amateur lapidaries who may be willing to help you out. There are also gem shows (one or more per year) in many cities that can provide contacts and even some first hand observation of someone cutting a stone. Explore a bit. You will be amazed what you might uncover.

Chapter 3

Cabbing Your First Gem

In this chapter I want to take you step-by-step through cabbing your first gem. There are many things to learn and lots of steps I have to explain in detail so you won't get lost. But hang in there…the task is far less daunting than the words needed to explain how to do it.

We learned in Chapter 1 that there were three basic steps in cutting a cab; planning, shaping and polishing. Here we will break the process down into easily accomplished tasks. Follow these steps and you will produce your first cabochon.

PLANNING

The first step in cutting a cabochon is planning, but like any step it can be broken down to make it easier.

Selecting Material to Cut. What stone should you cut first? There is no hard and fast rule here. It is okay to start with opal. Many successful cutters have never cut any other gem. However, most of us find a variety of stones beautiful. It is traditional that beginning cutters start with agate.

Agate has many advantages. It is readily available, inexpensive and easy to work. Agate

Agate Rough and Slabs

13

is found in chunks or seams. These are often big. The patterns inside them are not readily seen, so lapidaries use large saws to cut them into flat plates called *slabs*. These slabs expose the patterns in the stone. They are thick enough to be used to cut a stone. Usually they are large enough to cut a number of stones. It is also typical that the best patterns and colors are found only in one or more small sections of the slab. Let's start by cutting a gem from an agate slab.

Agate slabs can be obtained from several sources. Your local rock shop is the first place you should look. Gem shows often have dealers with large selections of slabs. Slabs can be purchased by mail or over the Internet, but this method leaves more to chance. At the rock shop you can select the slabs you find most attractive. Buying sight unseen means that you have to take what you get. People's tastes are different. Hand picking is always best.

It is far better at the beginning of your exploration into cab cutting to purchase pre-slabbed agate. This instantly gives you material to cut. Eventually, however, you may wish to do your own slabbing. Doing so allows you to obtain large chunks of agate that have not been high graded to remove the very best patterns. On the other hand, slab saws are big, dirty and expensive. Filling your garage with such equipment can wait until you are certain you want to continue cutting.

Now that you have selected a slab, study it carefully. Patterns and colors flow through it. Select a section of the slab that has a particularly attractive pattern and color combination. Think about the size and shape of the finished stone you might make from it. It may be helpful to use something like paper to block out other parts of the stone. This allows you to see the potential stone more clearly. Often people use a template of standard shapes to do this (templates will be explained in the next section of this chapter). Many times you will find more than one stone in a slab. Plan how you can cut these different stones out of your slab.

Having examined one side of the slab carefully, flip it over. The pattern will be different on this side…perhaps better. Select the side that has the best pattern to be the top of your stone. Sometimes the best pattern for one stone will be on a different side from another gem you find in the slab. There is no hard-and-fast-rule about which side of a slab is "top." Top is always the prettiest side.

Shape. A cab has three dimensions; length, width and height. Length and width produce the outline of the stone when it is laid on the table. Height is the thickness of the stone. When viewing a well cut cab from the side, you will notice that it is widest at the bottom. The edge of the stone curves up in a nice arc to the top. This is called the dome. Let us turn our attention first to producing the outline... or shape...of the stone.

You must now select the exact shape of your final stone. Cabs are cut into several basic shapes as well as some irregular ones. Figure 3–1 shows the typical shapes. The shape that is easiest to cut for your first gem is an oval.

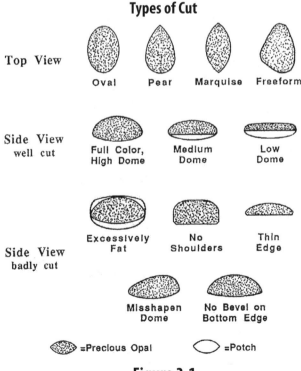

Types of Cut

| Top View | Oval | Pear | Marquise | Freeform |

Side View
well cut

| Full Color, High Dome | Medium Dome | Low Dome |

Side View
badly cut

| Excessively Fat | No Shoulders | Thin Edge |

| Misshapen Dome | No Bevel on Bottom Edge |

=Precious Opal   =Potch

Figure 3-1

Ovals can be cut with any length and width. However, there are some sizes that have become commonly used in jewelry. These shapes (with precise length and width in millimeters) are called calibrated ovals. Selecting and using one of these shapes has been made easier by the development of templates. Templates are sheets of plastic or metal that have openings the exact shape of various calibrated ovals (and sometimes other shapes). The advantage of cutting your gem into a calibrated oval shape is that it will make it easier to set into commercially designed jewelry.

THE CUTTING PROCESS

Cutting the Outline of the Stone. Let's make a calibrated oval stone for your first project. I have selected a slab of Arizona petrified wood for this first stone. Lay your slab down on the table. Place the template over the slab and move it around to put various size oval openings over the pattern you have planned to cut. Select a size and orientation that best sets off the pattern in your agate. You can start by cutting any size oval you desire, but I would recommend a medium size, like an 18x13mm, to start. This dimension is large enough for you to see the shape and dome as they develop but not so big that it takes you a long time to complete each step.

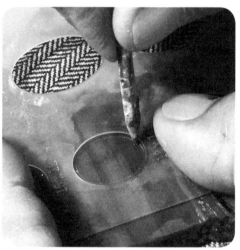

Outlining a Calibrated Stone

It is helpful in the cutting process to have the outline of the oval you are going to cut marked on the slab. This is accomplished by using a *scribe* which is an aluminum rod sharpened to a point on one end. Aluminum is used because it will not wash off while cutting, as a pencil does. Lay the template on your slab. It is helpful to keep the slab wet, as this makes it easier to see the patterns and colors. Orient the opening of the oval you wish to cut to best utilize the pattern of your agate. Hold the template in place and carefully trace the inside of the oval opening in the template onto the slab. Make sure the point of the scribe is sharp and snug against the outer edge of the oval opening. This will insure that the oval you produce is true to size and shape.

I have noticed that there are two types of cutters in this world. One does the job carefully and completely. He approaches the gem he is going to cut with respect and does his best to produce the most beautiful stone possible. Let's call him *Cab Cabaway*. The other type bulls ahead, bent on finishing the task as quickly as possible. I call him *Harry Leadthumb*. Cab has carefully scribed the oval outline on his stone. Harry has skipped the planning process completely. He has slapped the template on the slab haphazardly and scribed the outline inaccurately and is already grinding away some of the best of the pattern. You may think Harry is mythical, but I have had a number of people walk up to me and introduce themselves by saying, "Hi, I'm Harry Leadthumb." When I meet you I want to meet Cab…not Harry!

Sawing. The next task is to release the oval from the surrounding slab. Initially this is done using a trim saw. Again, planning is helpful. You want to saw through the slab in a way that releases the area you want to work while preserving as much of the rest of the slab as possible to be used later to produce additional beautiful gems.

Lay your slab flat on the trim saw table, top up, and initiate a cut near the oval mark…but not too close. You can tell where the saw will cut by the fine spray of coolant coming off the saw and hitting the slab. If there is no spray, you need more coolant. As you saw, keep even side-to-side pressure on the slab to

Proper Sawing Position

prevent the blade from bending. Near the end of the cut, reduce the pressure to prevent breaking the stone. Keep your fingers out of the path of the blade. Make several cuts to produce an angular outline with the oval well inside it. When you finish sawing your stone, you should have a basic block shape with the scribed outline of the gem you are going to cut well inside the edges as shown.

Blocked Outline

Grinding the Outline. You are now ready to move to the cabbing machine. When you do, remember my two rules; **Go Slow** and **Go Even Slower**.

The object at this stage is to produce a slab that has the outline of the oval. It should be somewhat larger than the aluminum outline and should have a square edge so that the bottom is the exact shape as the top. Why bigger? Because more material will be removed in the process of doming the stone then sanding and polishing it. If you cut into the oval outline with the grinding wheel, the finished stone will be smaller than you desire.

Grinding Outline

To produce this oval slab, grind the edge around the stone perpendicular to the top of the slab. Your mark should be to the right so you can see it as you work (unless you are left-handed, of course). Always keep one eye on the mark to prevent grinding too close to it. Work around the stone evenly, gradually approaching but not cutting into the outline. On the Pixie machine there are two grinding wheels on the left. Use the coarse wheel only to get a very general shape. Switch to the finer wheel as you approach the outline and reduce pressure to slow the grinding process. Cab Cabaway does this carefully, being as precise as possible, while Harry

Leadthumb has ground into the outline with the coarse wheel and is proceeding to transform an 18x13 oval into a 10x8. Once you have produced an outline on your slab that is precise and slightly larger than the aluminum mark, **STOP**.

Dopping the Stone. Before you produce a dome on your cab, it is convenient that you attach a handle to it. This makes handling and mov-

Ground to Outline ing the stone far easier.

To do this you need a *dop stick*. A dop stick consists of a wooden dowel cut about 4" long. Dop wax is melted onto one end to produce a "blob." Using an alcohol lamp, hold a stick of dop wax just above the colored part of the flame. Soften the wax until it is just starting to flow. Then scrape the wax onto the end of the dowel. Do this several times until you have a reasonable amount of wax sticking to the dowel. Now heat that wax slowly until it is slightly soft. Wet your fingers and shape the wax to produce a flattish ball that covers the end of the dowel. You now have a dop stick.

Dowel material comes in several diameters. You need to obtain several different small sizes. Dopping works best when the dowel is about two-thirds the diameter of the narrow dimension of your cab.

Alcohol Lamp & Dop Sticks

19

You now want to stick the dop onto the bottom of the cab. The bottom of your preform must be smooth, clean and dry. Usually slabs are smooth enough for the dop wax to stick. If not, you may have to sand the back with the coarse sanding wheel.

Place the preform, top down, on a piece of aluminum foil. Make sure the preform is clean, dry, and at least room temperature. The

wax will not stick on a cold stone. Some cutters like to warm the preform some before applying the dop stick. This makes the wax stick better. Heat the wax on the end of your dop stick until it is soft enough to move slightly, but not quite to the point where it drips. Place the molten wax onto the stone. Position it so that the stick is perpendicular to

Dopping the Stone

the stone and centered. It may be helpful at this stage to shape the wax to mold it to the back of the stone. Allow the wax to cool slowly as you hold the dop stick in place.

While the wax is still just a little soft, pick up the stone. Twirl it and observe if the slab wobbles. If it does, move the stone until it is exactly perpendicular to the dowel's length. Check this by placing the preform top down on a flat surface and observe the angle of the doweling. Getting the dop to stick without having melted wax dripping everywhere takes some practice. You will know if you get the wax too hot. It will run down the sides. If the dop does not stick to the stone, there are two primary reasons. The stone was too cool or dirty, or the wax was not warm enough. After the wax has cooled, test the stone to make sure it is firmly attached to the dop.

Correctly Dopped

Grinding a Dome. Now that you have produced the outline of your cab and have it firmly attached to a dop stick, it is time to grind the top into a dome. *Dome* is the shape of the gem when viewed from the edge. A correctly domed stone is flat on the bottom. The side is perpendicular to the bottom at the bottom edge. Then, working toward the top, the angle gets progressively flatter until the center is parallel to the bottom. The idea is to have a smooth arc.

There is an easy step-by-step process that insures that you produce exactly that type of dome. One of the most common problems in doming a stone is not leaving the bottom edge thick enough. The bottom one-fourth of the stone should be perpendicular to the back. This area is called the shoulder. The dome starts above this shoulder. Having a proper shoulder on your cab allows the prongs used to set it to grip the stone but not break the lower edge.

Start with the edge of the stone parallel to the grinding wheel. Now tilt the stone by rotating the dop stick slightly towards you. Grind a very smooth, flat edge from the top of the stone down three-fourths of the way to the bottom. This edge should be very shallow…say 15 degrees. When done, the bottom one-fourth of the side of your stone will

Grinding Angles in 3 Steps

21

be untouched, while the rest of it will have a very shallow bevel. Next, increase the angle and grind another bevel, stopping a little way above the lower edge of the first bevel. Increase the angle again, repeating this process. Using several successively flatter bevels, you can produce the desired dome. Do not increase the angle of these bevels too quickly. If you do, you will end up with a point in the top of your stone. Do this very gradually. You can always take more stone away. Cab Cabaway does this very carefully while Harry Leadthumb has ground down to the bottom edge, changed the shape of the oval and generally made a mess. To correct it he will have to make a smaller stone.

Once this basic shape has been produced, use the grinding wheel to smooth the edges of each angle until the entire surface produces a smooth arc. Be careful not to change the basic shape of the stone. Avoid the tendency to grind into the shoulder and produce a thin-edged stone. The result of this smoothing should be a stone that has a continuously changing arc. A very light pressure is used on the wheel to avoid changing the shape. The thin edges and points of a stone grind and sand faster than the main body. When working in these areas reduce the pressure you put on the wheel to slow the grinding or sanding. Some people find it advantageous at this point to slowly spin the stone and dop stick; changing the angle at the same time. Working from the edge toward the top will produce the nice, even transition you seek. To do this easily, point the dop stick to the right

Ground Dome

and parallel to the face of the wheel. Slowly increase the angle of the stone by bringing the dop stick away from the wheel, but retaining a light pressure on the stone, while at the same time slowly spinning the dop stick so all of the stone is covered. This can be a bit tricky at first, but a little practice will produce a nice smooth transition. There will still be a few little edges left by this process which will be removed in coarse sanding.

Cabbing Your First Gem

The end result of this step will be a cab-shaped stone with a precise oval outline just slightly larger than the opening in your template. It will have a smooth transition to its dome. But it will have various scratches and flat spots from the grinding wheel. These will be removed by sanding.

Sanding. Sanding your stone is a process of smoothing the surface using progressively finer grit wheels. Start with the coarse sanding wheel. With the dop stick parallel to the face of the wheel, start by sanding the shoulder of your cab. Be careful here. The coarse sanding wheel takes off a fair amount of material so a heavy-handed Harry Leadthumb approach will result in reducing the size of the stone and possibly even changing the shape of the oval and the dome. A steady slow process, punctuated with frequent stops to check your progress, is what is needed.

Sanding the Dome

Sand the shoulder and check the size and shape of the oval against the template, reducing it until the stone *almost* fits through the opening. Then transition up the side of the dome, smoothing it while keeping its basic shape. This can best be done by twirling the stone slowly in the same direction as the flow of the wheel while slowly changing the angle to cover the whole stone. Use only a moderate pressure; just enough to put a slight flex in the Nova wheel, and keep the stone moving. If you stop the twirling, you will produce a flat spot on the stone. If you twirl in a jerky, stop-and-go pattern, you will produce a number of flat spots.

Dry your stone frequently to check your progress, inspecting it with your *Opti*VISOR®. You should cover the entire stone. All heavy scratches from the grinding wheel should be gone and the surface should be smooth without any flat spots or sharp changes in angle. You are seeking the smoothest shape you can obtain. A soft surface such as that of a Nova wheel helps a lot in eliminating those annoying little flat spots. Once you have that smooth shape all over, you are ready to move on.

Sanded Dome

Medium sanding is just a repeat of the coarse sanding process. Again be careful. Even this grit can remove too much material if you aren't diligent. Keep the stone moving. Work up from the shoulder to the center of the stone. Once you have covered the stone well, **STOP**, dry it off, and inspect for scratches and flat spots. These will be more easily visible in the hazy reflection of the stone's surface. The object is to remove all the deep scratches from the previous wheel. If there are deep scratches still visible, re-sand. Once all deep scratches are removed, move on to the next wheel and repeat the process. Move on to finer and finer sanding wheels, checking frequently at each step.

There are two problems that frequently occur at this stage. Cutters seem to have a problem sanding the lower edge of the stone. This shoulder needs as much care as the rest of the stone. Get rid of the scratches from each previous step but do not work so hard on the shoulder that you make the stone smaller than desired. This edge is thinner and sands quickly, so go slow and check frequently against your template.

Also, cutters frequently cannot see subtle scratches on the surface of a stone that has been worked to the last fine sanding or pre-polish stage. It seems that people do not focus their eyes on the surface of the stone. Rather, they focus on the patterns and colors underneath it. Don't do this. Here is a trick to force you to focus on the surface. Hold the stone under the light and try to read the printing on the light bulb as it is reflected on the surface of the stone. When you do this you will be focused on the surface and any scratch will miraculously appear. Now hold the stone further from the light and move it. Watch the reflected shape of the bulb as you move the stone. The shape will change. However, these changes should be gradual, not abrupt. If the outline of the bulb suddenly changes as you move the stone, you have a flat spot or edge that needs care. Try going back to the previous wheel and sanding perpendicular to the edge or scratch you discovered. Often just a couple of swipes will do the trick. Then go back and re-sand the last step and inspect again.

I admit, passing the light bulb test is not easy. Many commercially cut stones, if cut by hand, do not pass. But your goal is to be better than that. Cab Cabaway will work diligently to make sure the surface is smooth and free of scratches.

Polishing. Once you have a pre-polished shape that is smooth and free of scratches, polishing is easy. Most machines come supplied with 14,000 diamond mesh for polishing. This is not fine enough for the superb, glassy polish we seek. I use 50,000 diamond on a Crystalite® Polypad (white). This felt-like pad holds the diamond well and produces a great polish on almost any gem with little effort. Charge (impregnate) the pad with diamond paste from a syringe. Work the diamond into the wheel with your stone while the wheel is stationary. Now turn on the machine and work the stone around the disc to

seat the diamond paste. Once the wheel is charged, it seldom needs additional diamond. If it does, I use diamond in a pump bottle to spray on the wheel (see SOURCE DIRECTORY).

Polishing

Spend a minute or so polishing the stone, then clean it off with a towel and inspect the surface. If there are spots that are hazy, more work is needed; not with polishing, but back at the last sanding wheel. Failure of a stone to take a glassy polish, especially a stone like your

25

agate, is most frequently caused by not removing all the scratches during the fine sanding steps. Go back to the sanding wheel just finer

Checking Polish

than the one that produced any scratches you can see, and do the whole process over again.

Once you have a polish you are pleased with, you are finished with the top of the stone. Take the stone off the dop in preparation for finishing the back. The easy way to do this is to place the stone and dop stick in the freezer for a minute or so. Not real long. Keep the stone itself from touching anything. Once the wax has cooled, the stone should easily pop off the stick.

Finishing the Back. There are differences of opinion on how to treat the back of a cab. Should it be polished or left frosty? The answer depends on the stone. Generally a well cut cab is perfectly polished on the back. But, some people argue, "Why bother? The back is not seen anyway." In opaque stones leaving the back unfinished has no effect on

Dop Stick in Freezer

the look of the stone as worn. However, stones like chrysoprase are a little less translucent and, therefore, less attractive if not polished on the back. If you want to keep a stone less translucent, as for example some crystal opals, finish the back only to a medium sanding. For most stones, polish the back to complete the cutting process correctly.

Finishing the back is just like finishing the front except that you will keep the back flat or at least almost flat. Depending on the slab, you may have to do some minor grinding to get the surface smooth. Then proceed through coarse, medium, and fine sanding to a high polish. Note that scratches are harder to remove on a flat surface so this process can take some work. A very slight arc on the back can make it easier to polish.

If your stone is big enough, working the back can be done by hand. If this is hard for you, dop the stone on its top before proceeding.

Bevel the Edge. Once the back is finished you will have a sharp edge where the back meets the shoulder. This thin edge could break as the stone is set. To eliminate this problem, cut a very small 45 degree bevel around this edge. I use the coarse sanding wheel for this.

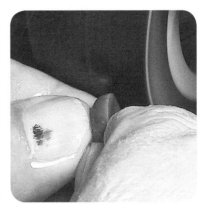

Beveling Bottom Edge

Now you have finished your first stone. Congratulations! Remove any dirt or dop wax by soaking the stone in alcohol for a few minutes and rubbing it with a clean towel.

Freeform Gemstones

Lapis

Fire Agate

Petrified Wood

Jasper

Chapter 4

Cutting Freeform Cabs

Okay. Here's the deal. I hate to waste good gemstone material. When I look at a piece of rough…be it opal, chrysoprase or agate…I think about the beauty to be released in the cutting process. Most gemstones are naturally irregular in shape. Their beauty is best released when they are cut to utilize that natural shape. Unfortunately, the gemstone industry is hung up on ovals!

There are good reasons to fashion gems into ovals. Primary among these is the economy generated by cutting many stones to the exact same size and mass producing settings that use that size. In China I have seen rooms where over one hundred workers sit at benches popping identical stones into identical setting all day long. Very efficient, but wasteful of rare gem material. And, in my opinion, boring.

In Lightning Ridge, the home of the best black opal in the world, stones are routinely cut into ovals. True, most rough is in the shape of a roundish nobby, but irregularities in the formation of the opal inside the nobby create a naturally freeform stone, not an oval. Still, Lighting Ridge cutters are convinced that they can only sell ovals, so thousands of carats of beautiful flashing black opal are ground away to accommodate the straightjacket of the oval cab.

The same is true with other gemstones. Cutting chrysoprase into standard size oval stones wastes over 30% of the stone. A freeform stone would save all that beauty. It is easy to see where that waste comes from. In this photo I have marked a standard oval shape onto a slab of chrysoprase. Note all the extra

Freeform vs. Oval

29

material outside of the black oval. I will save a little of it by sawing off the points and making small stones from them, but a large part of the stone would have to be ground away to accommodate the oval configuration. Instead, why not use the natural shape of this stone to produce a unique gem.

Candling the Slab

Now that I have convinced you to cut at least some of your gemstones into freeforms, let me tell you how to do it.

Inspect the stone. Look for cracks or imperfections that will alter the final shape of the stone. Candle the stone, as shown, to reveal any internal flaws. When I did this I discovered a crack. If you look closely at the photo you will see an irregular line just below the shadow on the top end of the slab.

Saw through any cracks, then grind the outside edge of the stone to remove rind and other imperfections. As you do this, the stone will take on a basic shape. It is almost as if the stone is telling you what shape it wants to be.

The stone now has a preform shape. You do not necessarily have to remove all the imperfections.

Sawing Through Crack

Rather think of them as beauty marks to be worked with in your jewelry design. If these imperfections are horribly distracting or threatening the strength of the stone, you have little choice but to remove them by making a smaller stone. If they are minor, live with them. A well–placed leaf or prong can reduce the visual impact of a beauty mark, thus saving the material around it.

Cutting Freeform Cabs

Once you have a preform shape you are reasonably pleased with, prepare the back of the stone. Grind it to near flat with just the slightest curve, then sand it smooth with the coarse grit sanding wheel. Dry the stone and dop it.

Starting on the edge with the shank of the dop stick parallel to the surface of the wheel, grind the edge all the way around the stone so that at least the bottom half is perpendicular to the bottom of the stone. This insures that you maintain a shoulder for the stone. It is now time to produce the dome. As you did with the oval stone in the previous chapter, begin at a very shallow angle, cut a series of circles around the edge of the stone working up from just above the bottom edge producing a smooth curved dome. Smooth the transition between the circles to generate an even flow using the fine grinder. Continue perfecting the shape of the stone and its dome using the coarse sander. Work in one direction, then work at right angles to that direction to generate a smooth transition.

Test the smoothness of your dome as you remove scratches with the fine sander. Dry the stone and observe the reflection of a lamp on the surface of the stone. Sharp transitions will become obvious as jumps in the reflection when you move the stone. Make sure the curve is smooth all the way to the base of the stone. Also, make sure the dome does not form a knife edge at the base. I insure against this by always starting on each successively finer sanding wheel with the dop stick parallel to the surface of the wheel. I sand the lower edge (shoulder) first then work up to the top of the dome. Don't forget to inspect the surface for scratches. Remove any irregularities with medium sanding, then repeat the fine sanding and polishing steps.

Once the top of the stone is completed and polished, remove it from the dop. Sand and polish the back. Be sure to put a little bevel at the bottom edge to help prevent chipping as the stone is set.

Now you have a unique stone with an attractive freeform shape, a smooth dome, and a bright polish. You are ready to set it into that special piece of jewelry.

As jewelry artists, our goal should be to produce a piece of jewelry that melds the design elements to compliment the gemstones we employ. A freeform stone offers the jewelry designer the opportunity to employ unique shapes to create an integrated design unlike any other. Don't be stuck with the same old boring oval stone. Cut a freeform and design around it. Techniques for designing your own setting are offered in Section Five.

Finished Freeform

We are now finished with the basics of cutting a cab. As we have seen, it is a three-step process which is applicable whether you are cutting a standard oval or a freeform… or any other shape for that matter. You must plan, shape, then sand and polish no matter the stone or its shape.

When cutting most cabbing material, there is little additional you will need to know. Some stones, like turquoise and lapis, are softer and work faster so extra care is needed not to go too fast. Other stones, like malachite and shell, can produce toxic dust so you need to make sure the stone is always worked wet. Stones like jade and chrysoprase are particularly tough so they take extra time. Some nephrite jade can be difficult to polish, even with 50,000 diamond. If you have a problem, consult someone who polishes nephrite to learn alternative methods of getting the polish you desire.

In short, there are some specialized techniques needed to finish a few cabbing materials, but for the vast majority, the techniques I have outlined will produce a marvelous stone.

It may prove useful to follow along with me in the next chapter as I cut several cabs. My discussion offers reasons why I do what I do and includes lots of new tips.

Chapter 5

Several Cab Cutting Projects

Each gemstone is unique, offering a different collection of patterns and color. And each contains various *imperfections* that must be worked around or incorporated with minimum adverse effect. In this chapter, I work through cutting several stones, commenting on how I have approached them and adjusted to what I found. In essence, I am attempting to give you the experience of watching me as I cut these stones. Come along. It will be fun.

MOSS AGATE – SUBTLE RESHAPING

I found this piece of Montana moss agate in a pile of tumbled stones at a gem show. The stone had a great moss pattern but it had a couple of problems; probably why it was put through the tumbler rather than cabbed. On the lower right in the starting stone photo you can see an indentation. This was a hole and crack. Not visible on the left corner, I found another small fracture.

Beginning Tumbled Stone

Final Freeform Shape

It took minimal reshaping to work around these problems. Grinding away the cracks left me with an "almost" finished freeform outline. Some minor refining produced the outline shown here.

Ready to be Set

Notice how a subtle reshaping of this stone transformed it from an unattractive clump of rock into an attractive gem. I cannot impart any great secret to achieving this. Just experiment and in time it will become almost automatic.

Montana moss agate is a translucent stone. The light passing through the stone makes the black moss inclusions stand out. For this reason it is important that the back of this stone be polished to bring out the translucency.

BRAZILIAN AGATE – NATURAL SHAPE

A slab of Brazilian agate came my way. It had beautiful tan and white stripes going across it and a natural long triangular shape. Someone had scribed an oval over the bottom third of the stone. What a waste! This stone was beautiful just as it was. All it needed was a bit of straightening of the sides and removal of some junk on the bottom edge. In the accompanying photo you can see that natural shape as I look for cracks in the stone.

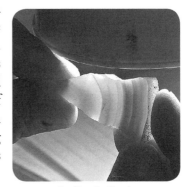

Looking for Cracks

Shaping the stone was simple. I just followed the natural contours, keeping the dome fairly flat to accentuate the triangle shape. Dopping, sanding and polishing were easy except that the fairly flat dome meant that I needed to be more careful to remove scratches in the middle of the top. If you look closely at the photo of the shaped stone, you will note scratches through the middle where the top white band is seen. These were scratches from grinding that I had not completely removed in coarse sanding. I went back to the coarse sanding wheel to remove them.

When cutting a low dome you must be particularly careful to produce a smooth arc. The tendency is to leave the middle perfectly flat rounding only the outside of the dome. In the accompanying photo note the reflection of the lamp and bulb on the polished surface

Shaped...Note Scratches

of the agate. The reflection is smooth, even, and mimics the triangular shape of the stone.

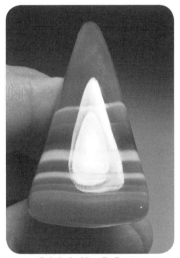

Polished...Note Reflection

LACE AGATE – CUTTING A PRECISE OVAL

Cutting a stone to precise dimensions takes a bit of extra care. Here I start with a beautiful piece of Mexican lace agate. I love this material. The intricate lacy patterns are fascinating and the bright earthy orange tones are most attractive.

I wish to cut this stone to a 25x18mm oval to fit into a standard bolo tie mounting. First I find the pattern I like and mark the stone by carefully scribing the outline using the template. Next I block out the stone with the trim saw. I proceed to grind the stone down to the general oval shape I want, but not too close to the markings. The reason for this is that I have a tendency to not keep the sides of the stone perpendicular

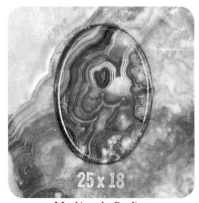

Marking the Outline

to the bottom. Hence, if I ground precisely to the mark on the top of the stone, the bottom may be too small. To insure against this I now re-mark the stone on the bottom, being careful to get the outline to reflect the outline on the top of the stone. I have ground the outline to the general shape but larger to make it easier to get the marking on the back correct.

Blocked Stone

Next I grind the outline of the oval close to the marking on the bottom of the stone. In doing so I find a small pit at the edge of the oval. Since this is on the bottom of the stone it will not be visible when set. I adjust the outline slightly and use a marginally thicker shoulder to make this pit as small as possible while still keeping the pattern I like

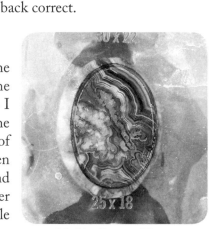

Marking Bottom of Stone

on the top of the stone. By the way, notice that the pattern on the back is far different from that on the top. In many agates the pattern shifts throughout the stone. Even as you grind the dome into a stone, the pattern can shift; sometimes only slightly, sometimes dramatically.

Outline Ground to Bottom Mark

This is where the precision starts. I dop the stone and begin by grinding the outline with the stone's bottom perpendicular to the grinding wheel, working carefully to make sure the edge is at right angles to the bottom. Grind close to the mark but not into it. This is because the outside of the mark is slightly smaller than the inside of the template. More important, sanding and polishing will remove more material so grinding too far now could result in an undersized finished stone.

Once the stone outline is down "almost" to the mark on the back of the stone and even all the way around, I start the dome. Careful not to grind into the bottom quarter of the side, I start with a shallow bevel and gradually work up. Once I have the basic dome, I smooth the whole stone with the grinder. As I do, I periodically check the

Fitting to Template

size and outline to make sure I have not changed anything. To check the shape I put the stone into the opening in the template from the back. I can now see if the shape is still true to the oval. The stone should not go "through" the opening. Instead the opening should hit the dome just before the straight shoulder. This will take several attempts at grinding a little and checking…grinding a bit more and rechecking.

Once the stone has been ground to a nice, smooth dome that "almost" goes through the template, it is time to start the coarse sanding. As usual, I start with the dop stick parallel to the coarse sanding wheel. This insures that I sand all the shoulder. I work up to cover the entire stone. Sand the edge just a little at this point.

Here is where we get the precise fit we are looking for. Sanding removes stone rather quickly. So, sand a little and check a lot! Sand using coarse grit until the stone "just" fits through the template. Once it does, go on to medium and fine sanding and polishing. Finish the back as you would any stone and we're done.

Precise Fit

TIGEREYE – ORIENTATION

I love phenomena stones. The best, of course, is opal with its ever-changing, flashing colors, but there are many more. There is an entire class of stones that produce either stars or eyes. Star ruby, star sapphire, and star garnet come quickly to mind. There are also several stones that produce an eye-like effect. All these stones produce the star or eye-effect because tiny inclusions bend the light coming back from the stone.

Finished Gem

The least expensive and most available phenomena stone is tigereye. Tigereye is an agate with asbestos inclusions which produce the chatoyant eye effect.

In cutting tigereye the orientation of the stone determines the look of the gem. In the example here I cut two identically sized stones.

Color Plates

Wyoming Apple Jade

CP-1

Brazilian Banded Agate

CP-2

Tigereye

CP-3

Mexican Lace Agate

CP-4

Lapis Lazuli

CP-5

Petrified Wood

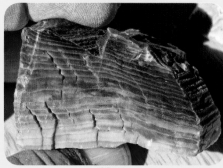

CP-6

Color Plates

Opal Rough from Coober Pedy

CP-7

Color Plates

Line of Fire

CP-8

Faced Bottom of Stone

CP-9

Color Plates

Candling the Stone

CP-10

Fully Faced Opal

CP-11

Color Plates

Sawn Into Three Pieces

CP-12

Sawing Alternative One

CP-13–A

44

Color Plates

Sawing Alternative Two

CP-13–B

Final Shape

CP-14

Color Plates

Dome Shape – CP-15

Preliminary Polish – CP-16

First Opal Finished

CP-17

However, the orientation, and therefore the look, is completely different. For one stone (the top stone in the accompanying photo) I have marked an oval on the tigereye slab that has its long axis parallel to the chatoyant eye found in the stone. For the second stone I have marked an outline that is perpendicular to the eye. As you can see in the photo of the finished stones, the look is quite different.

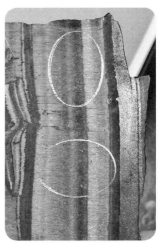

Two Orientations

Finished Stones

Tigereye orientation is fun to play with. Try angle orientations and combine them with complimentary freeform shapes to produce some truly unique gems. There are no hard-and-fast rules here. Use your imagination!

OOPS – ADJUSTING TO PROBLEMS

I found a piece of black and white Mexican lace agate (an increasingly rare treasure) among the same tumbled stones as the Montana moss agate. Upon inspecting the stone I found some very intriguing patterns on both sides of the stone. On one side I found the outline of an angel praying. Unfortunately, the stone had a crack right through the angel's head. Fortunately, on the other side I found the long neck and big eyes of an ET-like character. Searching for various orientations with my template, I finally decided on the 18x13mm oval as shown in the accompanying photo.

I blocked out the stone with the trim saw and proceeded to grind to the oval marking. As I did, I ran into a problem. There was a hidden

Side One

Side Two

crack in the upper right of the oval. What to do? If I made a smaller stone in an oval shape I could avoid the crack but I would cut into ET's eyes. I finally decided to slowly grind away the crack to see how deep it went. As I did, a simple freeform shape that kept the character of the stone suggested itself. I could cut this somewhat teardrop shape, avoid the crack, yet save ET. Again a subtle reshaping of the stone transformed disaster into a unique gem.

Selected Pattern

Final Shape

CHRYSOPRASE – FINDING A UNIQUE SHAPE

Not all rough can be found in convenient slabs. I obtained a chunk of beautifully colored chrysoprase from my friends Richard and Mary Lou Osmond, owners of the Candala Chrysoprase Mine near Marlborough in Queensland, Australia. This mine, recently reopened, produces the best gem chrysoprase in the world. See my article "Candala Mine Chrysoprase" in the November 2007 *Rock & Gem Magazine*, for the story of our visit to the mine.

What to do with a chunk of chrysoprase? It has beautiful green, translucent color on the edge but a thick crust prevents me from seeing into the stone. Time for some judicious grinding! This will take some time, even with the coarse grinding wheel, because chrysoprase is a tough stone. It takes a lot to wear it away.

Rough Chunk

Working with the coarse grinding wheel, I remove the crust on both sides of the chunk. As I do, I stop periodically to inspect the stone. I am looking for any fractures, deep pits or inclusions that would cause me to adjust my thinking about how the stone should be cut. This stone contained a deep pit on one side but fortunately the chunk was thick enough that I could grind the stone to a thinner profile and remove most of the pit.

Grinding Off Crust

When most of the crust is removed, I switch to the fine grinder. The finer scratches allow me to see into the stone so I can detect potential problems. Sure enough, just when I thought I was heading toward a roughly triangular freeform shape, something flashed in the stone. I candled the stone by holding it next to the opaque shade of my cutting lamp. This allowed

49

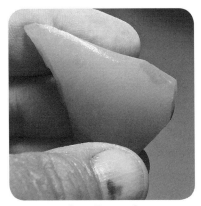

Crust Removed

the light to pass through the stone and illuminate any fractured surface inside. Candling revealed a long crack completely through one corner of the stone.

There is nothing to do but to saw through the crack and work with the remaining stone. When I do, an entirely different shape for the stone emerges. The stone seemed to want to be a large teardrop but a uniquely shaped one. The stone came to a natural point at the top but what makes it unique is the inward curve of the left side. The Pixie's 4" wheels allow me to preserve this inward bend as I grind the outline of the stone. Slowly working with the fine grinder, I remove the remaining crust and smooth the shape. The final outline emerges not so much from my will but from the natural characteristics of the stone.

Candling Crack

Sawn Through Crack

Doming the stone adds to the shape. To make it look more like a teardrop I make the top end of the dome thinner. The bottom is nicely rounded so as to simulate a drop of water just about to be released from a leaky faucet. Fat on the bottom with a flat back and thin at the top, it looks like a teardrop. The inward curve of the left side is accentuated and complimented by the curve of the right side. The result is a truly unique and beautiful chrysoprase gem.

Suggested Shape

Final Shape

Well, there you have it. You have followed along as I cut several different stones. This is by no means the end. There are lots of different stones for you to cut. Each one will offer a unique opportunity and special challenge. Work with the stone…not against it. When you do, the results may truly amaze you.

We are now ready to turn to cutting my favorite of all gemstones… the ***Opal.*** Like other stones, each opal offers unique opportunities and challenges. It also requires some special attention, but the rewards are worth it.

Finished Gem

Section Two
Cutting Opal

Cutting Rough

Chapter 6

Cutting Your First Opal

In this chapter I take you through the process of cutting your first opal. It is not difficult and will be quite enjoyable. Remember, your job is to uncover the hidden beauty locked inside each piece of rough and to make the most beautiful gem possible. "Haste makes waste" is certainly true in opal cutting. I presume that you have cut at least a couple of agates so that you are familiar with the general cutting process. However, if you have not, you can still be successful in cutting opal. I do suggest that you read Chapters 3 and 4 before proceeding. Within this chapter I have divided the cutting process into more steps than in Chapter 3. This is because special care is needed to ensure that the opal's color is shown to best advantage. This chapter is divided into two parts. The first provides detailed step-by-step instructions for cutting your first opal. The second takes you through the cutting of an example stone, complete with color reference photographs.

Part I

SELECTING MATERIAL TO CUT

Almost any opal will do for a start, but there are some that might be better. I recommend that you use an inexpensive material that comes from Coober Pedy, Australia, called *potch and color*. This is a material that has one or more lines of fire intermixed with a white opal that has no color or fire. Such material is pictured in CP-7. The common opal with no fire is called *potch*. Potch and color material is available from almost any rock shop (see SOURCE DIRECTORY).

It is always difficult to describe opal, so I may not be able to adequately outline the best material to begin cutting here, but I will give it a try. I suggest that you select material that has a bright line of color. This is because the finished stones you cut from it will look better. You will then be encouraged to continue. With poorer material that has only a faint line of color, you may cut the stone correctly, but the finished product may not be very attractive. You may think you did something wrong when you didn't. The better material is more expensive, naturally, but usually not too much so. Perhaps the rule you should use is to select rough that is not so expensive that you are afraid to cut it, but not so poor that it gives you no satisfaction when the opal is finished. This rule will be interpreted differently by each individual, which is fine. However, I do recommend cutting several relatively inexpensive opals before attempting that special stone you paid a ridiculously low price for three years ago and have been itching to cut ever since.

Material from the Mintabie (or Mintubi, the Aboriginal spelling) and Lambina fields in Australia also work well for a beginner. Much of it has color throughout the stone. If you are starting with such material, read Chapter 7 before you start cutting.

Mexican opal is more difficult to cut correctly and I do not recommend it as a starting material. Nor do I recommend the Honduras material as it works very differently and will not help you learn how to cut opal. American opals offer various unique challenges which are better left for after you are comfortable. Finally, inexpensive Lightning Ridge material is lots of fun to cut, but very frustrating for a beginner, so avoid it too.

For more ideas on rough material see Chapter 12, which contains a discussion of the types of materials coming from various mines.

CUTTING OPAL STEP-BY-STEP

The cutting technique is a simple step-by-step process which anybody can learn. In essence it is no different than cutting any other cab material. It just takes some added care. Your success is just a matter of using your head and cutting with love.

STEP ONE: Pre-grinding. Select a piece of the potch and color material you have obtained. Any size will do, but it would be best to find a piece with at least one good strong line of fire and enough thickness to enable the stone to be worked into a solid cabochon, and large enough to make at least a 10x8mm finished stone. Anything as large as 18x13mm is acceptable, but when you get larger than this you may find your first stone a little more time consuming; perhaps discouraging you. The rough should be at least 4mm thick with at least 3mm between the color line and one of the outside edges. This makes certain there will be enough thickness in the finished opal. Thicker is better...within limits. You can always remove extra potch, but you cannot add it! Well you can, but that gets us into doublets and triplets which are covered in Chapter 11 for more advanced cutters. Remember, you must learn to walk before you can run.

Inspect the stone for the *line of color* (called the color or fire line). The fire line is the area with flashes of different colors (see CP-8). It may be quite thin or fairly thick. Thicker is better. Inspect the wet stone under a strong overhead light. I recommend a 100 watt frosted bulb in a desk lamp. A color-balanced daylight bulb is ideal. Don't use fluorescent light as it kills the colors, especially reds. Economy or long lasting bulbs and the new energy saver bulbs produce very unnatural light and should not be used.

Look carefully to determine the direction and pattern of the fire line. The fire line will show on what will be the edge of the stone and may show on the face of the rough as well. Here we need to adopt some common terms. Think of this book as the line of fire in the opal. The book has length, width and thickness. Looking at the cover of the book is like looking at the face or top of the opal. Looking at the bound edge of the book is like looking at the edge of the opal's fire line. No matter how the rough opal is shaped, the face of the fire line is like the cover of the book and the edge of the fire line is the thickness of the book. Figure 6–1 shows a typical stone from the top (or bottom—at this point you haven't decided which side is the top) and from the edge. The line of fire is generally straight as in the figure. If it is not, select another stone with a straight line of fire for your first experience at cutting.

Having selected a stone, inspect it further to determine the full extent of the line of fire. Sometimes two fire lines are easily visible on the rough exterior of the stone. Often the fire line is not completely

Selecting Rough

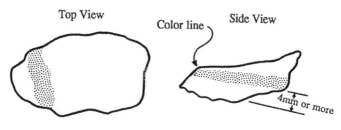

Top View   Color line   Side View

4mm or more

Figure 6-1

visible because of the potch (the opal with no color) and the brown material (sand) commonly associated with opal from Coober Pedy. In such cases it may be necessary to expose the side of the fire line.

Coober Pedy Rough Opal

Holding the opal in your hands, use a fine grinding wheel (220 grit) with plenty of water to grind away some of the sand and potch around the edge of the stone. Do not grind on the faces of the rough just yet. Remember, all you are doing in this step is determining the location of the line of color, so you do not need to remove very much material, and almost none of the fire line should be cut away. Stop frequently to inspect the stone. When you are able to determine the extent and direction of the line of fire, **STOP**!

STEP TWO: Planning (Orienting the Stone). Now you must decide how to cut your opal. You will want the line of color at the top of the stone and enough material under the line of color to give the finished opal strength. If you have enough material on both sides of the color line, you must decide which face is to be the top of your finished gem.

This can be accomplished by looking at the color line from as close to the plane of color as possible. This is done while the opal is wet and with your 100 watt desk lamp. The light should hit the line of color in the same way it would in a finished stone. Thus, the light should be as close to directly overhead as possible and your eyes should also be as close as possible to the same location as the source of light without interfering with it (see Figure 6–2).

Deciding Which is the Top of the Stone

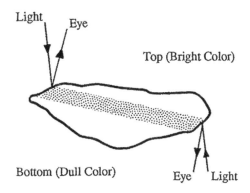

FIGURE 6-2

Move the stone around so that you can see how the color changes as the angle of the light varies. The object is to determine which face will show the brightest color without actually cutting away any opal. Looking at one face of the opal, the color line is usually visible around some of the outside of the stone. If it is not, move the stone slightly in the light until it is visible. Notice how bright the color is in the fire line. Now flip the stone over and look at the fire line in the same way. Is it brighter? The brightest face should be the *top of the stone*, assuming that the "bottom" is thick enough. Repeat the process a couple of times to make sure you have made the correct choice.

Occasionally, you will find a stone which shows very bright color when viewed on the edge, but virtually no color when viewed on the faces. For some reason this seems to happen more in the blue-green stones. When this is the case, there is not much that can be done. This type of stone will not be bright if finished with the color line flat as in the book's cover. Instead, if the color line is thick enough, the stone can be cut on edge. Of course, the finished stone will be smaller. If you find a stone that shows good color on the side but not much color when the line of fire is 90 degrees to your eye, set it aside for now and select another stone.

If the color line is close to one surface of the stone, your choice is made. The thin layer of potch is the top.

These instructions assume that you have chosen a piece of potch and color opal to cut. If you have a solid piece that shows color throughout, the orientation of the color is more complex. Refer now to Chapter 7 on orienting color, then return here.

At this stage inspect the opal for cracks. They are best seen by allowing the opal to dry (water hides the cracks) and then looking at it in a strong light. Use your desk lamp with the opaque shade and

Searching for Cracks

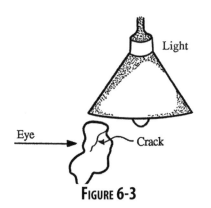

Figure 6-3

frosted 100 watt bulb...the same one you used to decide on the top of your stone. Place the dry opal so that it touches the edge of the shade and position your eye so that it is about 90 degrees from the light bulb, allowing you to see light through the opal. Move the opal so that you can see the cracks (see Figure 6-3). They will show up as opaque lines that sometimes look like the edge of broken glass. When the light hits them just right, it will reflect off the crack's surface with an orangish hue. Take note of each crack and cut your gem in the next step so that all cracks are removed. You may find it desirable to use your *Opti*VISOR® to see into the stone more effectively.

Opal Lover, Cab Cabaway's significant other, has taken her time at this step. She realizes that the more you look and plan, the better the finished product. Harry Leadthumb skipped this step completely and is busily grinding away the fire!

STEP THREE: Exposing the Fire (Facing the Opal). This is the most fun in the whole process. Holding the stone in your hands, carefully grind away the potch covering the top of the fire layer using a fine grinding wheel. Do this carefully and slowly, stopping to inspect your progress. *Don't* cut into the fire layer. Stop just before you get to it. This is particularly important if the fire line is thin. In a thin line of fire the scratches produced by grinding will cut deep into the color line. As you sand to remove them, you may remove much—sometimes all—of the color line. You can always go deeper later. Your stone will look like Figure 6-4.

This is the point where Harry Leadthumb really gets into trouble. He grinds into the fire. Noticing that the color gets brighter the more potch he removes, he reasons that he should remove even more to get to the really good fire. He grinds too deep, either removing all the fire at this step, or not leaving enough for finishing. Sometimes Harry is right... there is better color deeper in

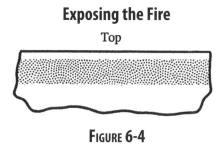

Exposing the Fire

Top

FIGURE 6-4

the stone. When uncertain about this, a thinking cutter like Opal Lover will select a small area on the edge of the opal which will probably not be in the final stone and grind at an angle into the fire layer there. In that way she can judge whether she needs to go deeper without risking the whole stone. The safest way to do this is to use the medium sanding wheel. This forces you to go slow. I like to think of it as "sneaking up on the fire."

STEP FOUR: Pre-shaping. Having exposed the fire, you now need to do two things. The first is to flatten the bottom of the stone and adjust the thickness. The bottom can be ground down by holding the stone in your hands and grinding on a fine wheel. The bottom should be parallel to the top of the color line, or as close as possible if the color line is not straight. Continue to grind away the bottom until the distance from the top of the color line to the bottom of the stone is approximately 4 to 5mm. It can be thinner or thicker, depending upon the size of the final stone to be cut. If there is still a little brown material on the bottom, you may want to make your opal a little thinner, but it is better to leave a little poor material on the back rather than ruin the opal by making it too thin. Imperfections on the back will not show in the finished stone in any case. The bottom need not be perfectly flat at this point and the stone can be left a little thick, as you will return to it later. Table 6-1 provides a general guideline to ideal thickness of various size stones.

Ideal Thickness

THICKNESS	APPROXIMATE DIMENSIONS OF FACE			
	18x13	16x12	14x10	10x8
Too Fat	8	6	5	5
Ideal	6	5	4.5	4
Too Thin	3.5	3	2.5	2

Table 6-1

Once you have adjusted the thickness, sand the back with the coarse wheel to remove grinding scratches to prepare it for dopping.

So far you have been cutting your opal while holding it in your fingers. This, you may have noticed, is hard on the hands. But cheer up, those little nicks will heal and you should feel better knowing that you are not getting the stone too hot. But do hold tight, as the wheel may grab your stone and fling it against a wall. There is one opal somewhere in my shop which slipped from my hand over 20 years ago. If you ever visit me and find it…it's yours. And it is a good one!

With the opal faced and the bottom roughed out, it is time for another inspection. Dry the opal thoroughly and inspect for cracks. Sometimes cracks are hidden in the stone and appear only after you have cut into it. If there are cracks in the stone now which didn't appear before, they were probably there all the time but not visible. If you have kept your stone cool and used a true wheel, as Opal Lover will, the cracks are not the fault of your cutting. These cracks were formed in the ground or during the mining process. Many cutters, upon finding a crack at this stage, get discouraged. Don't be. Just work around them. Not all opals will contain a crack, but such imperfections are not uncommon. Cracks are an indication of poor quality rough *only* when they are so numerous that they prevent cutting any reasonable sized crack-free stones from the parcel. If the crack is near the outside of the stone, a shape can be chosen which eliminates it. Just plan to grind it away as you shape the stone. If the crack is in the middle of the stone, it may be desirable to saw through the crack and make two stones. However, if you have treated the opal roughly, let it get hot, or dropped it, you are a relative of Harry Leadthumb! The crack just may be your fault. And, of course, it usually cracks at the very worst place.

You are now ready to decide on the final shape of your opal. Opals can be cut into standard oval shapes or into non-standard shapes such as pears, triangles, or totally irregular shapes called *freeform* cuts (see Chapter 3). The advantage of cutting to standard sizes is that settings are readily available and can be relatively inexpensive. Unfortunately, these settings are often designed for faceted stones and are not good settings for opal, as they offer little protection for the delicate edge of the stone. The disadvantage of cutting to a standard size is that you will loose some of the potential size and full beauty of your finished gem. For this reason, I hate to cut standard size stones. I learned to do custom-made setting in self defense and you will too in the Section Five of this book. Now we can avoid wasting opal.

I do not recommend cutting a standard size opal on your first try. Doing this correctly complicates the cutting process, making your first opal more difficult than necessary. Cutting opals to standard sizes is covered in Chapter 10.

The shape you choose should be pleasing and take advantage of the color of the opal. It should also eliminate any cracks you discovered. This shape can be roughed out while holding the opal in your hand. Again, use a fine grinding wheel. The shape can be cut with the top of the stone facing up, but don't do it. It is far better to grind the shape by placing the edge of the stone on the wheel with the top facing to the right or left. The advantage of this latter method is that it effectively eliminates the little chips that tend to form at the bottom of a sharp edge. At this point you are only grinding an outline. Do not grind any on the face of the stone.

You need not be really close to the final shape at this stage, since you will do your final shaping after your opal is dopped. Remember not to go too far in pre-shaping, as the sanding process will remove some more material.

STEP FIVE: Dopping. The purpose of *dopping* is to provide a handle on your opal so you can work it more effectively. There are probably more ways to dop an opal than there are cutters. Several of them work well. There are special cold dops that have been developed. Some people use 5 Minute® Epoxy or SuperGlue. Some even use double-sided carpet tape. All can work. But let me tell you how I do it. You'll be surprised.

Select a dop stick about one-half to three-quarters the diameter of the stone. Make sure the wax is fresh as each heating removes some of the shellac that makes the wax sticky. If you are using an old dop stick, add a little fresh wax to the end. There should be enough wax to leave a layer between the end of the dowel and the opal with some around the edge to mold to the back of the stone.

The bottom of the opal should be sanded with your coarse wheel, as the grinding wheel leaves the surface too rough. The wax won't stick. Also do not sand beyond this, as the surface becomes too smooth and again the wax does not stick as well.

With the opal dry and at room temperature, lay it top down on a flat surface right next to the alcohol lamp. Heat the wax on the dop stick over the lamp until the wax on the end is starting to drip. This is somewhat softer than you would get the wax when dopping an agate. Place the dripping dop stick on the back of the opal. Do not put pressure on the stone, as this will squeeze out the wax on top of the wood, reducing the strength of the bond. Using your other hand, wet your fingers slightly and shape the wax around the back of the stone bringing it out almost to the edge of the stone for support. The moisture on your fingers will prevent the wax from burning you and will cool it some so it starts to solidify. As it does, lift the stone so that the top is face up. Rotate the dop and gently shift the stone so that the fire layer is at a 90 degree angle to the dop stick. This can be checked by looking at the edge of the stone as you rotate the dop stick. If the color line wobbles as you turn the stick, it is not flat. When you are satisfied that the opal is positioned correctly, cool the stone and wax by moistening it with water. I find sticking it in my water tray the best solution at this point. Presto, you have a dopped opal.

On occasion you may find that the opal does not stick. This could be caused by several factors. The opal was not clean and dry. The bottom was not properly sanded. The wax was not hot enough. Or the wax is old and losing its stickiness.

As I explained to you earlier, opal is a lot tougher than people think. I have never cracked an opal using this method.

STEP SIX: Final Shaping. Having dopped your opal, you can now use the fine grinder to further finish the shape. First, true the edge of the stone by grinding it with the dop stick's wooden dowel parallel to the grinding wheel. Grind so that the edge is perpendicular (90 degrees) to the fire line. Support the stone with your left hand and rotate the dop stick with your right hand (or the other way if you are left handed). You do not need to flatten the top third of the side as this will be removed by the doming of the top. If you do flatten all the way to the top, you may remove a little opal that could have been left.

At this point you will finalize the shape of the stone. Be sure the side is perpendicular to the fire line. If an error is made, try to keep the top a little smaller than the bottom. Angling the other way...which makes the bottom smaller than top...will result in a smaller finished piece, unnecessarily wasting opal.

Next, using the fine grinding wheel, the top should be domed to the maximum extent possible consistent with the fire line and the preservation of a thick edge and adequate shoulder. If

Author Discussing Opal Dome

the fire line is very thin, the stone should have very little dome as in Figure 6-5,A. The thicker the fire line, the more doming can be done as in Figures 6-5,B and 6-5,C. If you put a high dome on a stone with a thin line of fire, as you would in your properly domed agate in Chapter 3, most of the fire will be ground away and the finished stone will show color only in the middle as in Figure 6-5,D. This is wrong.

Remember that rough sanding will remove some more material, so do not fully complete the outside dimensions and dome shape of the stone on the grinder, switch to coarse sanding. Complete the shape in the coarse sanding process or even in the medium sanding, if possible. This is a spot where Harry Leadthumb can get into even more trouble. The tendency is to grind too much before sanding. Sanding takes more time, but it is far safer. You may be surprised how fast a thin edge on an opal disappears even using medium grit sanding. When in doubt, use the finer grit. Also use a moderate touch. At this point Harry Leadthumb is in full swing and has just made a 18x13mm into a 8x6mm!

In the process of finalizing the shape during rough sanding, you will almost automatically remove the remaining potch on top of the fire layer. The way to tell if all the potch is removed is to look at the top of the opal as you dome it. If it is brighter around the edge than in the middle when viewed directly from the top, there is some more potch in the middle. Reduce the degree of dome by sanding the middle of the stone until the potch is removed.

Final Shape

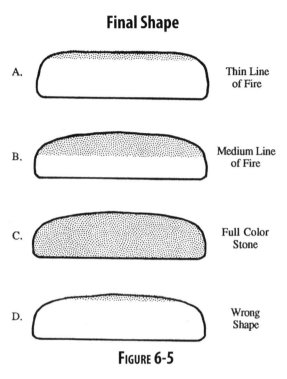

A.   Thin Line
of Fire

B.   Medium Line
of Fire

C.   Full Color
Stone

D.   Wrong
Shape

FIGURE 6-5

Also, pay attention to the shape of the edge. It is necessary in setting an opal to have a slight inward bevel to the edge. The bottom should be somewhat larger than the top so that the prongs can get a grip on the stone. The degree of bevel will depend upon the degree of dome on the finished stone. The transition from flat (perpendicular to the fire line) to the bevel should be gradual and rounded so you do not leave a thin edge which could crack in setting.

STEP SEVEN: Sanding and Polishing. The process of finishing the opal after finalizing the shape is just the same as for other stones. Be sure to keep the opal cool by using a lot of water or by dipping the opal in room temperature water periodically. Use a moderate touch. A heavy hand can heat an opal very fast. Too light a touch leaves flat spots and scratches. Sand across the scratch marks left by the previous wheel. Check to make sure that all scratches are removed from the previous grit before proceeding to the next step. You have to dry the stone before inspecting it as water hides scratches and flat spots. Also, make sure all the flat spots are removed during medium sanding. Opal, being soft, has a greater tendency to flat-spot than other stones. If you are using silicon carbide or the syringe-type diamond, the opal must be cleaned and dried between steps to avoid contaminating the next wheel. Harry Leadthumb does not clean his opal and puts a big scratch across the stone. He will have to go back to remove the scratch and may remove the last of the fire line in the process.

As you polish the opal, be sure to work the entire surface of the stone. Do not neglect the edges in your haste to see the great color on the top. I always start at the shoulder and work up to the top.

Clean the opal and check the polish by looking at the reflected light of a bulb on the surface. No scratches or dull spots should be visible, even with some magnification. Remember to focus on the surface, not the fire below. Flat spots appear like magic as distortions in the shape of the bulb. Opal Lover has taken her time and carefully moved from step to step. Her opal shines without a trace of flat spots or scratches. Harry Leadthumb's opal looks like the rough grading of a bulldozer.

STEP EIGHT: Finishing the Bottom. After you have finished the top of the stone, remove it from the dop stick. This can be done by placing the opal and dop stick in the freezer as with agate. (Hang in there…I'm not as crazy as I sound! Well, maybe I am, but it works anyway.) Make sure that the opal is not touching anything. Within a minute or two the dop wax will become brittle. Simply force your fingernail (or a pocket knife) between the opal and the dop wax. With a small amount of pressure the opal should pop off. If it does not, leave it in the freezer a little longer and try again. Once the opal has popped off the dop, set the stone on the counter and let it warm to room temperature. I have left opals in the freezer for over an hour. As an experiment I left some for weeks, never cracking one, but I do not recommend it.

After the opal has warmed, dop the top of the stone using the same method. Align the stone so that the top is at a 90 degree angle to the dop stick. The back of the stone was prepared with coarse sanding and should be parallel to the top. If for any reason it is not, flatten it using the coarse wheel. Be careful here as the polished surface of the stone does not stick to the dop wax as well. Use only a light pressure. Some cutters will put a dome on the bottom of the stone. This increases the weight of the finished stone, but does not add to its true value. I prefer to keep the bottom fairly flat because the stone is easier to set, but I do leave a slight dome as this makes the back easier to finish. Once the back is properly prepared, move on to medium or fine sanding. The back may actually be polished. It makes a nice finished look if you do, but it's not necessary. I do find that transparent stones look better if you stop at the medium or fine sanding step. This reduces the transparency of the stone slightly and intensifies the color of the finished product.

Having finished sanding, it is necessary to take the sharp edge off the bottom of the opal. Put a 45 degree bevel on the bottom edge with your medium sanding wheel. The bevel need not be real deep. All that is needed is to remove the sharp edge of the stone. Failing to do this will almost certainly cause the opal to chip or crack as you push the prongs down in the setting process…ruining all your work; not to mention God's.

Remove the opal as before. Soak it in fingernail polish remover or alcohol for a few minutes to remove all traces of dopping wax. Wash it off with room temperature water.

STEP NINE: Enjoy. You have now completed the first of many fine opals. If you are like me, you are fascinated by the play of color. It changes with the direction and intensity of the light, making the opal the most fascinating gemstone in the world. If you agree, you are an *Opalholic*. Welcome to the group!

SUMMARY

The key to cutting opal is to go slow; listen and inspect frequently, keep the opal cool and use your head. Remember that each opal is a unique gem. Your job is to unlock the beauty hidden within the stone.

Be an Opal Lover, not a Harry Leadthumb. Cut with love and you will be sure to succeed.

Part II

CUTTING AN EXAMPLE STONE

In this section we are going to go step-by-step through cutting an opal. The material is a potch and color stone with a modest fire line in a white potch typical of Coober Pedy. You can follow along visually by referring to the Color Plates 7 through 17.

Before we start, a note about opal photographs. It is very difficult to get the fire in a white base opal to show true to the actual stone while keeping the base color white. Hence the photos for this section understate the true fire intensity of the stone. I have kept the white base to better represent the stone you are likely to start with.

CP-7 shows a parcel of nice white base opal from Coober Pedy. This parcel is typical of the material from Coober. The tan is the outside edge of the seam of opal. Usually, but not always, the fire line is more or less parallel to this surface. These stones are mostly full color and probably better than you would use for your first stone.

CP-8 shows a piece of potch and color from Coober Pedy with a distinct fire line about one-third of the way down from one face. The fire line is fairly thin. Inspecting the stone I find another fire line just under the brown crust at the bottom of the stone. That fire line is so close to the surface that it may be full of imperfections. Let's find out.

Grinding a little on the "bottom" of the stone exposes some of this close fire line. Sure enough, the fire is mixed with brown sand and little cracks (CP-9). Candling the stone (CP-10) shows that the sand and cracks go into the stone pass this bottom fire line. Clearly this fire line will not make a good stone. As I suspected, we will have to work with the line in the middle of the stone. It was an interesting experiment that proved what I suspected without endangering our ability to cut a stone out of this center line.

Cutting Your First Opal

Now we flip the stone over and work on facing the opal. CP-11 shows the top of the stone ground down "almost" to the fire line. Drying the opal and candling it, it's obvious that there are several cracks to work around. Still, there is enough crack free opal to make at least three stones. The primary one…and the one we will work on…is the clear area in the upper right.

I use a saw as little as possible in cutting opal, but this is a prime example of where a saw can save some good material. Before sawing, I plan carefully. The idea is to saw through parts of the rough that will not cut stones due to cracks or sand and to leave as large an opal as possible. Do not saw right next to where you think the stone will be. Saw a bit away from it. We will work into the stone with the grinding wheel to remove any remaining cracks or sand as the stone is shaped. CP-12 shows the stone sawn into three pieces.

The larger piece in the middle is our main stone. Notice that there is a brown streak about one-third of the way into the stone. This is a crack. I knew it was there before I sawed. I left some of it so that I would have the freedom to work around it. CP-13, A and 13, B show the stone in two orientations with a line scribed down the stone to show two alternative ways it might be worked. With CP-13, A the stone would be sawn in two to make matching stones. With 13, B the stone would be one large piece with the left area ground away to remove the crack. In analyzing the two alternatives, I find that the one large stone not only offers a bigger opal, but the stone has better color when oriented as a pendant. So, the bigger stone it is!

Grinding away the crack and producing a preliminary shape, I discover that the crack goes a bit deeper than I could see. This is fairly common. The final shape shown in CP-14 is a pleasing "almost" rectangle. The stone is now ready to dop.

Once dopped, I straighten the shoulders and produce a dome. Note that the dome is fairly flat as shown in CP-15. This is because the fire line is fairly thin so a flat dome is needed to preserve the most color.

As I sand and polish the stone I make sure to keep this "almost" flat top. The center of this flat top will not sand as fast as the edges of the stone so extra time must be spent on this area.

After polishing I check the dome for shape and scratches. The top has a nice, even, gradual bend as is evidenced by the reflection of the lamp on the surface in CP-16.

The finished stone shown in CP-17 has a nice orange red fire with some less bright blue and green fire to give it depth. The color is definitely better when oriented as a pendant.

We have finished our first stone. It came out pretty well, I think, certainly worth making into jewelry. There is a lot to remember, I know, but as you work a few stones, referring back to this chapter as you go, the process will become much easier.

Chapter 7

Orienting the Color

You have now cut one or more opals; discovering that it is a simple, enjoyable pastime. The next step is to go on to more advanced cutting. This includes cutting more valuable material and specialized cutting such as the making of doublets and triplets. There is a lot more enjoyment ahead. In this chapter we present some of the finer points of cutting opal.

All opalholics are aware that opal shows different color when the light strikes it at different angles. It also has more intense fire from some directions. Your objective when cutting or setting an opal is to pick the best possible orientation for the stone so as to maximize its potential.

Some opals want to be rings while others want to be pendants. This has to do with their orientation. A stone which is brighter when looking down on it from above wants to be a ring. A stone which looks brightest at about 15 degrees from perpendicular wants to be a pendant. (We are not built straight up and down after all.) When oriented as a pendant most opals look best at one particular rotation. Play in the light of your lamp with the first stone you cut. It is trying to tell you what it wants to be...ring or pendant.

The issue of the best orientation for an opal comes up even in the case of a thick stone which has fire completely through it like the piece of rough in the upper left of the front cover. Such a stone can be cut from several different directions. Before you go through the orientation procedure you may find it advantageous to grind away some of the potch or sand on the outside of the stone so as to be able to see the intensity of fire. Be careful not to grind too much as this could reduce the size of the finished stone you could produce. The object is to remove only enough material so that you can see into the stone and properly orient it, no more. A quick pass over the ground areas with the coarse sanding wheel will help you to see the true color.

Orientation can dictate how you shape and cut your opal, so it is part of Step II (planning).

ORIENTATION TECHNIQUE

To properly orient a stone you need the same strong light you used to check for cracks, a frosted 100 watt bulb in a desk lamp with a solid opaque shade. Any background light is acceptable but it should be general all-around light rather than strong from one direction. If you have a strong light, rotate so the source is directly behind you. Try to avoid fluorescent light or energy saver bulbs as they kill the color.

Develop the proper orientation as you finalize the opal's shape. To identify this proper orientation, place the opal about 20" below the bulb. Position your eye as close as practical to the edge of the lamp shade without casting a shadow on the stone (or burning your eyelashes) and look directly down on the opal. The object is to try to get as close as possible to looking at the opal in the same direction as the light is hitting it (see Figures 7-1 and 7-2). Now, move the opal around in the light. The fire will change intensity as you move it. Keep the stone wet while you orient it. This makes it easier to see the color. Note how the color and intensity of the fire changes as the opal moves. This is one of the great wonders of opal. Select the position of the stone which shows the best combination of color and intensity. You have discovered the best orientation for your stone when cut for a ring. You probably can remember the orientation of the stone by looking at it in this position. However, you can mark the stone to aid your memory by drawing a line around the girth of the stone at right angles to the imaginary

Orienting for a Ring

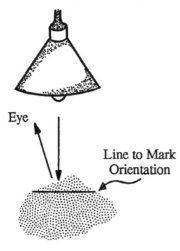

Eye

Line to Mark
Orientation

Figure 7-1

line from your eye to the opal. I use an indelible felt tip pen. This line then tells you how to orient the base of the stone if you are going to cut it as a ring stone.

To determine the orientation of the stone if worn as a pendant, place the stone 20" below the light and about the same distance behind it. With your eyes slightly in front of the light and about 6" below it, look at the fire coming from the opal. Remember that the stone lays about 15 degrees back from vertical when worn, so tilt it accordingly. Now rotate the stone in a full circle with the face always at 15 degrees to your line of sight. Note how it is brighter from some directions. Usually, one direction will be best. This tells you how to cut and shape the stone if it is used as a pendant.

Now you must decide which is best—ring or pendant. Generally, I choose the orientation which produces the brightest fire and cut the stone that way. I also allow the stone to dictate its rotation. This has sometimes led to peculiar shapes such as points at the bottom of a stone rather than the top. I will either reshape the stone or leave it as a challenge to the jewelry designer (me).

Orienting a Pendant

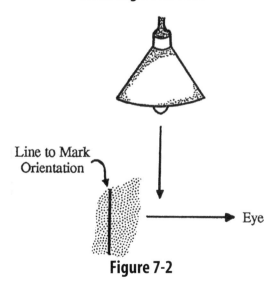

Line to Mark
Orientation

Eye

Figure 7-2

If the stone is thick, it may be possible to make two or more stones from it. This can be done easily by sawing the stone parallel to the line you have marked (or imagined that you have marked) on the stone, but before you do any sawing, see Chapter 9. Having sawn or ground the base of the stone, you are now prepared to cut and finish it as you would any other opal.

ORIENTATION AND YIELD

While the above is the standard method of orienting opals, there are special circumstances which may cause you to modify this technique. (Actually many opal cutters pay no attention at all to orientation and their stones suffer for it.) One problem you might encounter frequently results from having the brightest color in the stone showing in such a way that the size of the finished stone would be quite small. This might occur, for example, in a fairly flat stone that shows more color from the thin edge than from the larger face. You now have a frustrating decision. You want that bright color. You also want the larger stone. There is no real guide I can give you without seeing your particular stone. Clearly, if the edge is only a little less attractive, go for the bigger stone. If there is almost no color when the stone is oriented for maximum size, you may be better off going to the smaller stone. Alternatively, you may find that by changing the orientation slightly from the ideal, you can significantly increase the yield. This may be your best compromise. Part of the fun—and I must admit the frustration—of cutting opals is making this choice. Consider carefully the yield versus quality issue before sawing or grinding. You cannot go back once the saw has done its work.

ORIENTATION IN SETTING THE STONE

In setting an oval stone in a pendant mounting, the same trick is used. Play with the orientation of the stone so that it shines as bright as possible when you look at it as someone would when standing in front of the wearer in conversation, then mount it with this orientation. If you do, you will be pleased to hear many compliments on the quality of your work.

Chapter 8

To Dome or Not to Dome

Most cabochon cutters begin with inexpensive agate. They learn, as we have in Chapter 3, to form a perfectly proportional, smooth, symmetric high dome. When we turn our attention to opal cutting it's important to adjust our outlook. In opal, cutting a smooth, symmetric high dome is almost always not the best way to dome an opal cab.

> **In opal, cutting a smooth, symmetric high dome is almost always not the best way to dome an opal cab.**

DOME AND LIGHT

We have learned one reason to use a low dome when cutting opal. A thin line or a thin bar of the best opal requires that the stone be cut with a low dome. But, it is not the only reason.

Bear with me now. This is going to be a bit technical. The play of color in opal comes from light entering the stone, then being diffracted into rainbow colors and returning out of the opal. The angle where the light comes out depends upon the angle it went in. If the light enters perpendicular to the surface, it will come out at the same angle…right back the way it entered. However, if the light enters the surface at an angle it will come out at the opposite angle.

To understand how this works see Figure 8-1, A. The light strikes the surface of the opal perpendicular or 90 degrees. It comes back out

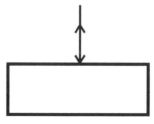

Figure 8-1, A

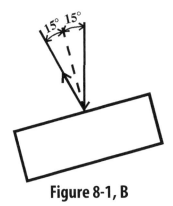

Figure 8-1, B

the way it entered, 90 degrees to the surface. In 8-1, B, the light strikes the surface 15 degrees from perpendicular and exits at the opposite angle. This is exactly the same physical phenomena you use in the rear view mirror of your car. It is set at such an angle that the view to the rear strikes the mirror and is reflected at an angle to your eye.

We can apply this phenomena to opal's play of color. Suppose that your eye is along the axis of light in 8-1, A. The diffracted light inside the opal would come straight back to your eye. However, suppose your eye was in the same spot along the axis of light, but the opal was tilted as in 8-1, B. Then the diffracted play of color would escape at 30 degrees (15 degrees plus 15 degrees) from your line of sight. You would not see the play of color. This is exactly the reason why opal changes its colors and look as it is moved in the light. All those colors are still there. They just aren't visible from the angle at which you are viewing them.

The shape of the dome on an opal affects how much of the diffracted light comes back to your eye. In 8-1, C, a high domed stone spreads the diffracted light. Your eye does not see most of it. But in 8-1, D, a low domed stone, more of the diffracted light comes back at an angle your eye can see.

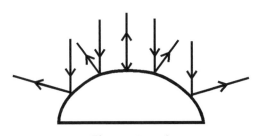

Figure 8-1, C

This physical phenomena suggests that low dome stones would be preferable to medium domes stones and certainly high domed stones. More of the diffracted light, and thus the play of color, would come back to the viewer's eye in the low dome stone so it would be more beautiful.

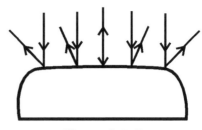

Figure 8-1, D

True, but too simple. Light does not strike the opal from only one direction. It comes from many angles. Light that strikes the surface from the side will come back to your eye as diffracted play of color. To see this, just mentally reverse the arrows for light direction in the figures.

Understanding this brings the medium and high domes stones back into our good graces. The higher dome allows the opal to gather light from different sources thus bringing the play of color to the viewer's eye. This is true but it is only one part of the equation.

DIRECTIONALITY AND DOME

For some reason I only faintly understand, some opals show a play of color only in one direction. As such a stone is turned it is very bright from one direction and loses all its play of color when the stone is turned even slightly. Such a stone is considered highly direction (see *Opal Identification & Value*, pp. 71). Other stones show a play of color no matter how you turn them. These are called non-directional. Other things being equal—which they never are in opal—the non-directional stone would be preferred. It looks good no matter what angle the light strikes it. Opals range in a continuum from non-directional through somewhat directional and very directional to highly directional. The look of the finished opal depends upon both this directionality and the shape of the dome.

The highly directional stone is the worse case. Since it produces diffracted light only at one angle, to see the play of color the light coming from the stone must be parallel to the light going into it. Now think about how this applies to the shape of the dome. A low dome such as shown in Figure 8-1, D, brings more of the light back to the eye from the one direction that produces a play of color. In the most highly directional stone, the best dome would be a perfectly flat one. A medium dome would collect light from side angles and bring it to the eye, but the directional nature of the stone would mean that this light would not be diffracted into fire colors. A medium dome on a directional opal will cause it to show color in only one section of the stone at a time. Moving the stone in the light would cause this section of color to move across the stone like an eye. The rest of the stone's face would have no color. Not very attractive.

Fortunately, very few stones are this directional. The less directional stones will gather light and play of color from more angles. A medium to high dome allows these stones to gather this light more effectively. All this complicated directionality and angle of light discussion leads us to a simple rule. The more directional the fire in an opal, the lower the dome should be cut. Very few opals are not directional at all. Thus, very few stones should be cut with a high dome. Most stones will look better with some variety of medium dome.

> **The more directional the fire, the lower the dome.**

The degree of dome you wish to put on a stone can be judged once the stone has been faced to expose the fire. Move the stone in the light of the cutting lamp at comfortable arms length. Does the brightness of the fire change dramatically as you move the stone? If so, head for a low dome. If it remains relatively consistent, just somewhat better from some angles, use a medium dome. Only if there is virtually no difference as the stone is moved in the light do you want to cut a high dome…and only then if the brightness is consistent at various depths of the opal. So you can see why so few stones should be cut with a high dome.

Chapter 9

Sawing Opal

I hate to saw opal and do so only when it cannot be avoided. A saw can get you in serious trouble very quickly, so use it sparingly.

WHY SAW?

Sawing opal is done for a couple of reasons. One is to remove large quantities of unwanted potch from a stone. For this purpose any trim saw will do a reasonable job because the saw is only removing potch. The gem opal is not cut into. The second reason to saw opal is to separate a piece of precious opal into two parts. In this case you want to save as much valuable opal as possible. Consequently a thin blade diamond saw is used. I use a saw with a 4" blade which is .012 inches thick. Such saws are commonly used to split faceting material. The saw uses water for its lubricant and coolant.

I prefer a high-speed saw as the speed helps prevent the blade from wobbling. A wobbling blade can produce a much wider saw cut and more waste. Blades thinner than .012 tend to bend and wobble even when used in a high-speed saw. In my experience a .006 blade will produce a thicker cut than a .012 because of this movement.

The **Ameritool 4" Trim Saw** fit with a .012 blade will be serviceable for sawing opal as well as agate and other gemstones. Use it on its top speed. Alternatively there are specialty high-speed saws that work very well. The one I have was made by **Rocks**.

HOW TO SAW

Sawing opal is simple, but I do have two hints for you.

1. Use plenty of water and go slow so as to not overheat the opal.

2. Use water as the lubricant, not oil. Opal is porous and oil can soak into it. Oil dulls the fire and hides cracks. If you do use oil, wash the opal with soap and water, rinsing all traces of soap from the stone.

Sawing Opal

The blade will sometimes grab the stone, causing it to chatter. This rapid hitting of the opal on the saw table can crack the stone. To prevent this, I hold the opal in my hands. My fingers are used to absorb the small shocks created by sawing. Place the opal between the first finger and thumb of each hand, leaving the area to be sawed free between the fingers of each hand. Place your hands on the saw table so that one or more fingers of each hand are between the opal and the table. Holding the opal firmly suspended in your fingers, you can now saw it along the desired line. Your fingers absorb the shock. Make sure there is enough space between the fingers of both hands to allow the blade to pass. While thick 10" table saw blades do not cut fingers, a thin saw such as this will! By the way, this is another reason not to use oil, as an oil soaked opal is very difficult to hold on to. As you saw through the opal, rock the stone back and forth a little. This gives the water a chance to cool the cut, saving both the opal and the saw blade.

WHEN TO SAW

Now that you know how to saw, let's talk about when. Suppose you have a thick stone with two or more good lines of color. Wishing to get as much as possible from the stone, you may be tempted to saw through the potch between two lines of color. This could work out fine, but in many cases it does not. The opal in one line will be oriented differently from the other. One of them is probably wrong.

I have adopted a sawing rule which has worked well. Before you saw, analyze, orient and face the best line of color in the stone. This insures that you will get at least one good piece from the stone. You can then saw behind this face at the appropriate thickness—a little thicker than you expect the finished stone to be. If there is another stone in the piece you have sawed off, great! I feel it is much more important to get one good stone than to take a chance, saw, and get two poor stones or none at all.

Face One Good Stone Before Sawing. A full–color thick stone— or a stone with one thick line of color—can also be sawed to produce two stones. One is tempted to saw through the middle of the fire line. This is a typical Harry Leadthumb trick. It has been my experience that the saw will go right through the best color, leaving some of it on one side of the stone and some on the other. The best color will now be in the bottom of the saw tray. It's like the saw has eyes.

As with multiple lines of color, it is far better to face the stone and insure that you get at least one good stone before sawing.

Sawing is an effective method of removing cracks or imperfections in a stone. Before you saw through a crack, analyze the resulting shapes of the opals you will produce. I find it useful to candle the stone and mark each crack with a scribe, as we did for our first opal in Chapter 6. Then I plan the saw cuts to remove the cracks *and* produce the best set of stones the piece allows. In this way you get the best the stone can offer.

Remember to saw only when absolutely necessary

Cutting Opal Into a Standard Oval

Chapter 10

Cutting Standard Sized Opals

Many of us have not learned the art of designing and constructing mountings for our stones. Instead, we purchase mountings designed for standard sized gems. The art of *lost wax casting* has rapidly expanded the available mountings over past years. It is now possible to produce jewelry with a custom design look you can take great pride in while using commercial settings. To utilize these mountings, obviously we need to cut opals to standard dimensions. Easy task, right? Well actually, no. There are two potential problems. Suppose you have acquired a pendant mounting that will require a 12x10mm oval and you have a piece of opal rough big enough to cut such a stone. The problem is that the stone still may not cut a desirable 12x10mm oval. It must produce the required size in the proper orientation without cracks or pits. This is not always easy. I cannot count the times I have picked out a stone to cut to a specific size only to have it not work out. There is a simple solution to the problem. Cut the stone to a standard size first; then pick out the setting. This approach eliminates one of the problems, but it is not always practical. You may not find a setting you like that uses that size stone, or you may have fallen in love with just the right setting but you do not have just the right stone to fit it. In either case, you may decide you need to cut an opal to size.

THE TECHNIQUE

Now, how do you go about cutting the opal so it fits? The basic technique is the same one we used to cut your first agate in Chapter 3. (See the precise size discussion for lace agate in Chapter 5). Because opal has some unique characteristics, additional care is needed. The tendency is to end up with a finished stone that is too small. Special care must also be taken to insure that the top of the opal has all the fire you want. The following simple procedures can eliminate these problems.

STEP ONE: *Obtain a Template.* Employ the template containing the standard size ovals that you used in Chapter 3.

STEP TWO: *Mark the Opal.* Once the opal has been faced with the best color just below the surface, mark the shape you desire on the face or top of the stone using a sharp aluminum scribe, getting the line as close as possible to the edge of the opening. Make sure the area you have marked is free of cracks and inclusions that would weaken the stone or produce an undesirable look (see Photos page 84).

STEP THREE: *Rough Grind the Shape.* Rough grind the shape, leaving a substantial margin around the marked outline of the opal. Be sure that as you grind the outline, you make the back of the stone slightly larger than the front. Also, grind with the stone on edge so as to reduce the tendency for the bottom of the stone to chip (see Figure 10-1).

Preshaping

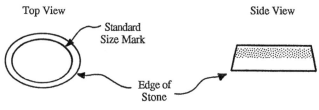

Figure 10-1

STEP FOUR: *Dopping.* Dop the stone, making sure that the top is perpendicular to the axis of the dop stick.

STEP FIVE: *Rough Sand the Shape.* Using your course sanding wheel, not the grinding wheel, slowly sand away the edge of the stone toward the marked shape. Stop periodically to check the size against your template. When you get near the proper size—but not to it— move to medium sanding. The reason for this is that opal is removed quickly, even with coarse sanding, and the thinner edge goes away very fast. Go slow and sneak up on the size you want.

Cutting Standard Sized Opals

STEP SIX: *Medium Sand the Shape.* At this point the top of the opal should not quite pass through the opening in the template. Continue medium sanding of the edge of the stone…employing the 15 degree shoulder angle…until the top of the opal passes through the opening but the bottom does not quite pass. If the shoulder gets below the middle third of the stone without allowing the top to pass through the opening of the template, you have left the base too big. Sand it down with the edge straight (90 degrees from the top) and continue the shoulder until the stone passes about one–half of the way through the template. Make sure the shape is as true to the oval template as possible.

STEP SEVEN: *Doming the Stone.* You are now ready to dome the stone. Either a high or medium dome can be cut. Use coarse or medium sanding to shape the stone but *do not* sand the lowest part of the edge yet. This size is what you are seeking. Also, make sure you retain a shoulder for proper setting.

STEP EIGHT: *Medium Sanding and Final Shaping.* Move to medium sanding. Finalize the shape of the dome and smooth the transition of the dome into the base of the stone. At this point the small amount of material you remove from the lower edge should allow the opal to "just" pass through the opening in the template. When you have smoothed the dome…retaining a proper shoulder…and the opal barely passes through the template, move to fine sanding.

STEP NINE: *Final Sanding and Polishing.* Fine sand and polish the sides and top of the opal. The stone will get slightly smaller here, but if properly prepared it will not lose enough to change its shape. At this point the stone should move easily through the template with just a little room to spare.

STEP TEN: *Finishing the Back.* Remove from the dop and bevel the bottom edge. This last step protects the stone from chipping during setting.

In summary, the secret of cutting an opal to size is to stop coarse and medium sanding before the stone is down to size. The additional sanding you do to finalize the shape and remove scratches will bring it down to size. Check the size periodically to make sure. Finally, remember that you can always remove more, but if you cut too much you can't put it back!

Chapter 11

Cutting Doublets and Triplets

Doublets and triplets consist of opal (usually crystal or highly translucent) glued to one or two layers of non–precious material. There are two purposes for producing a doublet or triplet. The backing adds intensity of color to the stone since the back is usually darkened in some way to provide a contrast to the flashes of light coming from the stone. The backing (or cap) also adds strength and thickness to stones which would otherwise be too thin to use effectively. Triplets are made for these reasons, plus the fact that the clear top protects the opal, making triplets stronger for such "rough wear" situations as men's rings. In addition, triplets use very thin slices of opal, thus conserving valuable materials and making pieces useful that are even too thin for use as doublets.

Construction of Doublets and Triplets

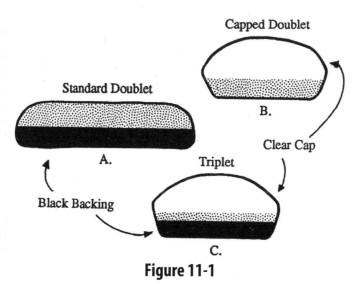

Figure 11-1

DOUBLETS

The typical doublet is a combination of a gem opal top and a non-precious bottom such as is depicted in Figure 11-1, A. Such stones can be truly spectacular. Let us suppose that you have a bright but thin piece of opal you wish to cut into a doublet. Use the following steps.

STEP ONE: Orienting the Stone. Orient the stone as previously discussed in Chapter 7. In this case all you need to do is decide which side is going to be the top of the stone. This will be somewhat of a guess since you will be working the back before exposing the color on the front of the opal.

STEP TWO: Flattening the Opal. Grind the *bottom* of the opal to a flat surface using a flat lap. Some people argue that the surface should be lapped down to 600 grit. I have found that 220 is preferred because it gives the glue more surface area to adhere to. This is the perfect application for the flat grinding wheel on the **Ameritool** machine. All imperfections such as sand spots and pits should be removed from the back. Also, if the thin color line is associated with opaque potch, all the potch should be removed from the back. This is because the dark background which is used to intensify the fire and make the stone look like a black opal will not do so if there is an opaque white layer between the precious opal and

Flattening the Opal

the dark background. The more transparent the fire line, the more important it is to remove the potch from the bottom of the stone. The best guide is to grind the back down until you are just barely into the fire line you will use for the top of the stone. Use water as a coolant. Be careful when grinding the opal to insure that the back is perfectly flat and parallel with the line of fire. There is a tendency to put more pressure on one side of the opal, causing uneven grinding.

Cutting Doublets & Triplets

STEP THREE: Flattening the Backing. Select a non-precious backing and grind it flat on a 220 grit lap. There are many materials which have been used. It is common to use some black colored backing. Materials used include black potch (non-precious opal), obsidian, basenite, black onyx, black jade, and even black Honduras matrix opal (a basalt). The primary requirement is that the back be strong. I personally prefer black jade, but it is more expensive than other alternatives. My wife's first wedding ring was a doublet I made backed with black jade. (Same wife, several wedding rings—all opal, of course.) It was once crushed in a folding bleacher. It took us an hour and a pair of pliers to get the ring off her finger, but the opal remained unharmed. The jade had added toughness to the opal. The finger mended in short order. The next most preferred backing is black common (potch) opal. The advantage of this material is that it has all the same characteristics as precious opal. It makes the doublet look more natural, but still is not as tough as black jade. I do not like basenite or basalt as they are quite soft and do not create tough stones. However, they are fine for the triplets we will discuss shortly.

STEP FOUR: Painting. I've got to be kidding, right? Why would anybody paint an opal? Ted Priester, a now retired opal cutter in Lightning Ridge gave me this trick. Clean and dry the back of the opal. Spray the back of the opal with a flat black paint. Be sure that the paint is compatible with epoxy glue. I use **Testors** paint for model airplanes. Apply a *thin, even* coat from a good 24" away (outside with newspaper to catch the extra paint). The paint need only be thick enough to give the opal a dark smoky look. Let the paint dry overnight in a place where the air is free of dust. Dust specks that settle on the paint can cause a problem with the seal of the glue. Be sure not to touch the painted surface. If the backing is not real dark, you can paint it in the same way.

STEP FIVE: Gluing. Glue the opal to the backing. I prefer using clear epoxy (Hughes 330), not the 5-Minute variety, as the latter dries to an amber color that can give a strange tint to your opal. I used to mix the epoxy with a black material called "Opaque Pigment for Polyester Resin" to darken the glue, but with painting this is no longer necessary.

Make sure that both surfaces are dry, clean, and free of all oil. This includes the natural oil from your fingers so never touch either surface after you have ground them flat. If you touch them by mistake, clean with denatured alcohol.

Before mixing the glue, heat the opal and the backing. Ted uses an

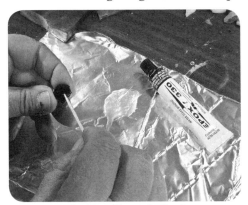

iron to do this. Jim Walch, a successful doublet maker in the United States, uses a lamp like the one you have used to orient the stone. Place the stones on a flat surface and position the lamp (with a 100 watt bulb) about 4" above them. Heat for a couple of hours until the stones are almost too hot to pick up.

Applying Glue to the Opal

Mix the glue. Try to get as few bubbles as possible in the mixture. Spread glue on the opal back and the backing using a wooden toothpick. Remove any air bubbles. Tilt the opal slightly as you set it on the back. Roll it onto the back slowly, allowing any air bubbles to escape (See Figure 11-2). Air bubbles are the bane of doublet and triplet making. The bubble looks like a round silver inclusion. It ruins the effect.

Press both surfaces together with moderate pressure and move in small circles until the excess glue is squeezed out. The proper amount has been removed when suction causes the opal to start to grab and be resistant to further moving.

Place the glued piece flat on the table and put the

Gluing Opal to Backing

light over it. This helps the setting process. Allow the glue to set 3 or 4 days. Don't rush it, as the pieces may separate in cutting if the glue isn't properly set.

Roll the Opal Onto the Backing

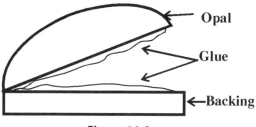

Figure 11-2

STEP SIX: Pre–grinding. Grind the top to a smooth surface parallel to the joint between the opal and the backing. Do not grind the stone too thin, as it can become quite fragile. Avoid creating too much heat as it may cause the glue to separate (see CP-18).

Doublets and Triplets Curing

STEP SEVEN: Shaping. Decide on an outline for your stone. Both standard shapes or freeforms are acceptable (see CP-19).

STEP EIGHT: Grinding the Top. Cut the top with a fairly low dome. To reduce breakage problems while setting the edge of the stone where the opal meets the base should be fairly thick as in Figure 11–3, B, rather than thin as in Figure 11–3, A. Such a thin edge will likely break during setting or, if not, it will chip when the piece is worn.

Thickness. The ideal for most Australian opal is an opal thickness of 2mm to 3mm. Typically the dome is fairly flat, but there are exceptions and potential compromises to be considered. A thicker, higher domed doublet will be stronger.

Edge Too Thin

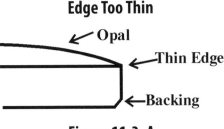

Figure 11-3, A

However, typically a thinner stone is darker thus looking more attractive.

An opal that has some base color, especially white, will look gray if left thick. The black behind the stone is mixed with the opal's base color. The thinner the opal is, the less of the base color there is to mix with the black. The stone darkens. The darkness provides a better contrast to the fire so the stone looks better.

Good Thick Edge

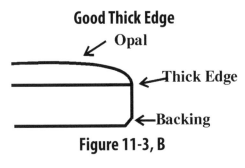

Figure 11-3, B

Thicker is better for strength. Thinner is better for color. Clearly a compromise must be reached. If you listen to the opal, it will tell you the best compromise.

Carefully and slowly grind the top of the opal (see CP-19). Watch the look of the stone change as the opal becomes thinner. If it still

Color Plates

Doublet Faced

CP-18

Doublet Preshaped

CP-19

Color Plates

Finished Doublet

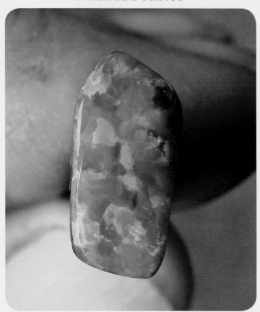

CP-20

Triplet Rough Glued to Base

CP-21

Color Plates

Triplet Pre-shape Before Cap

CP-22

Triplet Cap

CP-23

Color Plates

Triplet Side View

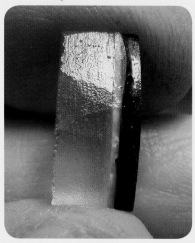

CP-24

Triplet Pre-shaped Capped

CP-25

Triplet Finished

CP-26

Color Plates

Rough Coober Pedy

CP-27

Rough Mintabie

CP-28

Color Plates

Mintabie Rough

CP-29

Lightning Ridge Rough

CP-30

Color Plates

Spencer Idaho Rough

CP-31

Ethiopian Rough

CP-32

Rough Simulant

CP-33

Simulant Colors

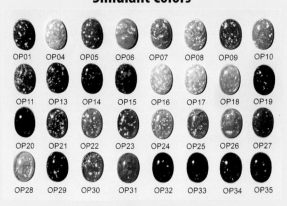

CP-34

looks gray or dull as you approach the desired thickness, grind a bit more. The opal should get darker and/or brighter. If, after a bit, there is no change, stop. If it keeps getting better, continue. However, keep the final thickness above 1mm if you can or consider a triplet. I find that many stones will improve rapidly in the first grinding but quickly reach the point where there is little additional change. The opal is saying "stop here!" A few seem not to change at all so the preferred thickness is best. Others get noticeably better after each little layer is removed. These opals may be saying "I want to be a triplet."

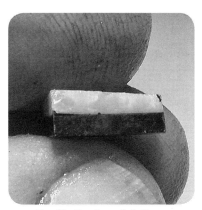

Doublet Preshape Side View

After the final thickness has been reached, shape the dome. Remember, in doublets it is very important to leave enough opal at the edge so that the finished stone will not be fragile. This means that the shoulder of the stone should begin well above the glue line.

STEP NINE: Sanding and Polishing. Sand and polish as you would other opals. Be careful not to heat the stone too much because excess heat could cause separation of the glue or cracking of the thin opal layer.

STEP TEN: Finishing the Back. Finish the back with a bevel as shown in Figure 11-1, A. Don't dop the top of the stone as it might crack. Hold the stone in your fingers. Don't worry, your nails will grow back (see CP-20).

Density of Fire. There is a type of crystal opal which does not have a great density of fire. Instead the color seems to float in the clear opal. This is typical in most Mexican opal but this lack of dense fire can be found in Australian and some American and British Columbian opal as well. When cut as a solid opal, the fire in such a stone is often almost lost as most of the light goes through the stone. Such a stone may be improved by making it a doublet.

To find out if such a stone wants to be a doublet, perform this experiment. Clear most of the junk and matrix off the stone on all sides. Now partially fill a black tray with water. I use the bottoms of Weight Watchers™ microwave dinners. Place the opal in the tray next to the bottom. Move it around and observe the color. If the color is far better with the black background, it wants to be a doublet.

> **If the color is far better with the black background, it wants to be a doublet.**

Before proceeding, determine which orientation produces the best color. Unless this orientation wastes a lot of opal, use it as the top of the stone. Sometimes a stone is very thick in one orientation and not good in others. In such a case consider sawing it in half and making two doublets.

Opal and Backing

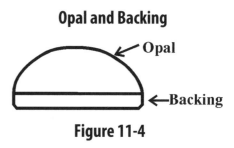

Figure 11-4

It is best to leave the opal layer as thick as possible when making doublets from these low density crystal opals (see FIGURE 11-4). Thickness allows as much of this less dense fire as possible to play off the dark background. Fortunately, these stones are normally completely transparent so the dark base shows through readily. These stones also typically look best in a high dome. The end result for such doublets is a thick opal layer cut in a medium to high dome with a fairly thin dark base. Jade is great for this as it stays tough even when thin.

CAPPED DOUBLETS

While the above is the standard way to cut doublets, there is another alternative. A clear cap can be glued onto the top of the opal as shown in Figure 11-1, B. The clear cap magnifies the color and strengthens the stone. The procedure is the same as used for the cap on a triplet.

Cutting Doublets & Triplets

There are two ways to cap an opal. One uses a pre-finished calibrated oval cap, the same type used for triplets (as explained later in this chapter). The second is to use a flat piece of unshaped quartz or other clear material. The instructions for a pre-formed cap are as follows:

STEP ONE: *Flattening the Top.* Flatten the top of the opal using a 220 grit flat lap, and continue grinding until you have reached a desirable color pattern. Clean and dry the opal.

STEP TWO: *Gluing the Quartz Cap.* Glue the quartz cap to the opal using clear epoxy. Heating the stone as explained above insures a better bond and reduces the chance of trapping bubbles. Pre-cut caps are available from **Teton Gems** (see Source Directory).

STEP THREE: *Grinding the Edges.* After the glue has set (3 to 4 days), grind the edges of the opal on a slight bevel toward the bottom of the stone. Leave the quartz cap a little wider than the opal as in Figure 11–1, B. This protects the opal when setting and wearing . Be careful not to grind into the cap, as that will reduce its size, making it not fit in a standard setting.

STEP FOUR: *Finishing the Bottom.* Finish the bottom, leaving the opal fairly thick if possible to add strength.

The instructions for an unshaped cap are basically the same as for a triplet (see below). The bottom of the cap must be flattened and cleaned before gluing. While it is traditional that this cap be made of optical quality quartz, it is acceptable to use lab grown quartz, or even plate glass. Once the glue has set, shape the quartz creating a medium to high dome. Make sure the edge of the quartz has some thickness above the surface of the opal. Shape can be oval or freeform. Again, leave the quartz cap just a bit wider than the opal to prevent chipping (see instructions for triplets in this chapter).

The advantage (or disadvantage) of this form of doublet is that it does not change the base color of the stone because there is no dark background.

TRIPLETS

Triplets consist of three layers; a dark (or darkened) base, a layer of precious opal, and a clear top (see Figure 11-1, C). Triplets intensify and magnify the color pattern of the opal. They produce a very strong stone as well. Triplets can use pieces of opal that are even too thin to make into doublets. Because they produce stones of superior beauty and strength, and because they use much less precious opal per finished stone, they have taken over a large portion of the commercial market from doublets. The disadvantage of triplets is their tendency for the glue holding the layers together to separate, producing an opaque spot in the stone which the quartz cap unfortunately magnifies. In addition, some people feel the effect of the quartz cap and the dark background makes the opal appear artificial.

For years opal triplets were produced in huge volume in Coober Pedy, Australia. These stones used low quality white rough. The result was a moderately bright stone with a distinctively gray base color. These triplets were then set into cheap jewelry and sold to the tourist trade. This has given triplets a bad reputation. However, if you get a chance to see some of the triplets produced from the opal found in Spencer, Idaho, your opinion of triplets will change dramatically. These stones show rich red multicolor fire on a dark background. In short, they look as good as the top black opals from Lightning Ridge. So do not think of triplets as junk. Cut one using good quality opal and you will be amazed at the beauty you have brought out of the stone. Cutting such a triplet may be the closest you or I will ever come to cutting or owning a magnificent black opal. And such a stone can be cut from quite inexpensive material, if you are lucky and careful.

To cut a triplet, all you need is a thin line of fire. The commercial triplet manufacturers in Australia produce thin layers of opal with a multi–blade saw which cuts the opal into slides so thin that there are 50 slices to the inch. This gives you an idea of how thin a piece of opal you can use. You can produce the same effect from inexpensive opal with a good line of fire.

Instructions. The following is an explanation of how to cut a triplet from an opal with a thin line of color surrounded by potch. Such stones are found in the low cost material coming out of Australia. They are also found in abundance in the outstanding opal from Spencer, Idaho. What you are looking for is a line of fire that is straight so that a large flat area can be produced. It is also advantageous if the fire layer is clear opal. If it is white base opal, the finished triplet will have a grayish cast to it. An advantage of the Spencer material is that it forms in thin, flat layers of crystal opal surrounded by white potch which must be removed as the stone is flattened for best results. Alternatively, thin pieces of opal with full color can be used to cut triplets. Wherever the source, the cutting procedure is the same.

The first five steps are identical to those for producing doublets. They are briefly repeated here. See the full explanation in the section on doublets.

STEP ONE: Orienting the Stone. Orient the stone by deciding which face should be the top.

STEP TWO: Flattening the Opal. Grind the bottom of the opal flat with a 220 grit lap, making sure to remove all the potch and imperfections. Leave the potch on the top of the opal.

STEP THREE: Flattening the Backing. Grind the black backing flat.

STEP FOUR: Painting the Back of the Opal Slice. Paint the back of the opal flat black.

STEP FIVE: Gluing the Opal to the Backing. Glue the opal to the backing with epoxy. Use heat as in the doublet instructions (see CP-21).

STEP SIX: Exposing the Fire. After the glue has set for a day or two, grind down the top potch layer with a flat lap (220). It may be advantageous to dop the opal to give you more control of the stone as you grind. The top of the stone must be parallel to the bottom like a very thin agate slab. You must grind into the fire line of opal, removing all potch. An even pressure is needed to prevent grinding the opal at an angle to the base. You will find that the deeper you grind, the darker the opal will appear. Leaving a thin line of opal is fine. Just be sure you don't go too far and grind it all away. A paper thin layer of opal can be sufficient to produce a beautiful stone, but grinding a stone that thin can be tricky and you may lose some of the color. Stop cutting when the opal looks good. Dry the surface and keep it free of dirt and oil (see CP-22).

STEP SEVEN: Flattening the Quartz Cap. Select a clears material for the top layer. Optical quartz is the most common choice, but synthetic spinel, glass and other materials are often used. Grind a flat surface on the clear material with a flat lap.

STEP EIGHT: Gluing the Opal to the Cap. Glue the clear cap to the top of the opal using Epoxy 330. Heat the stone as described above. Move the top in a circular fashion while putting modest pressure on it to remove excess glue and air bubbles. It may also be helpful to avoid air bubbles if you mix the epoxy gently so as to reduce the number of air bubbles in it. I also find it advantageous to coat both the quartz and the opal with glue. A thick layer of glue allows me to get air bubbles out more easily. But be sure you leave only a thin layer of glue. The series of photographs show how to roll the opal onto the cap material to help prevent trapping air bubbles. Allow the glue to set for 3 to 4 days (see CP-23).

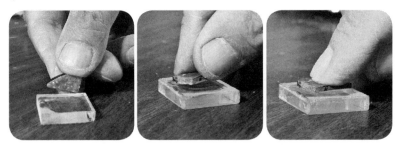

STEP NINE: Shaping the Stone. Decide on the shape of your finished stone. Inspect the stone carefully to determine the existence of imperfections such as air bubbles. Standard shapes and freeforms are perfectly acceptable.

STEP TEN: Shaping the Dome. Cut down the quartz top to the thickness desired. A medium dome is preferred to a high dome as the finished stone looks more natural. Adjusting the thickness can be done by sawing or by grinding (see CP-24 and CP-25).

STEP ELEVEN: Finishing the Cap. Cut the top into a natural dome shape such as is shown in Figure 11-1, C. A low dome is acceptable, but it will reduce the magnifying effect of the cap. A high dome produces an artificial looking stone. Don't allow the stone to heat up as the glue might separate. Leave a good shoulder on the cap itself. Do not use the opal as part of the shoulder (see accompanying photo).

Triplet Dome

STEP TWELVE: Finishing the Back. Bevel the back at approximately 30 degrees so that the quartz cap is the widest part of the finished stone. The opal line should be below the widest part of the cap, but not so far down that a ring of clear material is seen from above. Bevel the bottom edge as you do all stones to prevent chipping when the triplet is set.

You now have a completed triplet (see CP-26). Do not soak it in solvent to remove wax or unwanted glue, as this could cause the layers to separate. If needed, place a small amount of solvent on the affected spot and wipe it off as soon as it has done its job. Then flush the triplet in water to remove all the solvent.

Pre-cut Quartz Caps. In the above I have assumed that you are making your own caps. There is another alternative. Caps are commercially available. They are polished on the top and lapped on the bottom. They are usually made of glass, as they are cheaper than optical quartz. They come in standard shapes only. Alternatively, purchase pre-cut calibrated oval caps. Charlie Smith (see **Teton Gems** in the Source Directory) also carries basenite for the backing and rough Spencer opal.

To use these caps, do Steps One through Seven as above. Next decide which area(s) of the opal will be used to make a triplet. This can be done by wetting the opal, placing caps of different sizes on the opal one at a time, and moving them around until a size and location for each cap is chosen. Dry off the opal and the caps to be used. Don't get finger prints on the surfaces to be glued. Glue as in Step Eight. After the glue is set, trim the excess opal from around the caps with a saw. Finally, shape the back as in Step Twelve. Be careful not to cut into the cap and change its shape, and don't forget to leave the cap a little larger than the opal.

Chapter 12

Rough Opal Sources

The opal you are likely to encounter when buying rough will probably come from one of several areas in Australia, or from Mexico. There are many other locations where opal is found, some of which produce cutting materials which you might wish to work. Such materials are harder to acquire. In this chapter I will briefly describe the most common types of opal found in each of the main locations. Tips for better cutting of each type of rough will be offered.

Opal mining in Australia has hit hard times. There is far less opal coming out of the ground than when I wrote *Opal Cutting Made Easy* in the 80s. Coober Pedy is still producing, but the output is way below earlier years. The other major sources of opal…Andamooka, Mintabie and Lambina…are producing very little, as is Lightning Ridge.

However, this does not mean that there is no opal for you to cut. Several opal dealers have rough available in the United States and Australia (see SOURCE DIRECTORY). Much of it is old stock from the boom years of the 1980s, so you can still find rough that is worth cutting at a reasonable price (although, unfortunately, not as inexpensive as it was back then). Consult Chapter 13 before buying any opal rough.

COOBER PEDY, AUSTRALIA

Coober Pedy has been the largest producer of precious opal in the world for years. Located in the desert about 470 miles northwest of Adelaide, Coober Pedy is the town you have read about and seen on television where people live in underground homes which keep them cool in the extreme summer heat. Stories abound of armed miners, midnight claim jumping, and the rugged life of an old western town. While modern conveniences have arrived in Coober Pedy, it is still a frontier town; if a bit touristy.

Coober Pedy produces most of the white opal you are familiar with. This material comes in all grades from very poor rough with almost no precious opal, to very valuable stones with bright color but still retaining a general white background color. In addition, the area produces a material with a gray base color. Often the color is very light gray, but on occasion it shades into darker gray and even occasionally into black, but this is quite rare. The area also produces a clear opal with no base color which is called crystal opal when there is a play of color and jelly opal when it is only an opalescent blue with no flecks of fire.

The white base opal you started on is probably from this area. The techniques you have already learned work well for most of the rough from this field (see CP-27).

MINTABIE, AUSTRALIA

Mintabie (Mintubi) is a more recent find, about 250 miles north of Coober Pedy. It was discovered in the 1920s, but in 1976 an area was uncovered where large quantities of gray base and black opal were found. When first discovered, this dark gray material was sold at very low prices. As more and more superior gray and black opals were cut from this material, the miners began to wise up. Mintabie also produces some outstanding crystal and semi-crystal opal. The rough pictured in CP-28 and the stone on the cover come from a fantastic find of crystal opal. At the moment, there is no active mining in Mintabie. Some rough is still on the market but it is getting rarer and more expensive by the day. The prices of almost any gray/black rough from Mintabie have increased and are well above the prices for comparable quality white based material from Coober Pedy. This dark based material came primarily from the first ridge area. Cutting of the black based opals will be discussed in Chapter 16.

Facing Problems. Some rough from Mintabie looks great on the thin exposed edge, but shows little color when the seam is exposed. Test for this facing problem before buying or cutting the rough. To do this, look at the line(s) of color from the edge under good overhead light. Now turn the edge away from you and observe the fire as you do. Does it stay bright, get brighter, or get very dull? If it gets dull or disappears before you lose sight of the edge as you turn the stone, it may not show color when faced. Perform this test from several angles, turn the stone over and perform the test again. If the fire consistently gets dull, the stone almost certainly will not face. In this case, you have two choices: don't buy the opal, or if you do, cut the opal on edge to take advantage of the brightest color.

Swirling Lines Of Fire. The bending and swirling lines of fire found in some Mintabie rough require some special attention (see CP-29). Imagination is the key for this rough. Look for areas where the natural rounded shape of the fire line can be used to produce an effective shape for a cut stone. The line must curve like the dome of a cabochon and face well when observed from the rounded side of the fire line. This may require that the piece of rough be cut into several smaller cabs. Alternatively, the swirl can be used as part of the pattern of the stone, perhaps producing a picture stone.

LAMBINA, AUSTRALIA

Lambina is another area near Mintabie that has been producing a fair amount of opal. Most of this material is in thin seams of crystal or semi-crystal opal with full color. It will cut solids or doublets, depending on thickness. Because of its full color, crystal rough is more expensive than the Coober Pedy potch and color. Lambina orients and cuts easily.

LIGHTNING RIDGE, AUSTRALIA

Lightning Ridge, nestled in northern New South Wales, is the site of the most valued opal in the world. This is where most of the famous natural black opal is found. Black opal is usually found in small round stones called *nobbies* (see CP-30). These stones have a black or gray potch and, if the miner is lucky, some precious opal. It used to be that all nobbies with promise were cut on the field. Recently, rough has been available, even though the total output of rough from Lightning Ridge has dwindled to near nothing. Even now, however, the best pieces are cut for the miner, especially any potential red on black stone. This is because the finished stones are of such value that a miner does not want to take a chance of letting several thousand dollars worth of opal slip through his hands because he did not cut one stone. Much of the material from Lightning Ridge is crystal or gray base…not true black. Still there may be blacks hidden inside.

Discussion of cutting black nobbies is found in Chapter 16. If you have gray or crystal nobbies you can follow these same instructions.

ANDAMOOKA, AUSTRALIA

Andamooka is almost due north of Adelaide and southeast of Coober Pedy. This area is famous for its blue-green fire stones in a crystal base. It is claimed by Andamooka dealers and miners that, because of the way it was formed, this opal will not crack or craze as some opals from other sources do. However, I know of material from this source that has crazed.

While the blue-green crystal opal is the most common material found in Andamooka, there are many other types of rough found. This is the home of the famous *painted ladies,* a variety of boulder opal with a thin layer of opal on cream colored quartzite. It acquired its name because people often painted scenes on the opal to enhance (?) its beauty. Some of this material may be cut or carved with the line of opal on the face with the quartzite producing a natural backing. It is tough and holds up well.

Andamooka is also the only source of a treatable matrix opal…a porous white matrix opal which can be treated (dyed) with sulfuric acid and sugar to make it look similar to a natural black opal (see Chapter 21). Another type of matrix opal has a honey base color. This matrix will not take the dyeing treatment but will sometimes cut good bright stones. Treat the honey based pieces as you would any solid opal. You may not be able to obtain a bright polish because the surface of matrix opal is porous.

The output of the Andamooka area is limited now and the opal sells at a higher price because of its claimed superiority. Once cut, however, it is impossible to distinguish from opal produced from other fields.

Rough Opal Sources

QUEENSLAND, AUSTRALIA

The typical Queensland boulder opal consists of thin layers or seams of opal formed in a massive dark brown ironstone. As it is mined, it often breaks on the opal seams because they are more fragile than the ironstone. The opal can produce some magnificent natural boulder-black gems. This is because the opal is usually clear and a dark thin line of potch has formed between the fire and the ironstone which gives it a natural black background. Some pieces make excellent displays. While most of the opal is of the clear or crystal type, it is sometimes found in white and, rarely, in a honey or caramel color.

Special cutting instructions for this seam type boulder opal can be found in Chapter 17.

Another type of boulder opal from Queensland consists of small specks of opal spread throughout the ironstone. This is called boulder matrix, or often Mainside matrix because it is found near the Mainside Station southwest of Winton.

A very special type of boulder matrix is found in an area called Yowah and now in Koroit (see SOURCE DIRECTORY). Formed in small ironstone nodules, this opal is famous for the swirling lines of fire mixed through it. Very interesting stones can be cut from this material. Special cutting instructions are also contained in Chapter 17.

Boulder opal is very difficult and expensive to mine. Once mined, it is expensive to ship. Consequently, there is little boulder rough imported to the United States. Most of what is now available is old stock that dealers have had for years. Recently a steady supply of material has been available from Koroit.

MEXICO

Queratero, Mexico is about 160 miles northwest of Mexico City. This area produces the orange base clear opal you are most likely to be familiar with. The opal is formed in pockets within rhyolite. It is mined by blasting the rock apart and then breaking up the pieces to expose the opal. Consequently, much of the opal is cracked. Also, this material has a tendency to craze after it has been cut. I cut a great deal of

Mexican opal over a two-year period in the late 1960s. My experience is that it always looks better in the rough than in its finished form. It cracks easily while cutting, and often cracks or turns milky several months after it has been cut. On the other hand, it can produce an outstanding gem which is totally different from the Australian opal. And, in its clear form, it can be faceted to produce a truly unique and beautiful jewel.

BRAZIL

Brazil has been producing some excellent opal over the past twenty years. Until recently, however, there had been very little reaching the United States because of financial problems at the mines and export restrictions. There is more activity now, so more material is available. The opal is usually of the clear or crystal type, but white and gray bases are also found. It is harder than Australian opal and can be as beautiful. However, because of the way it was formed, it is more difficult to orient and cut properly.

When cutting Brazilian rough, you must pay particular attention to orientation. Most stones face best when the stone is cut on an angle of about 15 degrees away from the fire lines. Each stone will differ, so play with the orientation carefully as you face the stone and decide on the shape.

HONDURAS

Honduras produces a black matrix opal which hit the American market in force some years ago. It is very lightweight and quite soft. Usually it does not take a polish, but cutters have developed ways to produce an acceptable sheen. The general technique is to shape and sand the stone through fine sanding as you would any other opal. Then clean and dry the stone fully. It is then soaked in Opticon™, a two-part polymer crack sealer. Once the cab has been removed and the Opticon™ has cured, the surface will be fine-sanded and polished. While it can produce some interesting stones, it is not gem quality opal. This material should be called *matrix opal* not *black opal* because the dark look comes from the basalt matrix, not the opal (see *Opal*

Identification & Value). There is also a crystal opal produced in this area, but it is very uncommon and often quite prone to cracking. Some dealers still carry the matrix material. It is a fun stone for hobby cutting if worked as I suggested here.

VIRGIN VALLEY, NEVADA

Virgin Valley, Nevada, about 300 miles northeast of Reno, produces some of the most beautiful black and crystal opal in the world. The opal is usually a replacement of wood. Unfortunately, most of this opal is an unstable material which cracks when exposed to the atmosphere. Once mined, this opal is stored in water to prevent cracking. Numerous attempts have been made to stabilize this opal, but with little success. There is some material available which has been stabilized to strengthen the wood still found associated with the opal. Called *conch*, this material may be cut and polished because the opal represents small pieces in the wood so, even if it cracks, the whole stone remains intact. Small pieces of cutable Nevada opal are sometimes available. These are from mine material that has been allowed to dry. Once it has dried and cracked, the remaining solid pieces are stable. Pieces which have not cracked during drying will not crack further when cut. Generally, however, Nevada material is strictly for specimens. The main problem is that once people see a specimen bottle containing some outstanding black opal which costs $100 to $200, they get spoiled. Remember, if this material were cutable it would cost $1,000 per carat or more (see SOURCE DIRECTORY).

SPENCER, IDAHO

Spencer, located in the southeastern corner of Idaho, produces opal which is formed in a tough parent rhyolite rock. It takes a lot of hard work and the help of a hammer and pry bar to remove the opal, as many who have visited the fee mines will tell you. Your reward can be some excellent material. While some solid opals can be cut from this rough, it is mostly used for triplets. This is because it is usually formed in very thin layers of precious opal in white potch. Some of the opal is cracked. But when the cracks are sealed and a triplet is completed, it can be the rival of the best gem quality triplet Australia produces (see CP-31). This material is not commonly available at shows, but there are occasional exceptions (see SOURCE DIRECTORY).

LOUISIANA MATRIX OPAL

An opal and quartz matrix found in Louisiana appeared on the market in the late 1980s. It is not generally available now, but you might run into an old piece. Cutting this opal requires special care. It is especially heat sensitive. The opal separates from the quartz, leaving a pitted area. Use plenty of water. The opal undercuts. This causes the surface to be uneven and look somewhat dull. Finally, the color in this matrix opal shows better when dry. Orient the stone dry, cut it wet, and dry it again. Keep it away from oil as it absorbs the oil and reduces the visible fire. Louisiana matrix opal is interesting and a challenge to cut. You can produce some unusual stones.

ETHIOPIAN OPAL

Ethiopian opal is starting to make its mark in this country. Some rough is available. Typically it is orange crystal opal associated with a rhyolite parent rock like a thunder egg. To cut the opal, it is usually best to grind away the rhyolite, then inspect the stone for cracks. In my experience, much of this opal is unstable, cracking days to months after being cut. However, the miner claims that the new material now coming out of the mine is very stable (see SOURCE DIRECTORY). Let's hope so, as this is some of the most beautiful opal in the world (see CP-32).

OTHER LOCATIONS

Other locations contain opal but not in sufficient quantities to find them regularly in dealer stocks. They include active mines in California, Arizona and British Columbia.

The blue-base opal, originally found in the **Jay-R Mine** south of Tucson, has now been found in several locations from Idaho to Mexico. There is some of this material on the market. It is cut like Coober Pedy white base.

Rough Opal Sources

Oregon produces a clear opal, some with *contra luz* fire. Contra luz literally means "against the light." In these stones the fire appears only (or primarily) when the light is transmitted from the back of the stone. It can be faceted and/or carved. Some unique stones have been produced from it. Use the same techniques as outlined for Mexican opal.

A new find in British Columbia, called *Okanagan Opal,* is similar in look to Mexican opal. Found in seams and vugs, it should be cut like Mexican. For a discussion of this new find, see my articles in the February 1993 issue of *Lapidary Journal* and October 1994 issue of *Rock & Gem.* To date this material has not been sold in the rough.

The general guidelines offered here will work for any opal found throughout the world. Just use your head and let the opal tell you its secrets.

SYNTHETIC OPAL

Synthetic or man-made opal is available for cutting. There are two types.

Gilson opal once looked very unnatural, but recent changes in process have produced a beautiful stone that rivals the best black opal. It is still a little too perfect and regular for my taste, but it is a relatively inexpensive way to cut a stunning stone. Rough is available from several sources (see SOURCE DIRECTORY). It cuts like natural crystal opal. Be careful on the orientation as the side patterns are a bit artificial looking.

There is another synthetic (a *simulant* really,) that is quite a bit different (see *Opal Identification & Value*). While it starts as lab grown opal, it is impregnated with polymers to prevent cracking. It is softer than natural opal. The pattern is very consistent with small patches of flash fire when viewed from the top. From the side it looks like needles of fire. The bottom has a broad, very directional, flash fire. All in all it has a quite unnatural look to me, but people seem to like it. It is used extensively in silver inlay jewelry. While most of the material you see is white, it comes in dozens of base colors, including black, green and pink (see SOURCE DIRECTORY and CP-33 and CP-34).

Cutting this material is easy. First, be aware that it can produce potentially dangerous fumes. Make sure you cut it wet. Second, be careful not to expose too much of the side pattern. Keep to a low to medium dome. Third, this material is soft, so it works faster than natural opal. Be gentle.

Chapter 13

How to Buy Rough Opal

There are many fascinating aspects of the opal hobby, but probably none quite as enjoyable as the process of buying opal to cut. Rough opal is full of promise. Trying to determine which material has the most promise for the money is as much of a challenge as is fulfilling that promise in the cutting process.

Judging the potential in the rough cannot be done without seeing the material. You should not purchase without seeing the stones or, if ordering by mail or online, having the right to return unaltered opal for a full refund (less shipping) if you are not satisfied. The best situation for an opal buyer is to have several opal dealers from which to select material. Such a situation is most likely to occur at a large gem show. This allows you to compare material and prices among dealers. If you are not able to do such comparison shopping, you still can exercise good judgment and obtain the best possible buy. There are some basic rules which you can use to make the outcome more certain. This chapter is designed to teach you those rules.

GRADES OF OPAL

You may hear dealers use various terms such as "gem grade", "top commercial" and "mine run" to designate the quality of rough material. This may lead you to believe that there are some fixed standards for various grades of opal. In fact, there are not. One dealer will call a given opal *mine run*, implying low quality, while another may call it *commercial*, implying that the same stone is good enough to be set in 14kt jewelry. Thus, it is not possible to know from a written or verbal description, or from a photo on the web, the true quality of the rough being described. I have attempted to produce some standardization of terminology and grading in *Opal Identification & Value*, but not all dealers follow it yet.

121

Price is not necessarily an indication of value. Different dealers may charge quite different prices for the same quality of material.

Given a lack of standards for quality, you might find a reputable dealer and rely on his or her judgment. But how do you determine who you can trust? Clearly, there is no substitute for forming your own independent judgment.

I have included a list of dealers in the SOURCE DIRECTORY. They are people I know and trust, but they are by no means the only ones , and new dealers arrive on the scene frequently. Do your own homework.

To help understand what you are likely to find when starting to look for opal to buy, let me tell you a bit about the rough opal business. Opal is never sold without grading. Therefore, when you purchase *mine run* opal it is not ungraded material as it is found in the mine. It is, in fact, the lower quality opal that is left after the grader has removed what he believes to be the valuable opal.

Typically rough opal has passed through several hands before it reaches you. Some dealers claim that they get the opal direct from the mines. That may be true, but it does not guarantee a low price. Judge the opal on *its* merits, not the quality of the dealer's story. Opal grading is very imprecise, so you may well find a real winner in low priced material (and unfortunately an occasional dud in high priced material).

Judging Quality. Opal is a stone of surprises. Your task in judging rough opal is to find the positive surprises and avoid the negative ones. Positive surprises…finding a stone of high quality in low priced material… are common enough to keep your hopes alive. Learning to find the surprises will increase their probability and your enjoyment in cutting.

There are many dimensions which determine the quality of rough opal. They are by no means easy to describe in writing, but I will summarize them here. Full discussion can be found in my book *Opal Identification & Value.*

Here is a summary of the characteristics you should consider:

Brightness of the Stone. The brighter the play of color (fire) in the stone, the better!

How to Buy Rough Opal

Base Color. While this is a matter of personal preference, generally black base color is most valued, followed by crystal, semi-crystal, then gray and white.

Fire Pattern. Again a matter of preference, but *harlequin* (a term often misused) is very rare and most valued with *flashfire* and *pinfire* less preferred, in that order. Generally a pattern that shows large chunks of fire closely intertwined…called *flashfire*…is most common. Dealers have a tendency to invent names for patterns to make their opal seem special. To become knowledgeable about all relevant opal characteristics, rely on *Opal Identification & Value*. It offers the most universally accepted terminology and will help you sort the reality from the hype.

Color of Fire. Also a matter of preference, but in the United States red is usually preferred. Multicolor (several colors of fire in the same stone) is more preferred than single color stones.

Size and Shape. Larger stones are more valuable as are stones which will cut high dome solid gems.

Orientation of Color. Stones that show their best color in an orientation which allows you to cut larger stones are most preferred.

Cracks. They are an inevitable part of any rough opal. Badly cracked opal should be avoided if possible.

DEALING WITH DEALERS

Your goal when buying rough is to find the best possible combination of quality and price. To do so you must exercise your own judgment. As I stated, there are no fixed standards in judging quality. Furthermore, opal dealers, like other retailers, range in their competence, and pricing. In this section I will suggest how you might proceed to select your rough from one or more dealers at a show. At this point you should be aware, if you are not already, that I was an opal dealer. I attended shows regularly, sold a lot of rough, and observed many buyers and other dealers. I bought rough in volume regularly. You might consider this section as insider's tips. I have found that most opal dealers are very nice people who love the gem and the people who cut it. They will treat you fairly and help you as much as possible. Still, each dealer has different sources for his/her opal. They also have some materials that are better buys than others. It pays to shop around.

Buying At Shows. Selecting rough to consider buying is an enjoyable process, or it should be. You arrive at the show with great expectations, pay your entry fee, and are pleasantly surprised to find two opal specialists and several other dealers who might have some opal. Now the process of selecting opal I am going to suggest to you will work great. Be aware, however, it will drive some dealers nuts as you move back and forth between them. Recognize that they are trying to make a living so they are under some stress. Be open about what you are doing, but stick to your plan. Don't be swayed by statements that "this rough will go fast" so you should buy immediately. In most cases, the dealer had that same rough for sale at last week's show and the one the week before. There are cases where something becomes available and will move quickly…but these are few. With more experience in buying and cutting you will recognize these special deals yourself. Remember, this process should be enjoyed so relax and have fun!

STEP ONE: Pre-screening. What do you do? First, get out the pad and pencil you brought with you to take notes. Approach each dealer in succession and look over the opal displayed. Get a general idea of the range of quality and prices as well as the types of opal a dealer has. If you are seeking a certain grade or quality, look for this in particular. If you do not see it, ask the dealer. Often dealers do not display all the material they have with them. This is especially true if you are looking for higher quality. Make notes of particular parcels (bottles, bags, or trays) which are most appealing. Having obtained a general impression of the material available from this dealer, move on to the next. *Never* buy from a dealer without looking at all the available merchandise at the show. Once you have visited all the dealers, find someplace to sit down, have a cup of coffee and look through your notes. At this point you may be able to narrow your choice of dealers and stock somewhat, based on quality, price and type of material you seek.

STEP TWO: Careful Inspection. The next step is a more intensive investigation of particular rough and provisional selection of particular parcels. Go back to each dealer who had material of interest and look through the full range of opal of the type and quality you find interesting. Examine the parcels and select the few that you find most interesting. Study each carefully, judging the full range of quality indicators we have listed. Once you have narrowed your choices, if the opal is in a bottle, ask the dealer if he would open any bottles you are interested in. The dealer should be willing to allow an inspection and will probably open one bottle at a time. Do not open the bottles yourself unless the dealer gives you permission. If the material is in a tray or bag, ask to see it up close.

There are two main purposes of looking at the rough out of the bottle. The first is to get a better idea of size and brightness. Bottles magnify size and intensify brightness. The second reason is to determine if the material is excessively cracked. This requires that the material be dry. During this intense looking process, the dealer will probably be talking to you. Ask questions and listen carefully to answers, but do not accept what the dealer tells you uncritically. At this point there might be some discussion of price.

You need to know the price of the rough in dollars per gram. If you have all prices on the same basis they are readily comparable between dealers. If the opal is in a bottle, it should have a weight clearly marked. A weight in ounces creates a bit of an issue. Is the ounce U.S. based (Avoirdupois) or Australian based (Troy)? The U.S. ounce is 28 grams and the Australian one is 31 grams. Ask the dealer which he uses. If the bottle has no weight, ask the dealer to weigh it.

Now get out your calculator and determine the cost per gram. A bottle costing $100 that contains a U.S. ounce costs $3.57 per gram (100/28). However if the ounce is Australian the cost is $3.22 per gram. Now you can compare on equal terms between dealers.

You now have about as much information on quality as can be obtained and a general idea of price. Make notes on quality and price before going on to the next dealer.

STEP THREE: The Final Decision. After you have carefully screened the most interesting material from the various dealers, sit down again and think things through carefully. You may have a specific budget. Figure out what you can afford to buy. Are you better off with more lower quality material or fewer high quality stones? Are there some choices which stand out in your mind as particularly good value? If so, they should be the ones you concentrate on in your third trip to the dealers.

STEP FOUR: Making Your Choice. Having narrowed your choices, you should be prepared to buy. If you are like me, you will want to take home much more opal than you can afford. If there is something in particular that is bothering you, talk it over with the dealer. Take someone else's recommendation only if you have confidence in them.

Never buy opal if it goes against your instinct. Your best guide is your own judgment.

> **Never buy any rough that is stored in oil.
> The oil can hide cracks in the opal.**

Prices. During this third trip you are ready to buy. While you have been gathering information on quality, you have also gathered information on price. Here is one way to get a good idea of whether the price is reasonable. The yield of finished cut opal is from 1 to 2 carats per gram, depending upon the economy with which the rough can be cut and whether you intend to cut standard sizes with consequent lower yields or freeform stones with higher yields. Determine the cost per gram for the rough. At a yield of one carat per gram, this is also the cost per carat of the finished gem. Convenient isn't it. If a stone costs you $50 per gram, you should be able to buy an equivalent cut stone for that price per carat or higher since you add value to the opal when you cut it properly. If you could buy equivalent finished stones for less than $50 per carat, the rough is probably too expensive. Of course, you would like to buy it for less and this is often possible. Allow some room for error in judgment, however, as values and qualities are not always that easy to determine.

Another point must be made about price. Each opal dealer has his own pricing policy. Some have low markups and stick to the prices they list. Others have very high markups and bargain with the buyer. And then, of course, there is the odd dealer who has high prices and sticks to them. You will hear him tell you how superior his material is, but by now you should know if it is just overpriced and, if so, you pass him by.

> **Generally the price per gram is equal to the cost of the cut stone per carat.**

Do not be misled by someone who offers you a big discount on some material. Big discounts usually mean that the material was substantially overpriced to begin with. The most important price is the final one you pay. Judge the quality versus the final price and ignore the discount and the "great deal" the dealer is offering you. No matter what this dealer tells you, it is not a great deal if you could buy the same type of material for less from another dealer.

Splitting Parcels. It is not uncommon to find one or two stones in a parcel which are of higher quality or more appealing than the rest of the lot. You may wish to purchase only those stones. Sometimes a dealer will separate a parcle, allowing you to buy just those stones. However, the norm is to not separate lots. The reason is quite simple. The dealer buys in large lots which contain substantial variations in the quality of individual stones. If he allowed purchasers to pick individual stones, all the good ones would be gone and he is left with the poorer pieces which he then cannot sell at the same price. In order to cover his costs, he has two choices. One is to charge a substantially higher price per gram for the material and allow customers to select, thus making his necessary return on the quality pieces. This is what a dealer is doing when he/she has trays of opal and allows you to select any stone you want at a specified price per gram. The other is to package the material together and sell it at a lower average price. This second option is the one most dealers prefer. If you are buying individual stones, you can expect to pay a premium over the price per gram of the whole parcle. Your task, if given this option, is to decide whether you are better off buying the whole bottle or just the stones you like best. In my experience most cutters are willing to pay the higher price for the opportunity to select only those stones they prefer.

Some dealers put their opal out in trays and allow you to pick just the stones you want. I prefer this. Being able to select increases the chances that you will get stones that work well for you. However, until you have some experience cutting, this opportunity may not be as valuable because you are not experienced enough to make the best choice. Still, selecting individual stones is great fun…so enjoy.

Wholesale. One last word on price. Every day of a show dealers are approached by several people who want to buy at wholesale prices. A very few of these people are legitimately buying for resale. If you are reselling opal and have a retail license and a tax number, you are a dealer and can seek a dealer discount. If you sell an occasional ring or pendant to a neighbor, or if you run a plumbing business and have a tax number, you are not. A true dealer should have his license and tax number with him to show that he is in the opal resale business and should expect to buy in volume (at least several hundred dollars) if a dealer discount is sought.

MAIL ORDER OPAL

Common Practice. You may not be able to visit a show to purchase what you seek. There are many reputable opal dealers who advertise in the gem magazines or the Internet, so you can get good deals when ordering by mail or online. There are a couple of rules which may help. Be as explicit as possible about the type, quality, and price you are interested in. Price lists are useful in giving you a general idea of the types of material a dealer has, but fancy words are not a true indication of quality. You have to order to find out. After a couple of experiences, you will learn a dealer's quality versus price. (Be aware that photos can be misleading.)

How to Buy Rough Opal

Prices are usually quoted plus shipping and handling. Each dealer has different return rules, so check *before* you buy. The general rule is as follows: If you receive the opal and do not like it, you can send it back *provided* you have not altered it in any way. You will be refunded your full purchase price, but not the postage and handling charge. And you must pay the return postage. Wrap the opal carefully and return it via the same method you received it. (If you add the small cost of a return receipt you will have proof of return.) Remember, you have still bought it until it is received by the dealer. You may get two or more parcels in a shipment. In this case, the general rule is that you can select individual parcels, but not individual stones unless told by the dealer that you can do so. You should expect a reasonably quick response to your order as well as a quick response to your refund request. If you have unreasonable delays with a dealer, write or call him. By the same token, you should keep the material for as brief a period as possible so that any you return can be placed back in the dealer's stock—2 or 3 days should be sufficient.

Direct From Australia. It seems logical to expect that you can get a better deal by ordering directly from Australia. After all, that is the source of the material, so you reason that you ought to avoid some middlemen and save money. Your reasoning is absolutely correct... sometimes. Often, unfortunately, the price you pay for material "direct from the miner" is higher than the price you would pay at a local show, or from an American mail order dealer, for the same quality of material. Why is this the case? First, the large United States opal dealers may buy just as direct as some of these mail order "miners" and be able to give you better prices than the "miner" might give you. Second, the opal you get from Australia may have gone through more hands and been subject to more markups than that of an American dealer. Third, many Australians have an exaggerated idea of what hobbyists will pay for opal. Their object is to make as much as they can so they charge high prices. Fourth, it is more difficult and time-consuming to return material to Australia, so you are more likely to accept a parcel which may be priced too high. In summary, then, it might well be the case that you can get a better price from an Australian dealer, but you may not. There are a couple, like Murray Willis of **Australian Opal Mines**, that have been in business for many years (see Source Directory). They are still operating because they treat their customers fairly. Some of the material I cut for this book came from this source.

Sometimes Australians will come to the United States and travel from club to club giving talks and selling opal. Treat them like any other dealer. An Australian accent does not mean that the person is an expert, although some clearly are. We in the business had a saying that an Australian accent was worth a 25% markup in the price. Typically miners know almost nothing about how to cut opal but they love to think they do. So, if you meet a "miner" find out if he really knows how to cut by asking probing questions. Then judge his authenticity and his deal for yourself. They may be offering material at lower prices than American dealers, but they may not. Just think about who pays for their travel costs. Judge the opal on *its* merits as you would with any other dealer. If buying from Australia, stick with well-established dealers who have a spotless reputation.

SUMMARY

Buying opal is an art, not a science. And it is fun. Develop your skill at judging the quality of rough material and the competitiveness of the price. Don't be rushed into buying or misled by "deals." Rely on your judgment and instinct and remember the old adage "Buy in haste, repent in leisure" (or was that "marry," I forget!).

In the Source Directory you will find a listing of dealers for rough opal. The listing is not complete, by all means, as dealers come and go. These are just some I know that I feel will treat you fairly.

Chapter 14

The Care and Feeding of Opal

There is more misinformation on the care of opal rough and finished stones than in any other part of the opal hobby. Opal is about 6% water. The fear most people have is that it will dry out and crack. In fact, under normal usage Australian opal will not crack. Rough opal need not be kept in water until cut. Even the highest quality gem rough is shipped from Australia dry. Finished opals need not be oiled or soaked in water periodically. Some people believe that oil protects the color. Actually oil hides the cracks in a stone and *can* discolor or dull the stone over time. The best care for your opals is to wear and love them.

WHAT CAUSES WEAR

The stories I have heard about cracking fall into three groups. One is the common one of hitting the opal and having it crack. I expect that many circumstances where an opal *just cracked* are cases where people hit the opal but were unaware of it. Set properly, this problem can be virtually eliminated (see Section Five).

The second is the situation where an opal has been left in a jewelry box for several years and is cracked when it is taken out. Again, it may be that the opal was hit by other jewelry over the years. My recommendation is that you wear and love your opal. The moisture the stone gets when it is worn may prevent any problems. Do not soak an opal doublet or triplet in water.

The third source of cracked opals is the bank safe deposit box. For some inexplicable reason, safe deposit boxes are death on opals. It may be the atmosphere or a change in pressure or those sonic motion detectors. I don't know. But I have seen more cracked and ruined opals coming out of safe deposit boxes than from any other source except abuse (hitting). Avoid them if at all possible. If you do keep *unset* opals in a safe deposit box, put them in water. Set opals can be placed in plastic bags with a little moisture to help prevent damage.

There is another source of cracking which you should be aware of. Jewelry store windows and display cases use very strong lights which get very hot. So do the opals on display. After a long period of displaying, the opal may crack. I have seen numerous cracked opals in jewelry store displays.

OPALS DULLED BY WEAR

Wear can reduce the brightness of an opal. The surface of the opal becomes covered with small scratches and pits caused by coming in contact with harder objects. In addition, detergent tends to dry the surface and make it opaque. Scratches and detergent reduce the amount of light which can enter and return from the opal, reducing the brightness. This is most common in rings. A properly set opal can reduce scratching by making it more difficult for objects to come in contact with the opal. Removing rings before washing your hands helps reduce exposure to detergents.

If an opal does become scratched and opaque, it can usually be saved. Using fine sand paper, with the opal still set, sand the surface of the opal. Do not sand the prongs of the setting. Then re-polish the opal with diamond on a flexible leather disc or a muslin buff, making sure the stone does not get hot. You may not be able to remove the deep scratches, but you will be surprised how much better the opal looks. Be careful that the setting does not grab the polishing disc and go flying. This process will flatten the top of the stone slightly and will not remove scratches on the sides. In order to do a complete job it is necessary to remove the stone from the mounting, something I suggest you avoid if at all possible, because there is always a chance that the opal will break as you lift a prong.

Opal is not as fragile as is commonly thought. Remember my dopping technique. A well-protected opal will last a lifetime. The secret is the setting. This will be discussed in the Section Five of this book.

Section Three

Advanced Opal Cutting Techniques

NOTE: While a lot of what I talk about in these chapters is oriented toward cutting opal, the basic ideas are often relevant to other gems. Read these chapters with the idea that the special stone (problem) sitting on your bench can be saved using one of these techniques.

Opal & Gemstone Jewelry

Color Plates

Opal with Beauty Marks

CP-35

Lightning Ridge Nobby

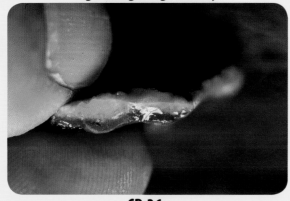

CP-36

Color Plates

Lightning Ridge Nobby Faced

CP-37

Lightning Ridge Nobby Finished

CP-38

Color Plates

Boulder Opal Rough

CP-39

Facing Boulder Color Line

CP-40

Boulder Opal Faced

CP-41

Color Plates

Boulder Opal Preformed

CP-42

Boulder Opal Finished

CP-43

Boulder Matrix from Koroit

CP-44

Color Plates

Lightning Ridge Opal Color

CP-45

Lightning Ridge Edge Exposed

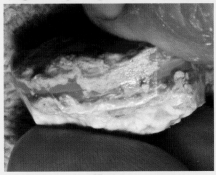

CP-46

Lightning Ridge Faced

CP-47

Lightning Ridge Fire on Black Potch

CP-48

Lightning Ridge Finished Black Opal

CP-49

Color Plates

Turkey Ridge Rough

CP-50

Turkey Ridge Lines of Fire

CP-51

Turkey Ridge Candling Inclusion

CP-52

Digging Out the Clay

CP-53

Big Piece Faced

CP-54

Turkey Ridge Finished

CP-55

Chapter 15

Loving a Gem's Unique Character

It is said that we are here to learn, so I try to learn something new every day. Yet sometimes I wonder why I have to learn the same things over again; probably because I didn't really learn the first time. Take cutting opal. I taught classes at Wild Acres in the North Carolina mountains and at my offices over the years. I started out each session by explaining to my students that opal is a unique stone and it doesn't need to be cut into standard ovals. I went to great lengths to show that freeform shapes are very attractive and save a lot of beautiful opal. My admonition always was to "let the stone tell you what it wanted to be; don't dictate to it." Sound advice which I still stick to.

One summer at Wild Acres I had a number of students who opened my mind and eyes to the true meaning of my statement. Fred came up with a stone in his hand that he just faced. In one corner there was beautiful color with a big splash of color covering most of the rest of the stone. But, in the middle of the stone there were black inclusions (called *feathers*) and some gray potch. Fred asked me what he should do. I suggested that he saw the piece, making two stones without the feathers. Fred retreated happily, but a half hour later he returned with the stone untouched. "You know," he said, "I really like the pattern of this stone the way it is. I think I'll keep it in one piece." Okay, it was his stone, so I agreed. About then my wife, Bobbi, came by. "Oh, what a neat stone," she said. "look at the pattern. It's like a forest with the sun rising above it," (she always sees scenes in the stones, or the clouds for that matter) so the forest was saved.

Later Ruth approached with a Lightning Ridge nobby she was working on. There was some nice color in it but it was quite irregular in outline. Lots of "ins and outs." If we sawed the stone to get rid of the irregular outline, each piece would be very small. We decided to work on another stone. The next day Ruth told me she decided to finish the stone in its natural shape because she hated to waste the color. It turned out beautifully.

Other students had similar experiences. In fact, such encounters are quite common, as any opal cutter knows. I used to be like Fred and Ruth but had become accustomed to cutting store type jewelry where "imperfections" like feathers, sand spots, and irregular rough shapes are not accepted. In short, I had developed a narrow-minded attitude toward what made an opal attractive and valuable. After all, such "imperfections" in the jewelry trade are severely penalized, but their market has nothing to do with the type of jewelry we wear and love.

My students tried to teach me to shed my straitjacket but only partially succeeded. It was not until I spent several days grading a large parcel of Mintabie potch and color that I finally learned the lesson; or re-learned it. Time after time I would pick up a stone to judge its potential and find a wavy pattern or some other unusual characteristic (I no longer call them imperfections)! Finally, instead of thinking that these unusual patterns ruined the stone, I began to see their beauty I then realized what I had been allowing myself to do over the last couple of years.

That started this chapter. I now look at the beauty of the whole stone as I did long ago and try to incorporate their uniqueness. I have been very pleasantly surprised to learn that a lot of people like these *character stones,* as "Willa B" calls them, proving the old adage, "By your students you are taught!"

I now use my admonition in a much broader sense. Opals can be cut with a combination of precious opal and potch showing on the top. They can also be cut from the edge. Some materials are much brighter from the edge but they show lines of color, perhaps mixed with potch. Still they make the most interesting stones (see CP-35).

In some cases the lines of color in the stone do not allow it to be cut on one line without having to make several small stones from the piece of rough. However, it may be possible to cut such stones so that a different line of color shows in each part of the surface. This may require that the top of the stone be finished as a somewhat wavy dome but the end result can be quite attractive. For example, one of the Mintabie pieces Bobbi appropriated and wears is actually three lines of color, yet nobody can tell. They are surprised when we tell them. The result is on the cover of this book…the pendant in the middle.

Recently, a cutter showed me a Lightning Ridge nobby which he was cutting like you would carve a fire agate or boulder opal. He carved away several pits, then followed the several lines of color to produce a bright stone with a highly irregular surface. It was a great idea which saved a difficult but attractive opal.

This carving of multi-lined stones has been brought to a fine art. A Lightning Ridge cutter has developed a technique for carving seam opal into elaborate irregular shapes to take advantage of all the color (see **Poor Boys Opals** in the SOURCE DIRECTORY). When approached in the traditional way, these stones would have been cut into many small ovals. Instead, they have been transformed into one beautiful work of art.

Harold, an opalholic who cuts all his stones by hand with a small Dremel® tool, showed me a brilliant red stone. It was one of the most beautiful opals I had ever sold. Finding an imperfection near the middle of the stone, he carved out the pit. It was stunning.

His sister, Dottie, wears a Lightning Ridge ring she cut by hand. It has two indentions in it but you never see them. After many trials and tribulations to convince the gold designer what she wanted, it was set with gold covering the "beauty marks". Dottie saved the stone and now people look at it without ever seeing any "imperfections," only a beautiful full color black opal. This lovely stone was completely and lovingly cut using no power tools. I could not have done better!

Over the last few years agate cutters have also begun using irregular carving to bring out patterns. The first examples of this I recall are some beautiful irregular shaped bowls that were carved in Idar-Oberstein, Germany. The fascinating patterns in the agate swirled and dipped.

Steve Walters and others brought this idea to the wearable jewelry level. They cut agate in irregular–shaped domes to expose different patterns. Teaching you to cut like Steve is not my goal here. Rather it is to get you to think about cutting in a more free-wheeling way. Who knows what you might invent.

Another great idea which I have been playing with is faceting the top of an opaque opal. The facets do not cause a reflection of light as they would on a transparent stone, but they do something else. The fire color of an opal depends upon the angle that the light enters and comes back out of the stone. So the different facets cause the stone to pick up different light. They seem to have more color. I do not use a regular pattern. In fact, since I don't own a faceting machine, I do each facet by hand. It requires a flat lap and a steady hand, but this technique produces an attractive final product. Be careful not to let the edges get too thin or sharp, as they become fragile.

There are many other possibilities for cutting a stone. Roger recently showed me a faceted opal which showed great color. Upon careful examination I found out that the opal was a thin line just below the girdle. The rest was quartz. Not only was it beautiful, but it was more serviceable than a faceted solid opal.

Everything I say about cutting opal here equally applies to other gems; integrating the imperfections into a cab can produce a unique stone.

So, loosen your straitjacket and look at each stone with an open and innovative mind. You will be able to transform an "unfortunate" or "disaster" stone into a thing of beauty.

It is also true that many stones are cut in one particular orientation. It has become traditional, for example, to cut petrified wood across the grain to show the pattern of the rings of growth. But as any woodworker knows, cutting "with" the grain can produce some uniquely beautiful patterns. Why not do the same with petrified wood?

The same is true for banded agate. Cutting across the outside edge of a rounded agate nodule can produce some unique patterns.

Chapter 16
Cutting Black Opal

Black opal is the most highly valued of all opals. To be called black, the opal must have a natural dark background produced by the opal itself, not from the matrix it is found in. (For a complete discussion of the criteria for black opal, see *Opal Identification & Value*.) There are two types of opal which produce most blacks. One is a seam type found in Mintabie and some areas near Lightning Ridge. The other, produced in various fields around Lightning Ridge, is formed as round stones called *nobbies*. Each must be cut differently.

DARK SEAM OPAL

Mintabie produced a seam opal with a black potch that oftten produced black opal. While very little rough is now coming out of Mintabie, some old stock is still available from various opal dealers. This material is fun to cut and can produce some outstanding black opals. However, not all rough containing dark potch will produce a true black opal.

To produce a true black opal, the fire line must be quite clear (crystal) and right next to the black potch. The black will then show through the crystal to produce the required dark background. If there is some lighter opal between the fire line and the black, the stone may not appear dark on its face and would not be called a black opal. Also, if the line of fire is opaque and light in color, the black may not show through and, again, it would not produce a true black.

Sometimes the fire line itself will have a black base color. If it does, it may face black even if the potch behind it is white. If it faces dark, it is called a black, even if the back of the opal is white.

Cutting Mintabie Seam Black. The Mintabie rough that is occasionally found in dealer stocks is formed in fairly thin layers. Some-

147

times the opal is relatively transparent. When it is transparent with no natural dark background, it should be cut as any other solid opal. If, however, this relatively transparent material is next to a dark layer of potch, you have a potential black or semi-black opal which is the subject of this section.

I will describe the cutting of an ideal stone. You may not be lucky enough to find such a stone, but this description should give you a start on how to approach the dark Mintabie you do find. The hypothetical piece you are going to cut has a solid layer of blue-green color sandwiched between two layers of black potch. Outside the black potch is a layer of soft whitish material that often looks and feels like hardened sand. This is the parent rock the opal is found in. Since the fire is all the way through the center of the stone (i.e., from one black layer to the other), you are very lucky. The stone may be cut so that either black potch layer can be used as the bottom. Looking at the edge of the stone from both faces as we have described in the section on orienting opals (Chapter 7) you decide that the stone will be brighter if oriented so that one side is the top.

Having decided which side will be top, you can now face the stone by grinding away the top black layer. As you get near the fire line, go slowly. You want to grind only to the point where the fire starts to show through the black enough to see any problems. It is now time to plan your stone.

Stop and dry the stone to check for cracks. These cracks are often not visible in the rough stone because the black potch hides them. You will need to cut around any cracks you find. Mark any cracks with your aluminum scribe. Next, wet the stone again and look at the color. Sometimes there are small black potch inclusions in the color layer, often called *feathers*. If they are bothersome to the pattern of the stone and can be avoided by shaping the stone, work around them, as they reduce the value of the stone. However, if these inclusions are very small or add an attractive pattern to the stone, leave them in. Sometimes these feathers are throughout the stone producing a spider web pattern. If this happens, all you can do is make the best of it.

Having decided on a shape, finish the opal as you would any other.

148

Cutting Black Opal

You can use a medium or low dome. The medium dome is unusual, however, because most material is fairly thin.

Additionally you may find that a thinner top fire layer intensifies the dark color and fire of the finished stone. This can be tested by grinding down an edge of the stone…slowly and without taking away any of the good opal…to see if the color is enhanced. If it is, grind down the top slowly. Be careful, you don't want to go too far. You especially do not want to make the stone thin and weak. Also, a thinner fire layer may cause imperfections in the back of the stone to become visible. Sneak up on the color. Grind a little and observe the color. If it gets a bit brighter, grind a little more. If not, consider stopping where you are. Low domes and relatively thin stones are common in finished Mintabie black and semi-black opals. Above all, always save some of the black potch on the back of the stone. If you grind it away you have just turned a valuable black opal into a less valuable crystal…a favorite trick of Harry Leadthumb. Remember that the back can have some sand and white spots on it. It need not be perfectly finished as the black potch is completely opaque. If all works as described here, you have just cut a beautiful black opal of high value.

Now suppose that the piece of rough contains a thin layer of color in potch. If the potch is opaque and white or gray, any black layer below it will do you no good. You may cut the stone with or without the black. It will make no difference. Treat it as you would any other potch and color stone. Note, however, that a gray potch base will intensify color and make the opal look darker. The darker the gray, the closer the finished produce will be to a natural black. If the fire line is near the black potch or if the opal between the fire line and the black potch is fairly transparent, the black can be used to advantage. If there is only one black layer, use it for the bottom unless it would produce too thin a stone or the color from this direction is very poor. The main idea is to use the black potch as a dark background.

CUTTING BLACK NOBBIES

The Lightning Ridge area produces roundish concretions of opal called *nobbies*. These nobbies can produce black opal, but often produce gray or crystal opal. Nobbies are a bit tricky to cut because they are difficult to see into. The following technique may help (see CP-36).

First, analyze the stone. Look for any fire that is showing. It is not uncommon to find that a nobby has matrix and/or white or gray potch surrounding the black opal in the center of the stone, hiding the black and the fire line. Such stones are often nipped to expose some of the black and fire. If you are lucky, the fire line is obvious, but in most cases it is not. To get a look at the fire line, *carefully* grind the sand and other junk off the surface of the nobby, all the way around the stone. It is like taking the peel off an orange. Look a lot and grind a little! As the fire line shows in one spot on the nobby, do not grind any more in that area. What you are attempting to do is produce some small "windows" in the nobby so you can judge where the line of fire goes. Once you have exposed enough of the fire line to see where it is going, **STOP!**

Now you must analyze the stone carefully. Does the fire line itself face black? If so, you are less concerned about the shade of the potch base for the stone. Test the stone to decide which side of the fire line is the top as you would any potch and color stone. Make sure that the fire line faces as dark as possible. As with Mintabie material, you may be lucky enough to find black on both sides of the color line. The nobby in CP-36 has black potch on one side of the stone and gray on the other. We will use the black as the bottom to make the finished opal as dark as possible. Choose the orientation that produces a good black gem with enough thickness for a strong stone. Never remove all the black potch from the back of the stone as this will turn a black opal into a crystal or gray opal, making it less attractive. Cut the opal with a dome no higher than the thickness of the fire line. Most nobbies produce fairly flat domed stones. It is traditional to cut nobbies with a round bottom. This adds weight, but don't allow the bottom to get too deep. Be careful to still leave a good shoulder on the stone for setting.

If the line of fire is crystal, which is more common in the lower value rough usually available, particular attention must be paid to the potch next to it. If one side is dark, that will be the bottom of the stone, unless the fire does not face well from that orientation. If both sides are gray…the most common situation in inexpensive rough…you must decide on which side to make the top by assessing the brightness of the fire and the darkness of the base. Darker is better; other things being relatively equal.

Sometimes nobbies will look gray on the outside but have a kernel of black in the center. This will be discovered as you face the stone. The black is much more valuable than the gray, so try to use the black exclusively for one stone.

Facing the nobby in CP-36 by grinding the gray potch, we find great color and a dark center patch (see CP-37). Analyzing the depth of this patch I see that a good sized stone can be made by sawing off the left side…close to the black center…and grinding down a bit at a slight angle to remove the rest of the black on top of the color. The end result is a stunning red multicolor black opal (see CP-38).

Nobbies are a real challenge. Success comes with a slow approach. You almost have to sneak up on the opal to win such a prize (see Chapter 19 for another example of cutting a nobby).

OTHER BLACKS

Some Ethiopian opal nodules have a very dark brown base color that borders on black. Likewise Virgin Valley, Nevada, blacks are really dark brown (see Source Directory). The color is so dense that it becomes black but in thin sections you can see it is brown. A cut stone from either source must be left thick so that the dense color retains its black appearance.

There are occasional blacks found in all fields. I have seen a half black/half white opalized snail replacement from Coober Pedy. If you find one of these rare stones, be sure to cut it to preserve the black.

Working Boulder Opal

Chapter 17

Cutting Boulder Opal

A fascinating opal found in Queensland, Australia is called *boulder opal*. Precious opal is formed in cracks in a brown ironstone which is usually hard, solid, and produces a natural dark background for the opal. This allows a cutter to produce natural boulder blacks although not all stones have the required dark base color. The opal is often of very high quality and is mostly the crystal type. Some of the most spectacular opals I have ever seen have come from this boulder material. I guess that there just has to be a drawback to such an ideal sounding rough, and indeed there is. The opal is usually formed in very thin and irregular shaped layers. It is not uncommon to find a paper thin layer of brilliant opal running through the ironstone. Often it will disappear, turn at right angles, or wave in and out. It is almost never straight for any distance. The problem the cutter faces is to expose this irregular surface and polish it without going through the opal.

CUTTING THIN SEAMS

Let me first discuss the general technique for exposing and finishing the opal. The ironstone cuts easily but be prepared for a real mess. As you grind and sand it, the ironstone combines with your cooling water to form a brown mud which gets onto everything. You can expect a brown face, brown hands and brown spots on your clothes. While it is a mess, the potential reward is worth it! But do change to your old clothes, as the ironstone stains and is very difficult to remove in washing.

Before you proceed with cutting a boulder opal you need to find the color line(s). This is more easily said than done. The seam may bend in unexpected ways. To get a good idea of where the seam goes, work around the stone with the 220 grinding wheel. Try to expose the edge of the fire line all the way around the boulder. This may require you to wash the mud produced off the stone so you can see what you have ground into. Once you have obtained a good idea of where the line of color goes you can start planning how to cut it.

STEP ONE: Orienting Boulder. Determine which side of the opal layer will be the top. The side you choose as the top will depend upon the shape of the opal layer and the thickness of the ironstone. The backing for the opal must be thick enough and solid enough to form a base for the stone. You will find the stone easier to work if the opal layer bows out toward the top of the stone than if it bows toward the bottom. Ideally, select as the top the face which bows toward you and which has a thick back. The boulder shown in CP-39 has a thin layer of ironstone on the top and the fire line bends toward this thin layer so that is the top of the stone. Often there is a very thin line of black potch found between the fire line and the ironstone, but not in this example. When such a line is present, leave it to darken the background just as you would in a Mintabie seam opal. In doing so you will produce a dark based boulder which is much more attractive. Such stones are called *boulder blacks.*

STEP TWO: Pre-grinding. Second, grind away the ironstone from the top of the opal to get close to the opal layer. *Do not grind into the opal.* If the ironstone is fairly thick, you may saw away the excess ironstone before grinding but don't get too close to the fire layer. Any grinding wheel (220 grit) will do for this job (see CP-40). The ironstone is removed easily so long as lots of water is used to remove the waste. If insufficient water is used, a thick mud will build on the grinding stone and it will no longer cut. The reason you must stop grinding *before* you get into the opal layer is that the deep scratches from grinding may go so far into the thin opal layer that you cannot remove them in the sanding and polishing process without removing all of the opal layer. When you complete this step you should see very little of the fire on top of the stone.

STEP THREE: Exposing the Fire. Use the coarse sanding wheel to expose the opal. Do this gradually, using lots of water to remove the ironstone waste. The object is to expose the opal while removing as little as possible. Keeping the opal very wet allows you to see how far you have gone. Stop frequently to check your progress. Keep the surface clean. If you do not use enough water the surface may remain covered with brown mud, hiding the opal. This may cause you to sand too much, thinking you have not reached the opal yet. Stop coarse sanding when most of the surface imperfections caused by the brown ironstone are removed. CP-41 shows the result of careful facing of this stone. Unfortunately a crack appeared through the blue color.

If the fire line is irregular, the face of the stone will now consist of both fire and ironstone. The fire under the ironstone can be exposed by carving the line with fine diamond wheels on a flexible shaft. Do this carefully using a wheel with a rounded edge. This prevents putting deep groves into the surface. Grind just enough to start to expose the fire. **Ameritool** produces a series of sanding wheels that are very effective at following and polishing these irregular seams. I have not done this in my example because inspection showed that the ironstone spots went through to the color line. Removing them would have just produced larger brown spots (see Photo on Page 152).

As you face the opal you want to remove as much ironstone from the face of the stone as possible. However, it is not uncommon for the line of color to become too thin to cut in some areas of the stone. In such cases some ironstone will be on the face. This is quite acceptable. Some of the best professionally cut boulders have some ironstone on the face. It cannot be helped.

STEP FOUR: Shaping. Shape the stone. It is common to find that there are areas in the opal layer in which the ironstone penetrates the opal from the bottom or the top. If the ironstone comes from the bottom through the opal, you have two choices. You can shape the stone so as to avoid the ironstone areas. Alternatively, you can incorporate the area into the finished stone as I have in CP-42. The ironstone will polish (usually to a dark, almost black, metallic shine).

STEP FIVE: Sanding and Polishing. Once the shape of the stone is determined, sand and polish the opal surface as you would any other opal starting with medium sandpaper. Leave the dome flat unless the opal layer is thick enough to dome without loss of size (a rarity). Remember that the thin opal layer is a little more sensitive to heat so don't overheat it or it might crack. Sand and polish the undulations which you cannot reach with your regular wheels using the flexible shaft. Sand the indented areas with discs of silicon carbide sand paper or with the diamond discs produced by **Ameritool**. While the rubber wheels made by **Cratex®** work, I have found them less effective. If you are using these wheels on a flex shaft, grinding and sanding can be done with the piece partially submerged in a pan of water. This keeps the opal cool and clean. Hard felt buffs work well for polishing.

STEP SIX: Finishing the Back. Grind the ironstone on the back to the final thickness of the stone—a little thicker than a solid opal back would be. Bevel the back edge because the ironstone will also crack if a prong is bent over a sharp edge.

The final product will consist of a thin, more or less flat, layer of polished opal backed by a relatively thick layer of ironstone matrix (see CP-43). The edges will be straight, relatively thick, and perpendicular to the opal on the top, with a beveled back edge and a very slight rounding of the opal on the top edge. A dome is used only when the opal layer is relatively thick, something you are not likely to find very often—not because it doesn't happen—but because most thick boulder opal is cut before it leaves Australia.

Boulder seams take a bit of extra care, but the end product is more than worth the effort.

NATURAL FACED STONES

You now know the basic technique for producing a finished boulder opal cab. There are a couple of special notes worth passing on. One is that on occasion, the ironstone cracks along the opal seam and exposes a beautiful opal pattern with a surface completely free of ironstone. When this happens, the stone may be used as it is. There is no need to polish the opal since the fracture will shine as much as any polish you could put on it. All you need to do is to shape the stone and adjust the thickness of the back (Steps 4-6). These natural faced stones have a character all their own, a sort of rugged beauty. Of course, if the opal layer is thick enough, you may prefer to flatten out and polish the surface instead. But there is no rule that says you have to.

Split Faces. Another special cutting technique is to use the natural tendency of this material to fracture along the opal layer to produce split faces. A split face is a pair of opals made out of two sides of a single opal seam. The two faces (tops) fit together perfectly because they were originally one piece which was split into two. Split faces can be cut as follows. Select a piece of boulder opal which has a moderately thick and straight opal seam. The thickness of 5 or 6 sheets of paper is probably sufficient. If this seam is in the middle of the ironstone so that enough ironstone is available on each side of the seam to make a solid stone, a split face can be made. Grind the ironstone away on the edge of the opal seam so that the layer of opal is visible and at least 5 pages thick all the way around the edge of the stone. When doing this, grind the stone to a pleasant shape.

Now comes the tricky part. What you want to do is to crack the stone along the opal layer. Place the stone on a hard surface with the opal layer perpendicular to that surface and the edge of the opal fire line on the surface. Next place a hard sharp object such as a screw driver or a knife in the middle of the opal layer so that it is pointing through the opal layer to the hard surface. Next give the screw driver a solid hit with a hammer. Don't overdo it. Make sure the opal is securely held. This will split the opal layer (if you are lucky) and expose the opal. You now have a matched pair of boulder opals called a *split face*. They will not need to be polished as they will naturally shine. As boulder opal has become more valuable, split face stones are less common. The Queensland cutters make them only when there already is a fracture line in the opal.

BOULDER MATRIX

The cutting of boulder matrix from Yowah and Koroit (see CP-44) is similar to cutting any solid opal, except for the mess. Orient the stone, then grind a face. Continue grinding the face until you have exposed a nice pattern with bright color. The stone can be shaped with a moderate dome. Polishing is just a bit tricky. The ironstone, if compact, takes a rich dark brown to black luster, but to obtain it you have to heat the surface a bit by allowing your polishing disc to be a bit dry. The friction will heat the stone. The trick is to heat it enough to polish the ironstone but not enough to crack the opal. A little practice may be needed to get the best results. If there are small pits in some of the ironstone, they can be held together by treating the stone with Opticon™ Sealer and Resin before polishing (see Chapter 22).

Boulder opal is a great form of this magnificent gemstone. All that is needed is a little care to uncover its beauty.

Chapter 18

Cutting Mexican Opal

The opal from Mexico is typically the crystal type with a light to dark orange base color. It can produce some of the most extraordinary gems you will ever see. It is also easily the most frustrating opal to work. It is softer than other opals so it is more difficult to cut without flat spots or ridges. Being a clear opal, it often looks better in the rough than when finished. Since it is mined by blasting, it is often cracked —usually in just the wrong place. But perhaps most frustrating of all, it is quite a bit more unstable than most Australian opal. I have cut many a gem only to have it crack or develop a cloud in it after a few months. Nevertheless, it is a fascinating stone to work with and it can be quite rewarding.

OPAL WITHOUT MATRIX

You will find Mexican opal in two forms in dealer stocks. The opal may be completely free of matrix or in its rhyolite matrix. First, let us discuss cutting the opal when free of matrix. Whether it is completely transparent or relatively opaque, treat it as any solid crystal opal. Orient it carefully. Cut with a high domed top and a low domed back. Do not finish the back. Stop at medium to fine sanding. Once you have finished the stone, set it aside for a year before setting it in jewelry to make sure it is stable.

Contra Luz. An interesting phenomena is found in some Mexican opal (and in opal from Oregon). This opal appears to be almost without fire when looking at it in the normal way. But when you hold it up to the light and allow the light to pass through the stone and then to your eye, intense fire becomes visible.

This type of opal is called *contra luz* meaning "against the light." It presents a unique challenge to the cutter. In order to bring some of the fire out of the stone, first orient the stone so that it shows the best color from the face of the stone with light coming through the stone. Next, cut the top to a high dome and the bottom into a medium dome. This allows some of the light entering the stone from on top to be reflected off the bottom and come back out the top again. As it exits it produces the contra luz fire. I have never been able to get the intensity of fire I see while holding a stone up to the light to show in a finished stone, but it does pick up some color when cut this way. The best use of this material is for faceting as, with careful attention to angles, a maximum return of light can be had, producing good color.

Thomas Harth Ames has developed another method of bringing out the fire which he developed while cutting Oregon opal that has a similar contra luz fire. He cuts the stone almost flat but places a bevel on the edge. When done with the correct angle, this bevel directs light into and through the stone, thus showing the contra luz fire.

OPAL IN MATRIX

Now let us turn our attention to the Mexican opal in matrix. The cutting process is quite simple. Once you have selected a piece of opal to cut, inspect the stone. Determine the play of color and the size of the opal. Try to decide if it would be better to cut the stone without matrix or with it. If the opal shows good color and appears large enough to cut as a solid opal, orient the stone and carefully grind away the matrix from the top and sides of the stone but not the bottom. As you remove the matrix, you expose more of the opal. This allows you to judge whether the stone would be better cut as a solid or in matrix. When you have removed enough material to enable you to pass light through the opal, **STOP**.

Let the opal dry and check for cracks. Next, wet the stone and check for inclusions. Sometimes the rhyolite parent rock will be mixed with the opal. If this is the case, you can either cut a smaller solid stone or a larger stone which incorporates some of the matrix. While solid stones are more valuable per carat, the larger stone may be preferred; especially if the matrix produces a nice pattern. Assuming the opal is large and free of cracks or matrix, remove the remaining matrix—not every speck but enough to see the stone fully. At this point you have created an opal free of matrix. Treat it like we discussed above.

If the opal is relatively small or cracked or interlaced with matrix, it is best to cut it with the matrix. The opal will show more color if you leave a solid backing of matrix on it, so try to cut it this way. The

Mexican Opal in Matrix

rhyolite matrix is softer than the opal. It will take somewhat of a polish but it is porous. After polishing the opal with a white powder such as tin oxide, you will need to scrub the surface to get the polish out of all the little pits in the rhyolite. Polishing with diamond works better. The matrix usually remains solid and adds strength to the stone. I find the finished product more appealing when opal covers most of the surface. A large cab with only a small area of opal is less attractive. A crack in the opal is not a problem, so long as it does not detract from the beauty of the stone, as the matrix keeps the opal together.

FACETING

Because of its transparency, clear Mexican opal, with or without fire, is sometimes faceted. Your faceting books can help you here. Not being a faceter, I am afraid I am of little help. However, remember that opal is heat sensitive. Heat can build up rapidly, especially when polishing small facets. The opal is especially prone to break when removed from the dop, so be careful. I recommend faceting if you can find appropriate material. I have seen some absolutely gorgeous faceted opals.

In general, Mexican opal is softer and more heat sensitive than other opals. Treat it with extra care to avoid cracking and flat spots.

Chapter 19

Finding the Beauty in Challenging Opals

People have asked me what is my favorite opal to cut. The answer is always a surprise to them. While I love top quality opal rough, I have consistently found more satisfaction cutting inexpensive opal. Material that shows promise, but has some serious drawbacks is a challenge. I love to make a nice stone out of rough nobody had much hope for. In fact, the highest compliment that I have received for my opal cutting was when another opal cutter told me I could get more out of a piece of junk opal than anybody he knew. I love to make a silk purse out of a sow's ear.

I hate to waste opal. It is far too beautiful and rare. Additionally, I have developed techniques for cutting stones that would otherwise be discarded or cut into small pieces. I have learned to bend the rules of cutting cabs so as to save the beauty of an opal. Sometime I even break them. Nowadays with rough opal prices up and supplies short, it is even more important to save those challenging pieces that are a part of every parcel. Here are some of the techniques I use.

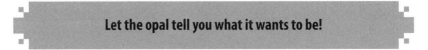

Let the opal tell you what it wants to be!

SNEAKING UP ON THE STONE

In my cutting classes, I continually advised students, "let the opal tell you what it wants to be." It will, if you look and listen to what it is saying. Now I don't mean that you actually can hear an opal talk with your ears. But as you study the stone, it will tell you: "I look better from this direction." "Look at this shape." "Aren't I bright from this unusual orientation?" "Think what I might look like if this second line of fire showed through the top line." "See this little corner, it suggests something special might be inside." It will also warn you: "I might be a heart breaker. See the sand pit." "Watch how my fire line bends and turns." "See my dark potch feathers, be careful." The challenge is to read and interpret them correctly. An open mind is the most important ingredient. Dictating to the stone what you want it to be is a sure recipe for failure, or at least less than satisfying results. Instead, listening to the stone and letting it tell you more as you work into it will lead to a more beautiful finished opal.

You will not always read the signs correctly. After more than 40 years of opal cutting, I find myself doing things that, after I have seen the result, I wished I had not done. When this happens—and it will—don't beat yourself up about it. Forgive your mistakes, but learn from them. Remember, this is supposed to be fun!

> **An open mind is the most important ingredient in successful opal cutting.**

Looking and listening involves little experiments which give you additional clues on how an opal is formed. Grind a bit then look. Then grind a bit more. This is the technique I call *sneaking up on the stone*. It's like trout fishing. If you go tromping into the middle of the stream and then look, all the trout will be scared away. Instead, a good trout fisher approaches slowly and observes as he or she goes. That's what I want you to do with your opal. Slowly unwrap the mystery of the stone by an incremental approach. Harry Leadthumb charges in and ruins the stone. Opal Lover sneaks up on the best of the stone and unwraps the beauty hidden inside.

An example. Probably the best way to show you how I sneak up on the beauty hidden inside an opal is by an actual example. So here, blow by blow, is my account of cutting a challenging opal. Each stone will be different, of course, for each stone has its own unique story to tell, but this example will explain the techniques I use.

There is no more consistently challenging rough than Lightning

Finding the Beauty in Challenging Opals

Ridge nobbies. The roundish shape and few chipped edges do not provide many clues as to how the fire layers sit in the stone. To make it tougher, most nobbies are opaque so you cannot see into them. Add the fact that some color lines and/or black may be hidden inside the stone and you have a challenging piece of rough. But with care that challenge can be met and an outstanding opal may be produced.

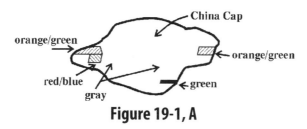

Figure 19-1, A

Let's cut one of these nobbies together. Here before us is a round-ish, somewhat flat stone with white clay covering much of the surface (see Figure 19-1, A and CP-45). Close inspection reveals some nice green fire in one area, a line of orange-green fire on an edge, and red-blue fire in one little section next to the orange-green. Turning the stone, some orange-green fire can be seen apparently continuing to the other edge of the stone. Dark gray potch is visible in a couple of places. Lots of potential and lots of mystery.

Does the orange-green go through? Is the red a line of fire that can be used? Red fire on black is very beautiful and valuable. Should we sacrifice the orange-green? Will the clay penetrate into the fire lines?

Inspection does not answer these questions, but some judicious grinding can. Let's start by grinding around the thinner edge of the nobby where no color is showing (use a 220 wheel). Grinding this edge does not remove any useful opal, as little color is taken off and the stone is too thin to use at the edge. Grind a little, look a lot. The opal cannot be replaced once it is gone (see CP-46)!

Gentle grinding reveals a great possibility. The red line lies under the orange-green line and there is dark gray potch under the red (see

Figure 19-1, B). As often happens in nobbies, above the orange-green line is a harder white clay called a china cap. Frequently, as in this case, the china cap is the top of the stone. It is also frequently true that the best color is just under this china cap. Let's hope it is in this case.

We have now ground off no more than 5% of the weight of the stone and no useful opal. But we have learned a lot. The red line goes

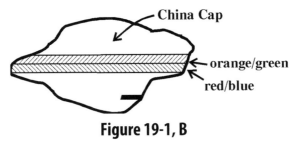

Figure 19-1, B

through the stone. The orange-green line is above it everywhere and dark gray potch is below it. There is some sand showing in the lines of fire, so we may still have a problem. In one section of the stone there is not much potch backing, so the finished stone will be smaller than what remains after this first grinding. Clearly the orange-green line just below the china cap is the top of the stone and the gray potch will help form the bottom. The other alternative would be to make a stone with the white china cap as the base. This would cause the stone to have a white base color which is far less attractive than the gray background available if we use the gray as the base.

Now that we know how we wish to approach this stone, we can grind away the china cap top and expose the fire. Careful now. Sometimes something special is hidden just under that cap so let's continue to grind a little and look a lot. I find it helpful to grind the top with a low to a medium dome. That way the color starts to show on the edges first, giving us more clues. Then as the color shows, flatten the dome to expose the fire over the entire top. Do not grind into the fire in the center of the stone. Stop when the white is thin and the color and structure are just visible. In that way you will preserve all the options instead of removing some at this stage.

Finding the Beauty in Challenging Opals

It is a challenging stone after all. The good news is that as the china cap was removed we could see that the orange-green line combines with the red line to produce some spectacular color. The bad news is that the china cap goes deeper in one section and there is a sand pit right in the middle of the best color (see Figure 19-1, C). CP-47 shows the piece with the imperfection visible in the face.

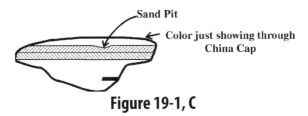

Figure 19-1, C

We are just about through the china cap, so let's grind some more off just where the china cap remains. Again we do this very carefully to remove just what we don't want (see Figure 19-1, D).

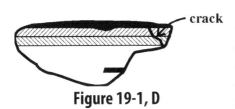

Figure 19-1, D

More good news and bad. Careful grinding removed most of the china cap and left lots of color. It also revealed a crack on the edge, right in the best red color. Grinding the edge to remove the cracked material showed (Figure 19-1, E) that the sand pit did not go as deep as we feared. However, the edge is thinner than we thought and contains sand, so we must work around this problem.

We are almost ready to establish the final shape of the stone. Before we do let's grind and pre-shape the back to see if there are sand problems or other hidden cracks we have to work around. Like the top, let's work the bottom with a low to a medium dome to gather clues and leave as much potch under the fire as possible (Figure 19-1, F).

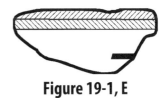

Figure 19-1, E

Figure 19-1, F

We now have another problem/opportunity. That green line we saw at the beginning opened up into a nice orange-green line of fire. We can't get two stones out of the piece because it is too thin. Perhaps we could get a double-sided stone out of it. Removing the remainder of the gray potch over the heart of the back line will not cause the stone to be too thin. So let's do that. At the same time we will remove some areas around the edges where sand is making the stone weak. As we do this, let's keep the top side firmly in mind. It would be a shame to ruin the top in hopes of getting something out of the bottom.

Well, that didn't work. The back line turned out to be far less attractive than the front and the sand spots were more extensive than it looked. To make a two sided stone, we would lose half the top. Too much beautiful opal would be lost. But we did find that the gray potch is now black and rests right next to the best color, giving us the potential for a great red on black stone (see CP-48). So we will round the bottom, leave a little of the green fire just for fun, and pre-shape the stone (Figure 19-1, G). Remember that we need at least 2 to 3mm of thickness from the top to the sand on the back to insure there is enough strength in the stone. Also we must keep in

Figure 19-1, G

mind the direction the stone looks best. The most important attribute of the finished stone is how it looks when worn. A freeform shape that is obviously best suited for a pendant is not very good use of the opal if the stone looks better as a ring.

In this case our stone looks best as a pendant. The shape that remains after having removed the thin parts of the back lends itself to a pendant. This opal was saying "pendant" all the way. We can now sand the back with the 220 (coarse) sanding wheel and dop the stone.

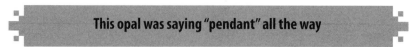
This opal was saying "pendant" all the way

As we coarse sand the top and sides of the stone, we finalize the shape. After sanding, there are two pits remaining on the top. Careful sanding with the medium grit in just those areas removes most of the pits. Fine sanding blends these areas in with the rest of the top but leaves the dome irregular. We will live with that, however, because we would go through the best fire to force the dome to be regular. Polish the top, sand the back with medium grit, and break that sharp edge between the side and the bottom with the same medium grit sanding, and we are done.

The end result is a beautiful red multicolor stone that will make a great pendant (see CP-49). To be sure, our problem child still has some difficulties. The dome is somewhat irregular. One edge is thinner than the other. The back is also somewhat irregular, has a sand area in it, and there are still two tiny pits on the top. This opal would never win a cutting competition, but you know what...once it is set, nobody will notice any of that. We have successfully found a very attractive usable opal in that challenging nobby. I'm proud of us, aren't you?

MULTIPLE BARS OF FIRE

What could be easier. A nice thick chunk of rough full of fire. You think you couldn't possibly go wrong cutting such rough. It's a no-brainer (see Figure 19-2, A). Careful! The best stone may not be obvious from casual examination. Look closely. Is the fire bar really

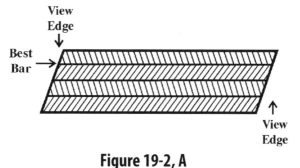

Figure 19-2, A

one line of fire or are there several bars stacked next to one another? If there are several bars, is one better than the other? Almost always, one bar is better. Even if there is only one thick bar of fire, some part of it may be brighter than another. Here is how you can get the most out of a stone with multiple bars of color.

The Best Line of Fire. Study the opal carefully. Look for differences in brightness, pattern, and color in these various bars. Remember also that the fire can look very different when viewed from the edge as compared to viewing from the top. You want to cut your stone so that the best bar of color, when viewed from the top, is on the top of the stone.

A lot of study and a little judicious grinding can help determine how best to cut such a stone. Frequently the edge fractures on most opals are at an angle to the seam. This allows you to look at the edge from the top and bottom to determine how each of the bars faces. If you cannot see the edge clearly, it may be necessary to grind it on an angle. Just a little though, you don't want to take off too much opal.

Now if you find there is no significant difference in quality or pattern in the various bars of color, then cutting is easy. Treat the stone as if it is full color.

However, if you find that one bar stands out, try to get that bar at the top of the stone so that it shows its best color. Assuming that each bar is fairly thin, less than 1mm, which is typical in such rough, the best stone will have a fairly low dome. This allows a large percentage of the top surface to display this best fire bar. Getting the best of the bar at the top of the stone will produce the most attractive stone possible. To see why the best stone will have a low dome, see Figure 19-2, B and 19-2, C.

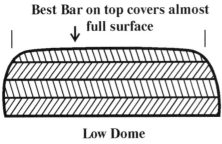

Best Bar on top covers almost full surface

Low Dome

Figure 19-2, B

If the opal is cut in a low dome as in side view 19-2, B, almost the full face of the stone will show the quality of the best bar of fire. However, if the stone is cut with a medium dome as in 19-2, C, only a small part of the top of the stone will show the

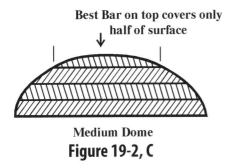

Best Bar on top covers only half of surface

Medium Dome

Figure 19-2, C

best fire. The rest has been cut away and is sitting in Harry Leadthumb's tray as dust. This is one of the reasons why low dome stones are the best choice for most opal.

Let's suppose we have been unlucky and the best bar of color is in the middle of the stone. If we were to grind down to that bar, the stone would be too thin. It's time for compromise. Is there another bar almost as good which will make a thick enough stone? If so, cut the stone with that bar on top as in 19-2, B. Be of good cheer, there almost always is a reasonable second choice. However, if the differences in quality are vast, your best choice may be to make a doublet with the good bar at the top surface and then make one or two other doublets with the material on either side of this line of fire.

MULTIPLE LINES ON TOP

Another challenging opal with multiple line of fire is one that is chunky and shaped so that cutting parallel to the lines of fire would produce a small stone. Look at Figure 19-3, A. Because of the angles of the breaks on the edges, this stone would be very small if cut parallel to the lines of fire (dotted lines). Instead, we could cut the stone at an angle to the lines of fire and produce a larger stone.

Is this the best solution? It depends upon how the stone looks when viewed from that angle. Move the stone around to view it from all angles. There will be angles at which it is attractive and some at which it is not. You may have to compromise between the best look and the most yield. Remember, it will look different when oriented as a pendant or ring.

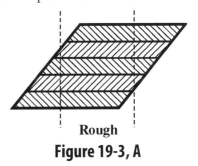

Rough

Figure 19-3, A

Finished Stone
Figure 19-3, B

Once you have determined the best orientation, cut the stone in a medium dome (see Figure 19-3, B). This dome usually blends the bars of color best. The resultant pattern may show the bars. This is acceptable. Some will find it objectionable, but others will love it. By the way, Brazilian opal almost always looks best when cut at an angle like this rather than parallel to the lines of fire.

CURVING LINES

Sometimes the lines of fire in an opal are not straight. They bend, usually in the most inconvenient and frustrating ways. The challenge is to find a way to take advantage of the bends. It may be possible to use the bend as part of the dome. This is what can be done with the stone in Figure 19-4, A. This is the stone pictured in the Mintabie Rough section CP-29. Changing the orientation slightly and allowing an irregular dome can produce a larger stone. Note how the orientation has been changed slightly. The arrow in the rough and cut opal (A & B) points at the same orientation relative to the line of fire. Also note the somewhat lopsided dome that resulted. Unless the uneven shape of the dome is severe, it will not be noticed in a jewelry piece.

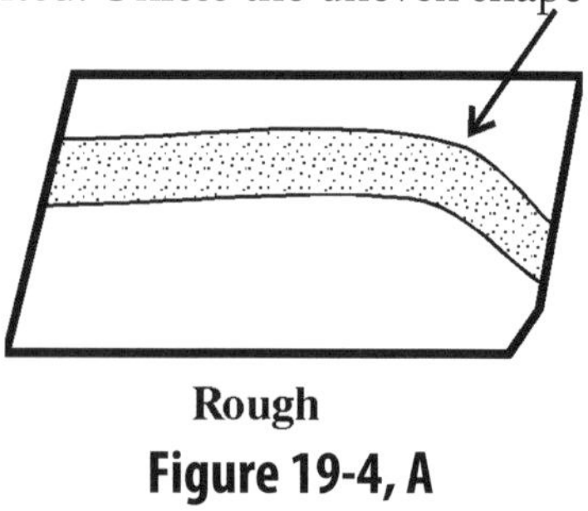

I received a chunk of gray base rough in one Mintabie parcel which provided an interesting challenge. The chunk had three lines of fire, one only on the left, one through the center and one on the lower right only. Between

Rough
Figure 19-4, A

each line of fire were thin bars of gray potch. The rough had an overall gray base color. The choice appeared to be cutting the stone into several small pieces. Instead, I rounded the left edge slightly to expose that line of fire. I then dished the middle of the stone slightly to get through the thin gray potch bar to the central fire. On the lower right I dished it further to get down to the third line. Fortunately the gray potch bars blended into the base color and were not visible from wearing distance. The result was a freeform stone with an irregular dome. From wearing distance it looks like one solid sheet of fire and the irregular shape is hardly noticeable. The end result is the pendant on the cover of this book.

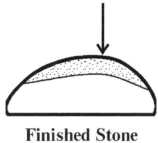

Finished Stone
Figure 19-4, B

Take advantage of the bends.

THICK OR THIN

I remember a parcel of fascinating rough from Mintabie. It was clear crystal opal made up of numerous thin bright lines of fire. Each line had a different pattern and color mix. One particular mix of lines made this rough unique. A strong line of red multicolor in a beautiful flashfire pattern was overlaid by a line of blue without much pattern. When the stones were cut so that the blue line remained over the red one, the stone had a floating blue opalescence that made the red fire haunting. If the blue was left too thick, the red looked dull. If the blue was almost removed, the opalescence effect was lost. It took some experimentation to determine how thick to leave the blue.

Blue fire needs to be thick in most cases to show to best advantage. This is true in crystal and sometimes in black. I had one parcel of Mintabie rough where there was a thick blue-green crystal opal with a black potch bar below it. Usually it is best to cut the fire line down so the top of the stone is close to the black. This intensifies the blackness of the base. This approach works great for red lines, but for this blue-green the closer I got to the black, the less the blue-green showed. Blue-green usually needs as much depth as you can give it.

The moral on thickness is: Look carefully as you work into a line. If it

Blue fire needs to be thick.

is getting better as you go, continue carefully. If it is getting worse, stop.

There are as many challenges in opal cutting as there are stones. Those discussed above are some of the common ones I encounter. Just remember to keep an open mind, sneak up on the stone, and listen to the opal. Meeting the challenge is the most rewarding part of opal cutting.

Opal Cutting Class at Wild Acres

Chapter 20

Finding Imperfections

Almost all pieces of rough…opal or any other gemstones…contain imperfections. Cracks may or may not be evident. Sand inclusions pose problems. Cotton (gypsum) inclusions can occur. Changes in base color can be disturbing. The ideal may be a perfect stone, but when such imperfections are found, your challenge is to find a way to work around them to make a better, if not perfect, stone.

FINDING PITS AND CRACKS

Not all pits, inclusions, base variations and cracks are evident when examining a piece of rough. In opal, most are hidden by the sand or clay skin. To find the stone's imperfections it is necessary to grind away most of the skin. Use my "sneaking up on the stone" technique from the previous chapter to get a better view into the stone.

Agate nodules are often difficult to see into as well. Using this same technique of grinding the rind off and sanding can reveal both patterns and imperfections before you saw and make a mistake.

Once your opal or agate has been exposed in this way, it must be examined closely for imperfections. In order to see pits and cracks, the stone must be dry.

To dry your stone, first wipe it with a towel. Then hold it under your cutting light—but not touching it—for a couple of minutes until it warms some. This will allow the moisture collected in the pits and cracks to evaporate. As this happens, the pits become irregular instead of smoothed over by water. The light is broken up and they become visible.

> Water hides cracks and pits. Dry your stone.

The same is true of cracks. A crack is most visible when the stone is held up touching the opaque shade of a lamp and viewing the light transmitted through the stone. As the stone is turned, light bouncing off the dry internal fracture surface appears orange. Notice the distinct shadow that represents the crack.

It takes some practice to recognize these pits and cracks. In my cutting classes I came upon an alternative method of finding these imperfections…the *magic marker trick!*

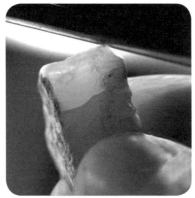

Candling a Crack

Dry the stone as above. Then paint the surface completely or just in suspected areas with a black magic marker. Allow the ink to dry. Dampen a finger slightly and rub the marker off the surface of the stone. The black liquid will have penetrated the pits and fractures that break the surface and dyed them black. They are now easily visible. This method will also point out deep scratches left behind by hasty sanding.

I should warn you that now those pits and cracks are permanently black. Unless removed completely, they will detract from the look of the finished stone. Although a great learning tool, I try to avoid it. I will sometimes leave a small pit on the surface of a finished stone rather than cutting through good fire in an opal or sacrificing stone size in an agate to remove it. The black magic marker will leave the pit black, making it visible and distracting.

It is also true that the technique does not work with all cracks. Some are internal and the dye does not reach them. Others are not open enough to accept the dye. The magic marker is a learning tool. Once you have learned what to look for you will not need it any more.

Some internal imperfections cannot be seen until you cut right down to them. For example, there are small white spots found in some chrysoprase rough. These spots are often invisible until you get just about into them. Once they are discovered, you will have to adjust how you cut your stone. In all types of rough there will be an occasional unexpected imperfection. The candling technique I explained will catch many problems, but not all. This is where going slow and observing carefully pays big dividends. Catching a potential problem early allows you more leeway to work around it.

HOW DEEP DOES IT GO?

Suppose that while grinding away the clay or sand and approaching the best fire in your opal you find that it has a patch of clay or potch that seems to penetrate down into the stone. How far does it go? This is really important to know. If it goes very deep the best choice may be to make the piece into two stones sawed at the penetrating imperfection. If it is shallow, perhaps the top can be ground down to eliminate it without removing all the best fire or making the stone too thin.

The first thing I do when I encounter such a situation is to examine the stone from the edge at the lamp shade as I would for a crack. Frequently the shadow of the clay or potch can be seen in the light showing through the stone from the back. Clean the edges first, as above, to get a better view.

If this does not work, there is another alternative. Employing a flexshaft and a small diamond ball bit, slowly grind into the imperfection. Alternatively, scratch out the clay with the sharp point of your aluminum scribe. Dip the stone in water periodically to cool it and remove waste. If the imperfection is a clay pit, the bit or point penetrates quickly. When it gets to the bottom of the pit it slows dramatically. A little experimenting will allow you to learn when you have reached bottom. You can also tell you are close if you look at the stone in transmitted back light and the bottom of the pit is translucent like the rest of the stone.

The following photo shows a chunk of rough opal that I have ground down to expose the fire line. I found several areas of clay in the fire line and a crack. Using a diamond bit I ground away the clay. The

Clay in Opal

result is shown in the next photo. Note that the clay went through the fire line on the right. However, removing most of the clay at the left and on top showed that the fire line is thick enough that the rest of the clay can be removed without going through the fire. Also the crack has diminished significantly. This means that it is fairly shallow and it, too, can be removed in final shaping without a major loss of stone size.

For potch inclusions, the bit is grinding through opal so there is no slowing. The potch is too hard so the scribe does not work. The bottom is found when the imperfection is no longer visible. The hole you are digging must be dry and clean to see this.

Now that the depth of the imperfection has been determined, it is decision time. If the pit is not too deep it may be best to grind down the rest of the surface to the bottom of the pit, thus eliminating the imperfection. However, if doing so would remove all the good color, it is time for the saw.

The beauty of this pit excavation process is that it does not remove any useful opal. It allows you to learn how serious a problem is and what to do about it before you remove opal you may wish later you hadn't.

Clay Removed

The bottom line on imperfections is simple. If it really bothers you, remove it. If it doesn't, leave it. Learn to love the imperfections that, if retained, allow you to preserve the beauty of the stone.

Chapter 21

Advanced Opal Cutting Hints

All opal is cut in the same manner, but some types require specific attention. In this chapter I offer some hints for cutting these special materials.

SEAM OPAL: HORIZONTALS AND VERTICALS

It may be helpful in orienting an opal and reading the line of color to know how seam opal is formed. Most of the opal from Coober Pedy, Mintabie and Lambina forms in seams or breaks in the parent rock. Many of these seams form more or less parallel to the earth's surface. Such seams are called *horizontal seams*, or just *seams*. Occasionally seams form at other angles and sometimes more or less straight up and down. These seams are called *verticals*. In Figure 21-1 these different types of seams can be seen. In all cases the lines of fire always form parallel to the surface of the earth. In horizontal seams the edges of the seam

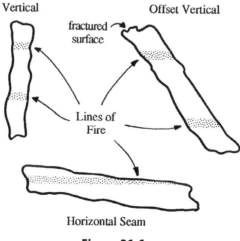

Figure 21-1

may not be perfectly horizontal. In such cases the line of color may run through the seam on an angle. Follow the seam to determine the orientation of the fire line.

Verticals are unique in that the fractured surface of the rough is the top or bottom of the stone...not the edge as in a horizontal seam. These stones should be cut with the line of fire oriented as in Figure 21-1. Verticals are usually thin seams that will cut only small stones. However, they are often very bright.

Sometimes verticals form with many lines of fire closely associated with one another. Instead of cutting these in the normal way, an interesting stone may be produced by cutting them *on edge*. The result is an opal with lines of fire running through it. This is found frequently in Brazilian rough.

Whenever you cut seam opal, check the direction of the line of color to make sure you are cutting it correctly.

CUTTING A VERTICAL SEAM

Enough theory, let's cut a real stone. The opal shown in CP-50 is a vertical seam from Turkey Ridge in Coober Pedy which I acquired from Murray Willis of **Australian Opal Mines** (see SOURCE DIRECTORY). The first step in cutting any stone is a careful inspection. As you can see in the photograph, there is a large clay inclusion in the stone. The surface had been sawed before I received it and showed some very good potential. But, is this the best face? When I looked at the side of the stone I found an interesting situation. The color showing on the sawn surface at the top of CP-51 is very thin. Below it is a green-orange line and below that a rich red line. Looking at it from the other side, I find the rich red line is almost at the surface. This means that the best line of fire...the rich red one...sits at an angle to the sawn face of the opal. To get to this line of fire I will have to grind the sawn surface at an angle.

But before we do this, let's address the clay inclusion. Candling the stone I find that the clay seems to penetrate fairly deep and at an angle (see CP-52). But how deep does it go? If it is not too deep, I may be able to grind down to the color line at the angle I could see from the edge and clear the clay. This would yield a larger stone.

To find out…without removing any good opal…I dug out the clay with the point of my aluminum scribe. Keeping the clay wet makes it soft and it can be removed easily (see CP-53). When I do this I find that, unfortunately, the clay penetrates through the best fire line. In fact it goes quite deep, as you can see in the photograph.

What to do? If I saw through the empty space where the clay was, I can produce two good stones. If I adjust the angle of the saw cut slightly from the angle of the clay opening, I can make the smaller stone a bit larger without reducing the size of the big stone since the material

Sawing Through Clay Opening

I would be sawing through is common potch that would have been ground away in shaping the big stone. Sawing seems the best option since it saves a nice stone and does not risk the big stone.

Once the piece has been sawn, I inspect the big piece again. The

Off-cut Rough

slant of the main color line is now clearly visible on the saw cut and is a bit steeper than I thought. Following this line I expose the full color face (see CP-54).

I then shaped the stone, using the natural contours of the rough

181

(see CP-55). I was careful to preserve that big splash of red at the upper left. The end result is a very attractive stone that will make a great pendant.

But what about the piece I sawed off? The fire line is right through the heart of it so all I had to do is follow the angled fire line. Again using the natural shape, I produced a very attractive pendant stone. Verticals are not difficult to cut as long as you recognize the natural structure of the rough.

CRYSTAL OPAL

Opal that is transparent is called *crystal* opal. When it is translucent rather than transparent, it is called *semi-crystal*. Because of this transparency, crystal requires some special attention. The clear base allows light to enter and escape from many angles. Often crystal looks better in the rough than when finished because cutting has removed material which was blocking light from entering the stone.

There are three things which can be done to reduce this problem to a minimum. First, be as careful as possible when orienting the stone. Keep the opal wet so that it will appear as transparent as possible, and avoid dark backgrounds when orienting the stone. Second, cut the stone as thick as possible. A thicker stone provides more background for the fire to play against. Third, cut the back of the stone in a low dome and sand it only to medium/fine grit. This reduces the amount of light which passes through the stone, resulting in more intense fire. Other than this, treat crystal like any other opal. However, high quality crystal is quite expensive, so you may want to pay particular attention to yield (see later section in this chapter).

Because of its transparency, and the fact that it loses its color in thin layers, thin pieces of crystal opal are often used for doublets or triplets (see Chapter 11).

MATRIX DYEING INSTRUCTIONS

The following instructions for treating Andamooka matrix to dye it black were provided by E. W. Liggett. Before you decide to treat

Andamooka matrix you should be aware that you will be working with dangerous acid. Know all the rules about handling acid *before* you start this project.

> **WARNING: Sulfuric acid is potentially dangerous! Treat it with care.**

"There are two major matrix categories of Andamooka matrix opal: opalized sandstone and opalized quartz. The *opalized sandstone* is further broken down into what Andamooka miners refer to as "proper" matrix and the less valuable "concrete." Proper matrix is the best material. It polishes well and only requires color treating. Concrete, on the other hand, requires color treating and stabilizing with Opticon™ Fracture Sealer.

"The color treating or dyeing process for treating matrix is possible because, unlike pure silica opal, matrix opal is porous. Matrix is treated by heating it in a heavy sugar batter mixture. During the cooking process the sugar penetrates and fills the porous space around the grains of the opalized host rock. The sugar-treated matrix is then cooked in pure sulfuric acid which carbonizes (blackens) the sugar, thus dyeing the host rock. Matrix opal has very little visible fire without this dyeing process.

"The treating process is very simple. First, you will need a two temperature crock pot (slow cooker), a five-pound bag of white sugar, and a quart of 90% or better sulfuric acid. Car battery acid will not work, nor will any other type of acid! Sulfuric acid is ready to use out of the bottle and is easy to deal with if you are careful when using it.

"Wash the matrix opal and place it into the crock pot. In a separate bowl pour in some sugar and add hot water, stirring as you pour until the sugar becomes a thick liquid glaze sugar batter. Now pour the mixture over the matrix, covering it completely. Turn the crock pot to high heat, stir the opal every half-hour. Each time you stir the opal the sugar batter will be lighter because the sugar is being absorbed into the matrix.

"Constant supervision and adding water as necessary is a must. Also, keep the lid on the pot whenever you are not stirring the matrix. I recommend a big wooden spoon to stir the matrix. The cooking time is a minimum of three hours. Remember, never let the sugar dry out, or you will have a glued together mess. When you feel the soup is done—usually 3 to 24 hours—the most important step begins. Unplug the pot and let the solution cool on its own **SLOWLY** for at least two hours (in the sugar batter). As the matrix cools in the batter, it sucks in the sugar. This is called "forcing the treatment."

"Many people tell me their matrix will not treat. I ask if they force-cooled the batter and they usually admit they only added warm water to cool it down quicker. **DO NOT DO THIS**! If you do, it will wash the sugar out of the surface of the matrix and may even crack the matrix.

"After cooling for at least two hours, rinse the stones and the crock pot in warm water. Dry the stones and the pot and place the matrix back into the pot. Make sure there is no water left in the pot as the water could possibly react with the acid and spit acid. Carefully add the sulfuric acid. **PLEASE WEAR OLD CLOTHES, GLOVES AND EYE PROTECTION.** Try not to spill or splatter any acid, as it will burn your skin and leave holes in your clothes. The process of cooking the matrix in acid is not different than when in sugar, except **VENTILATE THE ROOM WELL**! Never open the lid while bending over the pot, as the fumes from the acid will burn your nose. Cook the stones in the acid until they are dark, about two hours. **NEVER** add water to the acid. The acid is allowed to cool slowly as you did the sugar solution. Save the acid as it will work just as well a second time. I never use it more than twice because it gets weaker and wastes time by having to retreat again.

"The treating process is repeated as many times as necessary to obtain the degree of blackness. Treat the rough rock to observe the color bands for slabbing, or to face up the rough for the best color. Slab the rough then re-treat the slab. Then you can layout cabs. Do all the cabbing steps except the final polish. Check to ensure that any soft, cracked or crumbly surface material is ground off. Re-treat the unfinished cab using brand new sulfuric acid. This is the third treatment and usually the last needed. The unfinished cut cab will be treated throughout at this point. Allow the stone to cool in the pot. When cool, pour the acid back in its bottle. Add water and baking soda slowly to neutralize the acid. Soak the stones completely with this mixture for at least 8 hours. The acid will be neutralized at this point. The matrix will be internally hot and may sweat for a day or two after treatment. This is no problem. After the cut stones cool just wipe them off if they sweat until they don't sweat any more. At this point you may wish to treat the stone with Opticon™. Now polish the cab. Go back only to the pre-polish stage, then polish."

Color-treated matrix is a beautiful and far less expensive alternative to natural black opal.

You may find slabs of Andamooka matrix available for cutting. Often they have been pre-treated to show the fire against a dark background. Be aware that the treatment might not completely penetrate the stone. When you cut it, the stone will start to turn white as you grind away the pre–treated surface. In such cases the matrix will have to be treated again to dye it black. This can be done after you have fine sanded the cab. Treat, then polish to finish the stone.

Also you need to know that Andamooka matrix varies in its ability to accept this treatment. Even in a single slab there may be areas that take the treatment poorly or not at all. You will have to decide whether to cut the full stone and live with the variations in base color or cut smaller stones that treat well.

CUTTING FOR YIELD

The primary object of any opal cutter is to produce the most beautiful stone possible from each piece of rough. However, opals are valued by weight as well as beauty. (See *Opal Identification & Value.*) This means that the cutter must be aware of how his/her cutting choices affect the weight of the final product. Obviously you wish the most beautiful and heaviest opal possible, but these goals often conflict. We have addressed the potential for necessary compromise in the discussion on orienting opals, so it need not be belabored here. It is sufficient to note that the issue of yield (weight of the final product as compared to weight of the rough) becomes more important as you cut more valuable material.

When cutting a stone which you will use only for yourself, yield may be of less importance. But when cutting a stone which is to be sold, you have to pay attention to this factor. If you are cutting commercially, it can make the difference between profit and loss. *Cutting for yield*, as it is called, requires that the shape of the stone you cut be modified. Suppose that you have a piece of rough with fire completely through it. You could cut the piece into a standard shaped dome as shown in the dotted portion of Figure 21–2. Alternatively, you could make the stone heavier by keeping some of the material on the edges of the domed area, making the dome more flat and the edge thicker. In addition, you may decide not to completely flatten the bottom of the stone. This high yield shape is shown as the solid outline in figure 21–2. The high yield shape may weigh up to 20% more than the low yield shape shown.

Cutting for Weight

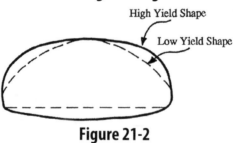

Figure 21-2

Personally, I don't like the shape of high yield stones. They look fat, losing the elegance which I feel a good opal deserves. While your preference may differ, I find that I can cut an opal to an attractive shape while being conscious of yield and be much more pleased with the result. A simple rule for cutting for yield might be to do so, to the extent possible, consistent with producing the beautiful stone you are seeking.

Advanced Opal Cutting Hints

Yield Factors. Yield (the final weight as a percent of the beginning weight) depends upon

1. The way you cut each stone,
2. The cracks and other imperfections found in the rough, and
3. The percentage of the rough which lacks color.

These waste factors generally average out over several parcels of rough so that a general rule of thumb can be stated. The yield of rough generally is 20%, but it can run as high as 40% or more, or as low as 10%. The 20% factor is very convenient because one carat is 20% of one gram. Thus, if you purchase a parcel of opal with 10 grams of rough in it you can expect, on average, to cut finished opals with a total weight of 10 carats. This gives us the rule of yield.

> ## RULE OF YIELD:
> You can expect to obtain one carat of finished opal for every gram.

There is a convenient corollary to this rule.

> ## COST COROLLARY:
> The cost per gram of rough is also the expected cost of the finished opal per carat.

For example, suppose you purchase rough at $20 per gram. You can expect on average that you will obtain one carat per gram of rough. Thus, your cost for the finished stone is $20 per carat. This allows you to estimate the value of the rough by comparing it to cut stones dealers have at that price per carat. You should have a better stone. Rough sells at a lower price than finished stones because the work of cutting is to be done by you and because there is always an inherent risk that the rough will not produce the stones it looks like it will. Cutting for yield can increase the yield 30% or 40%, but rarely more. A 40% yield would mean that stones costing $20 per gram would cost $10 per carat. Cutting standard size ovals reduces yield significantly, perhaps below 10%. For further discussion of the importance of yield in buying rough opal, see Chapter 13, *How To Buy Opal Rough*.

For convenience in determining the relationships among weights, refer to the following table. Note that there are two different ounces. Troy ounces are heavier. They are the measure used in Australia. In the United States, a dealer may weigh 28 grams or 31 grams; or something in-between as a measure. When in doubt, ask.

Weight Conversion Chart		
	Carats	Grams
1 carat	.20	1
1 gram	1	5
1 ounce Troy	31.1	155.5
1 ounce Avoirdupois	28.3	141.7
1 pound Troy	373.2	1866.1
1 pound Avoirdupois	453.6	2268.0

Chapter 22

Treating Cracks and Stabilizing Matrix

There are valid reasons for treating an opal to seal cracks and stabilize matrix. An opal can crack in wearing, although an appropriately designed setting can minimize this possibility (see Section Five). Some opals craze. An antique jewelry piece with a cracked or crazed opal is a good candidate for treating. Replacing the opal makes the piece no longer have the provenance of an antique. Treating the opal, instead of replacing it, preserves this provenance. Likewise, it would be a shame to throw away a beautiful opal you have worn for years because of a crack. Treatment can save such pieces. Cracked and crazed opals can be made wearable by treating them with Opticon™ 224 Fracture Sealer. The purpose in treating the opal is to stabilize the crack to prolong the opal's life. It is not to hide the crack, although treatment may reduce its visibility somewhat.

The matrix found with some opals may be too soft to be wearable. Other types of matrix are prone to chipping. Still other types of matrix contain pits that are unattractive. Treating the matrix with Opticon™ can save these opals.

Opticon™ will fill most cracks so that they are not visible when finished, so thin, cracked opals can be treated then made into triplets. This is an excellent way to use otherwise unusable cracked material.

THE TREATMENT PROCESS

Treatment for cracks, crazes and matrix stability problems, pits, and softness of the matrix can all be accomplished with the same technique. Opticon™, a two-part epoxy polymer, is specifically designed to penetrate into openings in gemstones. If used as follows, it will do the job as well as any technique you can do yourself. There are other methods and materials that have been used, but they are not

189

easily available. As with any chemical process, read and follow the manufacturer's directions.

Equipment. Treatment will be most successful if some form of vacuum can be produced as the stone is treated. A simple, relatively inexpensive vacuum machine can be found at laboratory supply stores. Treatment can be successful, however, without such a vacuum device.

Treatment. Prepare stones for treatment by cutting and sanding them to medium grit. Pre-cutting maximizes the probability that the polymer will penetrate into the areas to be treated. Be aware, however, that treatment will not affect internal flaws which are not connected to the surface. Set opals must be removed from the setting before treatment and cleaned with alcohol to remove any oils. They do not have to be sanded at this point. Soft, crumbly matrix may need to be treated before shaping and sanding to prevent breakage, then treated again after shaping and medium sanding.

Once the stones are pre-cut and/or cleaned, dry and warm the stones. Use a desk lamp or that old electric frying pan on low. Do not heat above 150 degrees.

Heat the resin portion of the Opticon™. Do not overheat. Warming makes the resin watery so it will penetrate into the stone better. Do this by placing the resin, but not the hardener, in a separate glass container and put it in the frying pan.

Place the warmed stones into the heated resin. Put both into a vacuum chamber (if available) and draw a vacuum. Hold it awhile, then release it. If you do not have a way to put the stone in a vacuum, just place it in the container with the warm resin and let it cool. Allow the stones to cool to room temperature in the resin. As the stones cool, the resin will be drawn into the stones. Once cool, clean off the excess resin.

Heat the hardener and resin required in the second step of the instructions on the label, then mix them together. At the same time heat the stones. When everything is warm, place the stones in the resin and hardner mixture. Draw a vacuum as before (if available).

Remove the stones and wipe the surface to remove excess Opticon™ before the mixture starts to set. The stones should be left with a film of Opticon™ so that the extra material can be drawn into the stone as it cools if needed. Allow the stones to cool and cure completely. Some Opticon™ may leak out at this state, so set the stones on aluminum foil to cure.

Once the stones have cured, re-sand with medium grit and pre-polish. For opals that you have removed from a setting, go directly to pre-polish, as medium sanding can make the stone smaller, thus causing the stone to be too loose when re-set. Use 50,000 diamond to polish. Cerium oxide can leave white spots in any remaining cracks or pits. Avoid excessive heat in polishing as this could cause the polymer to separate from the opal. Mark the back with a *"T"* to alert people that it has been treated, and the stone is finished. Avoid heat when setting or resetting treated opals.

TREATMENT ETHICS

There is no basic moral problem with treating opals. Treatment is common in many gemstones such as sapphires, topaz and emeralds, and becoming more common in others such as diamonds. The moral problem arises when a treated stone is sold as being untreated (natural).

Any gemstone treatment should be revealed to a prospective purchaser. Disclosure of treatment is required by the Code of Ethics of AGTA (American Gem Trade Association—the nation's largest wholesale colored gemstone dealer's association). It is, or shortly will be, legally required as well. By the way, any treatment may not be detectable by simple inspection. Polymer treated opals can be detected only by infrared spectroscopy as conducted in the GIA (Gemological Institute of America) gem laboratories.

In the past, misrepresenting treated material as natural has been a problem only with Andamooka treated (dyed) matrix (see Chapter 21). This material has been sold by some as natural black opal. However, treating with polymers to seal and/or disguise cracks is becoming more common in opal, so we can expect increasing problems with misrepresenting treated opal in the future. The problem of misrepresentation may arise from unscrupulous or uninformed secondary sellers. An honest person will reveal the treatment, but someone down the line may not know about it and sell the stone as natural. If there is a problem which requires treatment to save the opal, and there is a good reason to do so, go ahead. Consider carving a small "*T*" into the back of any treated stone with a diamond bit so that others—several buyers down the line—are warned.

Section Four

Advanced Gemstone Cutting Techniques

There are some specialized cutting techniques that can be applied to all cabbing material. While, to me at least, opal plays a central role in all of them, it is not necessary to use any opal.

Intarsia by Jim Kaufmann

Chapter 23

Intarsia

If you are seeking an interesting, innovative, and attractive way to present gems in jewelry, consider *intarsia*. This lapidary technique is fairly simple to do once the basics are understood. Endless design possibilities are available, limited only by the imagination. It's just plain fun!

Intarsia is the process of fitting pieces of gemstones together to produce a pattern. Each piece is angular and fits together like a jigsaw puzzle. Semi-precious stones such as lapis, malachite, and sugalite are commonly used, but almost any lapidary material in the same general hardness range will work effectively. I have seen agate, jasper, turquoise, chrysocolla and even jade used successfully. It is traditional to use opal as the center of the intarsia piece, but it is by no means necessary. Any combination of gemstones can create a stained glass window-like design.

Intarsia can be very precise with exact angles and exact thicknesses of pieces like the magnificent piece on the opposite page made by Jim Kaufmann using the rough opal from the upper left of the front cover of this book. Jim does his work on a faceting machine. It can also be less formal and still be fun and attractive.

BASIC PROCESS

The basic process is simplicity itself. Start with a center stone. Fashion this center stone so it comprises three or more straight line edges (triangle, square, irregular polygon, etc.) Next add strips of another material to each edge. These are glued onto the edges and ground down to produce a new outline. Once a second angular outline has been produced, add a third. After several layers, the design will be finished. This process of building out from the center makes adding layers and changing angles easy.

The center stone in an intarsia design is the key to its beauty and its color combinations. This center stone should have some uniqueness. I feel that stones with a unique pattern, such as opal or rhodochrosite, work well. Plain, single color center stones do not generally work as well, but that all depends on the side stones you use with it.

Opal has become a traditional center stone for an intarsia pendant piece. The opal pattern produces a focal point for the design. The colors in the fire can be complemented by selecting side stones in the pattern that pick up on the opal's fire.

Once you have decided on a center stone you must select various different materials to use for the other pieces of this intarsia puzzle. In order for the pattern you are carefully designing to be noticed, it is necessary that successive outlines be of somewhat contrasting color and/or pattern. Suppose you develop an intricate pattern of stones where all were lapis. Everything would be blue and the pattern would be lost. Suppose instead the pattern alternated lapis and malachite. Then the contrast between the blue and green would make the pattern obvious. Differing patterns of the same material can also work. For example, the bar pattern of rhodochrosite can be cut at different angles to produce a contrasting pattern.

The outside edge of the piece should consist of several pieces of the same material. This produces a frame for the design. To add strength to the piece and to produce a finished look, a slab of the same material as the edge is glued to the back of the piece. Then the whole piece is shaped, sanded and polished.

Designs can be very regular like squares or triangles; each successive layer larger than the one before. Or it can be as wildly irregular as your imagination allows with new layers taking off at different angles from the previous ones. I have made checkerboards, Z–shapes, crosses and wild freeforms. That is the fun of this technique. The combination of patterns and materials is limitless, bounded only by your imagination.

A SIMPLE PROJECT

To get started, let's go step-by-step through a simple project. It is best to work your pattern from what you intend to be the top of the stone. This way you know what the finished project will look like. The back can look like junk. It doesn't matter, it will be covered up anyway.

STEP ONE: *Select and Shape a Center Stone.* Select a center stone for the project. This stone should be 2 to 4mm thick. Use the best pat-

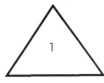

Figure 23-1, A

tern as the top or face of the stone. Grind the back parallel to the face. This need not be perfect since the back will be flattened and covered near the end of the project. The face should be nearly flat.

Now the edges must be established. The center stone can be of any angular shape you wish, but for simplicity, let's assume it lends itself to a triangle as in Figure 23–1, A. Each of the sides must now be ground to form a flat straight line. Start

with one side. Using a grinding wheel, cut this side to approximately where you want it. Keep the edge as close to perpendicular (right angles) to the top as you can manage.

Switch to the flat lap; if you have not already. The **Ameritool** grinding disc is ideal for this job. Lap this edge so that it is perfectly flat and perpendicular to the top. To check that the edge is 90 degrees to the top, use the inside corner of the movable center of a millimeter gauge. Remove it from the gauge and lay the long part on the top of

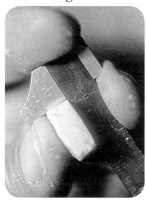

Checking Right Angle

the stone with the right angle of the head at the edge you are working. Move the head along the edge. Any gap at the top or bottom indicates that the edge is not perpendicular to the top. Get it as right as you can as this will make future steps easier. With the first edge established, cut the other edges the same way. Keep a pleasing triangular shape but do not be a slave to a perfect equilateral triangle. Such perfection can be worked on after the basic technique is mastered.

The end result is a chunk of material like 23–1, A with three straight edges perpendicular to the top. Don't be discouraged. It will take a while to be good at doing these 90 degree edges. Yes, a faceting machine head makes this all easier, so use it if you have one.

STEP TWO: Adding the Border. We are now ready to build out from the triangle. Select a material that compliments the center stone. Saw several strips from this material. Each strip must be long enough to overlap the center stone as in the dotted lines in 23–1, B. These strips should be thicker than the finished border around the center stone and deeper than the center stone.

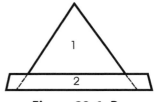

Figure 23-1, B

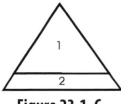

Figure 23-1, C

Starting with one strip, flatten the top if you have not already done so. Then flatten an edge so that it is at right angles to the top. Make sure the entire length is free of imperfections as any problems will end up very visible in the final product.

Glue this strip to one edge of the triangle. Use 5–Minute Epoxy. Do not use superglue as some adhesive will inevitably escape the edge and glue your fingers to the stone. Trust me, I know from personal experience. The top edge of the strip should

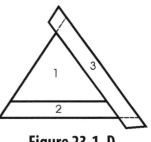

Figure 23-1, D

be just above the top of the center stone (see the edge view of B in Figure 23–1, I). Hold the two pieces together with your fingers until the glue has set well enough for the pieces not to move. Try not to let the two pieces

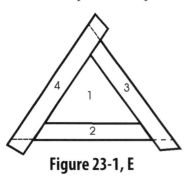

Figure 23-1, E

slip, as this will slow and weaken the bond. Once the glue has set enough that the pieces do not move, set them on some aluminum foil in a position where they will be stable. I usually squeeze the foil around them to brace the pieces. Let it sit overnight.

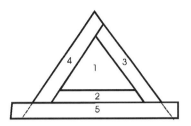

Figure 23-1, F

After the glue has set, grind away the excess to form a larger triangle as in Figure 23–1, C. Keep the edge perpendicular. The second strip (3) can now be glued onto the piece as in Figure 23–1, D. After this glue has set, grind a new triangle as in Figure 23–1, E and add the third strip (4).

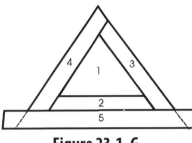

Figure 23-1, G

To complete the design add strips of different materials, including opal if you want, that complement the design. Use as many layers of strips as you wish. In our example, two borders have been added (see Figure 23–1, H). It is usually best to choose a darker material for the outside edge. This gives the piece a finished frame.

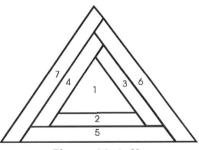

Figure 23-1, H

At this point the face of your piece will be a little disorganized (perhaps ugly) with each section you have added being of different thickness and at least a little bit above the face of your center stone. Don't worry, this is normal and will be taken care of in a bit.

Figure 23-1, I

STEP THREE: The Back. Putting a back on the piece is traditional but really a matter of choice. I prefer a back because it adds strength to the piece and gives it a more finished look. It also covers imperfections in the back of individual pieces. In the case of an opal center stone, the back also serves as a base for a doublet-like darkening effect.

To add a back, first gently grind the back of the piece parallel to the top. Be careful, the glue lines on the strips could part if uneven pressure is put on one side. Remember that some of the top will still have to come off later. Flat lap the back so that it is perfectly flat and parallel to the face of the center stone. The center area of the back can have some small gaps as these will be filled with glue and covered by the backing, but the outside edge should not have gaps as these will show in the finished product.

Choose a backing material. Traditionally the back is made of the same material as the outside border of the design. This makes the back blend into the sides for a more professional, finished look. The backing material should overlap all edges and be thicker than you wish the finished piece to be. Flat lap the side that is to be glued on the back and let it dry.

Glue it on and let it set. Oops, I forgot a trick you will need if you are using opal for your center piece. The finished center opal will be fairly thin (1 to 2mm). Therefore the back may show through. To prevent this and to enhance the look of the opal, spray the back of the opal with black paint before gluing the back on as you would a doublet. If you do not wish to have the opal or other translucent materials darkened, use a paint color matching the center of the intarsia piece. Once the paint is dry the two pieces can be glued together with epoxy.

After the glue is set, the back can be ground down to its approximate final thickness. The top should be from one-half to two-thirds the total thickness of the piece.

STEP FOUR: Finishing. Using a grinding wheel, work the top of the stone down. The strips that form the border will all be higher than the center stone (recall Figure 23-1, I). Grind these down parallel to the top of the center stone until the center stone is just reached. Tradition suggests that the entire top be flat lapped and polished. On the other hand, I like the look and ease of finishing with a *very slight* dome on the piece. To me it looks more like a piece of jewelry this way, but be a traditionalist if you wish.

Once the top has been established, sand as usual. The flat laps of the **AMERITOOL** machine work wonderfully for doing flat-topped intarsia. However, careful work with a wheel–type cabbing machine can do the job too. The edges should be ground and sanded at this time too. Be careful not to round the points of the triangle. A rounded outside outline to an otherwise very angular piece is not usually attractive if the final piece has very regular angles as in Jim Kaufmann's design. Put a little round break on the top of the edge to prevent chipping and a bevel on the bottom edge. The back can be polished if you like.

There you have it, your first intarsia. The triangle may not be perfect. The border strips may be thin or one-sided. Don't worry, each piece will get easier and better.

SOME DESIGN IDEAS

Intarsia designs are limited only by your imagination. Here are a couple of basic design techniques which will get your mind going.

Checkerboard. A checkerboard is a simple design. The basics lend themselves to other designs.

Start by preparing strips of two materials of contrasting colors; say for example white opal and black onyx. The strips should be of roughly equal length. Flatten the tops and grind the edges at 90 degrees. Make all the strips exactly the same width. This is so they

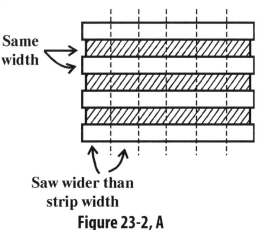

Same width

Saw wider than strip width

Figure 23-2, A

will form perfect squares. They should be longer than the set of them are wide to allow for lost material as they are worked to make a perfect squares. Glue them together, alternating materials as in Figure 23–2, A. Note that one more strip of one material is needed, in this case 3 opal strips and 4 onyx strips. This will produce a final 6x6 checkerboard.

After the glue has set, carefully plan to saw the piece into 6 strips. Each strip should be a little wider than the original strip width.

Grind the sawed edges at 90 degrees to the top. Adjust the thickness so that each of these new strips is exactly as wide as the original

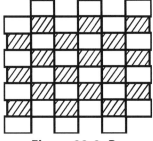

strips. Make sure that the cuts are perpendicular to the original strips' edges and exactly the same thickness. The object is to make perfect squares.

Now glue the strips together alternating their locations so squares are produced in a checkerboard pattern (see Figure 23–2, B). Take care to line the edges up properly.

Figure 23-2, B

I find that a foil frame helps hold all the pieces together. The gluing can be done all at once, but it may be easier to glue one strip at a time to ensure proper placement.

Once all pieces are glued together, grind the outside edges down so that the outside squares are exactly the same size as the interior ones. Make sure to keep the edges perpendicular to the top.

Prepare four strips to make an edge around the board. Glue on two sides, grind the excess length off and glue on the others. Finish the second set. You now have a checkerboard with a border (see Figure 23-2, C). Prepare and glue

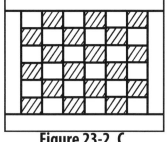

Figure 23-2, C

on the back. Finish front, sides, back and you're done!

There are many ways to vary this basic design. Sawing at an angle can produce unusual parallelogram designs. Uneven spacing can produce interesting rectangles.

Play with designs on paper before you start the work to make sure you know how all the pieces will work together. Try drawing strips on a sheet of paper. Cut the paper as if the rock it represents was sawed and play with putting the pieces together in different ways.

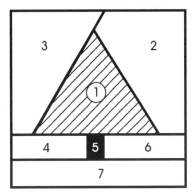

Figure 23-3

Tree. A simple tree design can be made with a complete boundary using seven pieces of stone. Start with a triangular shape that looks like a pine tree (Piece 1 in Figure 23-3). Now add border piece 2. Make sure the edges overhang so that it can be cut down to the shape shown in the figure. Now add Piece 3, again overlapping. Prepare Pieces 4, 5 and 6 to produce the trunk of the tree. The trunk material (5) can be the same as the tree but may look more natural if it is a brown material like petrified wood. Glue 4, 5, and 6 together. Flatten the bottom of the tree and the top of the tree trunk. Align the tree trunk and glue the two pieces together. Allow this all to set. Add a base to the design (Piece 7). Finish the sides, bottom and top. There you have a simple tree.

This same placing of pieces can be used to produce many patterns. Letters such as "T," "L,". "X," etc. are easy to do. Stars are possible too.

There you have the basics. Almost any design can be produced using this technique. It is just a matter of fitting the pieces together in the correct way.

> **A simple tree design can be made with a cosmplete boundary using seven pieces of stone.**

A FREEFORM INTARSIA

I had a nice, thin slice of white based opal from Coober Pedy. I decided to use it as the center of an intarsia piece. I have always liked the look of white opal next to green jade. I prepared and glued two strips of jade to the sides of the opal. I then found a similar-looking piece of white pal with more green fire which I prepared and glued to the top of the stone. For the bottom I had another piece of green

Photo 23-1

Photo 23-2

fire opal. I fit it to a piece of green jade then prepared it to glue onto the base of the center piece (see Photo 23-1).

Photo 23-3

Intarsia

As a border I decided to use black jade. The contrast of the black, green and white makes for a striking pattern. I fit strips of black jade to the sides first. Then I fit other strips of black jade to the top and bottom. The end result is the ugly mess shown in Photo 23-3.

After flattening the back, I fit a black jade slab for the back (see Photo 23-4). Once the back was glued I had a piece that looked like Photo 23-5.

Photo 23-4

Photo 23-5

I decided that, because all the angles were a bit irregular and the balance is not perfect, I would generate a shape that is less formal and softer. Thus, I rounded the points and cut the top with a low dome. The finished stone can be seen in CP-56.

Another simple design, this one a bit more formal, can bee seen in CP-57.

Not all designs have to have the outline made from one type of material. In Photo 23-1 the opal centerstone goes to the edge of th piece, giving it a unique look.

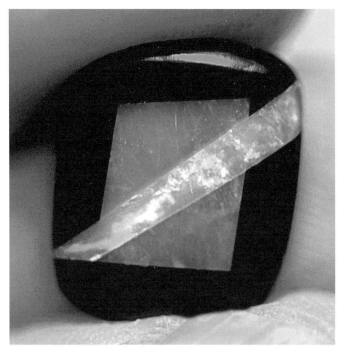

Photo 23-1

Chapter 24

Using Chips

In cutting opal and other gems, there will be small chips left over that are too small to cut useful single stones. I hate to waste these small beauties. Here are some suggestions.

THE CHIP JAR

This is the simplest solution of all. Just collect the chips in a clear bottle of water. I keep such a bottle next to my cutting machine. As I find a chip or saw a small corner from an opal or other gem, I clean it of matrix and dirt with my grinding wheel and deposit it in the chip jar. Over the years the jar fills. I find it fascinating to hold the jar in the light and slowly turn it. All sorts of colored gemstones tumble down to produce a kaleidoscope of color. The jar never looks the same and is always beautiful, but a chip jar is cumbersome to wear. A variant on the chip jar is the miniature liquor bottle. When the label is removed and the bottle filled with chips, it makes a very attractive display (see CP-58). Where can you get these bottles without drinking yourself silly? Try your next airplane ride. They go through a lot and may be willing to save empty bottles for you.

Is there another way to use chips? Actually there are several.

Bobbi and I saw a most fascinating use of opal chips one year in Andamooka. An opal dealer had gathered tiny chips of top grade crystal opal. These had been carefully graded into fire colors. Then they were placed in long glass tubes filled with mineral oil. A number of these tubes were placed on a revolving rack like an egg timer. When the tubes were turned top to bottom the opal chips that had settled in the bottom of the tubes now slowly cascaded down to the new bottom. The result was a spectacular flashing display of opal colors.

Opal & Gemstone Jewelry

FLOATING OPALS

These were popular years back but are not seen often now. Small chips of opal (and/or other gems) are placed inside clear glass vials filled with glycerine or mineral oil. The top is then sealed and a cap added. Floating opals/gems can be made into pendants or earrings (see CP-59).

The problem with this process is locating the vials to fill. At one time they were available commercially but I know of no source at the moment. A solution may be to find a glass blower who could make some up for you.

The seal at the top is crucial to success once the vials are found. Try to find a clear plastic that can be used as a top. Glue the top on with epoxy to complete the seal. Then add the bell cap.

Make sure that the opal/gem is clean and free from sand and clay inclusions. Dirt will make the mineral oil cloudy. Sand and clay darken when wet and become distracting.

CHIP TRIPLETS

A very effective method for using opal chips is chip triplets. The small chips are glued together and then used as the opal component of a standard triplet with magnificent color. Extraordinary opal chip triplets were made in Lightning Ridge years ago. The cutter carefully selected, flattened and placed each chip into a mosaic pattern. This carefully fitted piece is difficult to distinguish from a solid black opal at wearing distance (see CP-60). The process is as follows:

To start, a tray is needed that has a perfectly flat bottom and sides about 8mm high; just large enough so that all the chips completely cover the bottom and are touching it. I make these trays out of heavy aluminum foil. The tray will be destroyed later so it must be disposable.

Now the chips must be cleaned to remove any matrix, clay, or unattractive spots. If the chips are large enough, each can be flattened on one side on a grinding wheel. If you really want to do a fantastic job, the chips can be carefully flattened on top and ground on the edge to be fitted together. For best results, the edges of each chip should be at least 1mm thick. Allow the chips to dry completely.

Using Chips

Place the chips in a bath of epoxy resin to wet them and release any air trapped on their edges. Mix a large batch of Epoxy 330. Put a layer of epoxy on the bottom of the tray. This layer should be thick enough to allow the cutting of a thin mosaic slice once the glue has set. At least 2mm is needed so that the final slice is at least 1mm thick. Once the chips are wet and air free, place the chips in the tray and arrange them carefully with the flattened side down to cover the entire bottom of the tray. Use a wooden toothpick to move the pieces. Once everything is in place, more of the resin/hardner mix can be added if needed. Do this slowly to avoid adding air or moving the opal. If you don't cover the entire bottom with opal, the additional glue will cause the chips to shift. Part of the opal chips can be above the epoxy, but be sure all the flattened faces are next to the bottom of the pan. Try to get all the pieces to fit closely together. Use the toothpick to remove any air bubbles trapped between pieces.

Cure this tray like a doublet. After the glue sets, remove the tray. The aluminum will come off in strips and some may stick to the surface. This causes no problems. Now grind the bottom surface of your epoxy/opal mix on your 220 grit flat lap. This will be the bottom of the triplet. Use very gentle pressure to avoid breaking your slab of glued-together chips. Grind just enough to expose the opal chips. Next paint the bottom black. When the paint is dry, glue the opal onto your choice of base as in making triplets (see Chapter 11). Cure the glue.

Flatten the top with a grinding wheel. Do this very gently as the wheel could lift off a chip. Grind down so the entire surface is flat. Use your flat lap to make the top absolutely flat and about 1mm thick. Dry the top but do not touch it.

The cap can be made of any clear material. I use synthetic quartz or glass. Tempered plate glass works very well. Flat lap one side of the clear cap material and dry. Now glue the cap to the opal layer, being careful not to trap any air bubbles. Cure.

The final step is to shape and finish the triplet. Remember that the clear cap should be a little wider than the opal. This gives the triplet strength for setting. The dome should be low to medium.

The result will be an attractive triplet with spots of opal closely fit together. Careful work can save some terrific opal.

There are as many uses for chips, both opal and other gemstones, as you can imagine. One friend used our chips to make the leaves on wire trees. Let your imagination run wild.

Section Five

Setting Your Gems

In this section we will talk about setting your gem into a jewelry piece. This can be done using pre-produced commercial settings, which is fine. However, a piece of jewelry of your own design is truly unique. Fortunately, with some simple equipment, you can accomplish this quite easily.

Opal & Gemstone Jewelry

Faceted Setting

Photo 25-1, A

Cabochon Setting

Photo 25-1, B

Chapter 25

The Basics of Proper Setting

A piece of jewelry consists of a design made in some kind of metal with an opening where the gem is inserted. Permanently attaching the gem to the jewelry is the process called *setting the stone*. This can be accomplished in several ways. The gem can simply be glued into the opening. Alternatively, prongs can be bent over the gem to hold it in place. Finally the gem can be placed in a metal channel called a *bezel* and the sides of the bezel can be bent over the edge of the gem. Bezel setting a gem is actually a difficult process that requires some training. We will concentrate on the two easier alternatives.

There are two types of prong settings. One, used mostly for faceted stones, is designed to hold the stone up in the setting, essentially suspended in air such as is common in setting a diamond (see Photo 25-1, A). The other, used mostly for cabochon stones (cabs), is designed so that the gem rests on a metal base and prongs hold the gem to the base (see Photo 25-1, B).

Cabs can be set in jewelry designed for faceted stones, but the prongs do not hold the thicker shoulder of the cab well without excessive length that makes the finished piece unattractive. It is best to use a setting specifically designed for cabs.

COMMERCIAL CABOCHON SETTINGS

There are a number of jewelry supply companies that sell already designed jewelry pieces for use with cabs. Most are designed to fit calibrated ovals like your first agate cab. The least expensive settings use common metal plated with gold, silver, or some substitute. Other designs are produced with solid silver or gold settings. Which you use is completely up to you. While there is no rule about this, typically inexpensive stones are set in inexpensive settings. Logically the best gems are set in gold with silver being somewhere in-between. To some extent the metal color that best complements the cab should be considered in choosing what metal to use. For example, white-based opal gets a bit lost when set in a silver or silver color setting. A gold color setting is better for such an opal. Boulder opal, however, does well in a silver setting. Most agates and other opaque cabbing materials do well in silver color settings. Look at your cab next to gold and silver to determine which color is best for it.

There are two ways to proceed. You can cut stones in calibrated sizes you like, then search for a setting. However, it might be best, at least initially, to pick out settings you like then cut agate or other materials to fit the setting.

Here are a couple of mail order companies that produce cabochon settings (see SOURCE DIRECTORY). This is not a complete list, and new sources appear regularly, so check through the pages of the lapidary magazines, on the Internet, and with fellow lapidaries for new sources.

SETTING YOUR CABOCHON

Setting your cab into a commercial prong setting is very simple. Place the cab in the opening. It should fit with just a little space between the stone and the four prongs. The stone can be a little small but not so small that it looks lost in the setting. If you have cut your cab too large, the stone will not lay flat on the base of the setting. It is very difficult to turn the prongs over such a stone without the stone slipping and ending up crooked in the setting. It is better to recut the stone to fit correctly. Once your stone is properly sized, it is time to proceed.

With the stone oriented so the pattern is "right side up" when worn, align the stone in the opening. Now slowly bend one prong toward the stone until it *just* touches it. Bend the whole prong from the side so that it bends only from the base. Make sure the prong just touches the stone but leave it centered in the opening.

Prongs can be easily moved using a *prong pusher* or *jewelry pliers*. A prong pusher is just a piece of metal with a blunt, smooth end that is applied to the side of the prong with sufficient force to move the metal. Instead of a fancy prong pusher, you can use the blunt end of a wooden dowel. Select one that is as big or bigger than the prong to minimize the potential of the prong pusher slipping. Pliers have the advantage of extra leverage to help move the prong. Using your prong pusher, bend the prong that is 180 degrees from the first prong so that it just touches the cab. Once these two prongs are in place, bend the other two prongs to just touch the stone. At this point you will have the stone sitting on the metal and being held in place loosely by the four prongs. Make sure it is centered in the setting. If not, lift a prong slightly and push the opposite prong (180 degrees) in to center the stone.

Now use your prong pusher or pliers to bend a prong over onto the stone. Do this by applying pressure to the *tip* of the prong aimed directly at the stone. The prong should bend over the surface of the stone taking its curved shape. Do the same with the opposite prong making sure that the stone does not move in the setting (see Photo 25-2). Finally, bend the other two prongs in the same way. To prevent movement of the stone, I usually bend each prong part way then come back and bend each the rest of the way.

Photo 25-2

You now have a securely set cab. If the prongs were moved to just touch the sides of the stone, then bent, the stone should be tight and square in the setting. There is no way to lose it short of bending at least two prongs out until the stone clears them…a highly unlikely event.

Your finished piece is now ready to wear!

TO GLUE OR NOT TO GLUE

That is the question. Jewelry craft persons contend that a properly set gem does not need glue to keep it in place. This is true, but note the word *properly*. Commercial settings may have little rough spots on the prongs. A bit of epoxy on the inside of the prong will fill these spaces, thus ensuring a proper fit of the prong. Epoxy also provides a little cushion between the stone and the setting. This can help prevent damage to the stone if the setting is hit hard.

I find glue a useful addition to the setting process and do not in the least feel that I am unprofessional in using it. What I do is place a very thin coating of Epoxy 330 on the inside edge of each prong and on the base of the setting where the stone contacts it before I start bending the prongs. Just the tiniest bit is all that is required. Once the prongs have been bent into place, check to make sure none of the glue has squeezed out and is visible. If it has, wipe off the excess with a paper towel.

Glue adds a bit of insurance to your setting. Use it if you feel it is appropriate, or skip it if not.

GLUE-IN SETTINGS

Gluing a stone onto a setting that has no prongs, just an opening for the stone to sit in, is simple. But again, some care is needed. Be sure the stone and setting are clean and free of oil from your fingers. Cover the back of the stone with 330 Epoxy, then place it on the setting (see Photo 25-3). Make sure that it is centered in the opening. Leave the setting someplace where it will not be moved until the glue sets. You are done!

Photo 25-3

Chapter 26

Lost Wax Design

If you are like I was when I started, you will find commercial settings constraining in short order. You must find a commercial design you like with a setting sized for the gem you wish to set. I frequently found myself unhappy with the designs I could find or displeased that I had to cut a stone to a smaller size because the only design I could find was for a smaller stone. Then, as I cut more and more stones into freeform shapes, the cost of having someone else design a setting was prohibitive. In addition, others could not always produce the design I had in my mind…not that I blamed them. They are designers, each with their own style. Adapting to someone else's design ideas is very hard, even for the best designer.

There was nothing else to do. I had to teach myself how to design and manufacture jewelry. How to proceed?

There are two ways to make a custom setting. One is to start with various pieces of metal and fabricate them into a design. This requires a lot of cutting, sanding, fitting, soldering and finishing. This, in turn, requires a whole additional set of tools and a significant learning process.

The second alternative is to do your design in wax then cast the final setting. This is called the *lost wax process* and is much easier.

It is likely that local designers near you employ fabrication and/or lost wax techniques. Many designers are active in local rock clubs. Visit with them to learn a bit about each alternative. Classes may even be available to get you started. Alternatively you may decide to attend classes at a school. Some community colleges offer instruction. There are also special lapidary schools such as William Holland School of Lapidary Arts in Georgia or a class through your local Federation at Wild Acres in North Carolina. A little help, even a weekend seminar can get you started quickly. However, you can do lost wax design by teaching yourself with the instructions I offer in the following chapters.

THE BASICS OF LOST WAX SETTING

The lost wax process has been around for centuries. A design is created in wax. The wax has an attachment put on it to allow metal to flow...called a *sprue*. The wax is then encased in a mold material similar to plaster of Paris with the sprue left exposed. Once the mold has cured, it is heated in an oven to approximately 1400 degrees Fahrenheit. The heat causes the wax to vaporize, not melt, leaving a perfect impression of the design in the mold. Molten metal is forced into the mold. This can be done with steam pressure, centrifugal force, or vacuum. After the metal cools somewhat, the mold is placed in water where the mold material dissolves. Next the sprue is removed and the metal cleaned and polished. Finally the gem is set.

Photo 26-1

Photo 26-1 shows a ring design that has just been cast. The sprue is attached to the base of the ring. At the right end of the sprue is a large chunk of metal called the *button*. The button is generated by having more metal in the casting process than the setting requires. This is done to insure that the setting is completely reproduced in metal. There is nothing worse than to have all your work ruined because the casting was incomplete due to lack of metal.

Sounds involved and complicated. Fortunately, the casting and metal cleaning can be done by someone else. In fact, I recommend that you have someone else do this if you are not already set up for casting. Casting and metal finishing are another set of skills I will not cover here. I find that my time and money are better spent having someone else do the casting, but you may wish to get into it. By the way, there is a simple casting technique using steam and an electric hotplate which is inexpensive but works great. Look in old issues of the lapidary magazines for instructions on this system (see Source Directory for the company I use for casting and finishing).

My friend, Fred Sias, has produced an excellent, detailed book on how to cast and finish your lost wax designs. If you wish to expand your jewelry making to include casting, this book starts where I stop... at the point where the design is finished in wax and ready for casting. (See Source Directory for *Lost Wax Casting*).

Now that I have allayed your fears about getting a wax design cast and finished, you are ready to proceed. There are two approaches to wax design. One starts with a block of wax. This wax is carved, shaped and polished into a finished design. The other starts with pieces of wax which are built up into a design by soldering them together. Now don't be concerned, soldering with wax is very simple and only requires the heat of your alcohol lamp.

The technique I offer here uses the build-up technique.

WAX

Wax is the basic building block of a setting. The best wax to use depends upon what you intend to do with it. Waxes are either hard for carving or soft for fabrication. I use the soft wax exclusively in my system.

Each manufacturer has their own wax mixtures and color coding so it is best, at least initially, to stick with one manufacturer. The one I have found to work best for me is Ferris or Freeman (see Source Directory). Their lighter blue wax is soft and pliable. Once bent it keeps its shape reasonably well. I use rectangles, uncut bezel, and wire in my basic settings, then add design elements to this. To attach the wax pieces together I use Red Designer Wax.

TOOLS

Making a lost wax setting design using the build-up method requires only a few simple tools. There are more advanced ones that

Photo 26-2

can make the job go faster and easier, but they are not necessary, just nice to have.

Tools include an alcohol lamp to melt the wax, dental tools to shape the wax, a scalpel or knife to cut it, a glass surface to work on, and panty hose to polish the wax. A ring mandrel is used when designing a ring.

Photo 26-2 shows the set of tools I use to design my jewelry. Refer to the Tools for Wax Design & Metal Finishing Chart at the end of the chapter.

Basic dental tools are available in most jewelry supply catalogs. A straight probe or needle—fairly thick like a darning needle—is used to shape the wax (see Photo 26-3). A curved half-circle probe is used to solder wax pieces together and to build up designs. Compactors (tools with round balls on the ends) are used to smooth the wax.

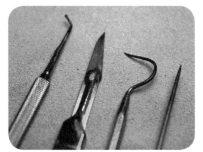

Photo 26-3

A scalpel or knife is used to cut the wax and for minor shaping. I use an electric waxer in addition since it has an easier, more constant source

Photo 25-4

of heat for soldering and design buildup. This machine is nice to have and makes many design jobs faster and easier. It is not necessary, however, as the same jobs can be done heating dental tools over a flame.

There are two types of electric wax pens. One has a changeable single point that is heated. The degree of heat is controlled by a rheostat. This tool allows consistent temperature and can be used to pick up and apply wax. It can also be used to smooth wax. The second type has a two-pronged or V-shaped point (see Photo 26-4). It, too, is heated with a temperature control and will perform all the tasks of the first type of wax pen. I prefer it, however, because the V–point is very useful for picking up red designer wax and applying it to the design. It saves time and gets results that cannot easily be obtained with the

TOOLS NEEDED FOR WAX DESIGN & METAL FINISHING

Wax:
      Ferris Designer Wax - Red (medium)
      Ferris Wax Wire Assortments - Blue
            Square & Rectangle
      Freeman Bezel & Uncut Bezel
             Round & Half-Round

TOOLS:
      Alcohol lamp and alcohol
      Glass or tile work surface
      Dental Tools
             Straight point (probe) or needle
             Curved point (probe)
             Compactors (various sizes)
             Scalpel or knife

      Wax Ring Mandrel - wood or aluminum
      Pantyhose

      Buckley Universal Electric Waxer
             or
      Giles Precision Waxer

other wax pen or dental tools. This second type of wax pen is produced by Buckley Electronics and is listed in the SOURCE DIRECTORY.

Photo 25-5 shows a waxer being used to add design elements to a ring.

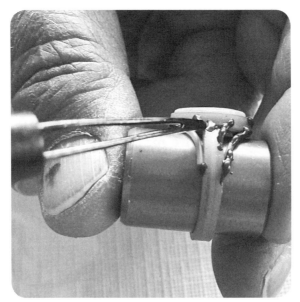

Photo 25-5

Color Plates

Finished Intarsia

CP-56

Opal and Jade Intarsia

CP-57

Color Plates

Chips Bottle

CP-58

Floating Opals

CP-59

Chip Triplet

CP-60

Color Plates

Lace Agate
CP-61, 62, 63, 64

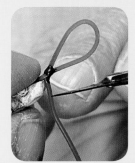

Moss Agate
CP-65, 66, 67, 68

Color Plates

Doublet Ring One Side

CP-69

Doublet Ring Other Side

CP-70

Triplet Design

CP-71

Agate Triangle

CP-72

Boulder Opal

CP-73

Color Plates

Book Cut Stones in Designed Settings

**Moss Agate
CP-74**

**Triplet Ring
CP-76**

**Triplet
CP-75**

**Intarsia
CP-77**

**Boulder Opal
CP-78**

**Lace Agate
CP-79**

Color Plates

**Paul's Designs
CP-80-84**

Color Plates

CP-85

Paul's Designs

CP-86

CP-87

CP-88

CP-89

CP-90

Have Fun!

CP-91

CP-92

Let Your Imagination Soar!

Chapter 27

Preparing a Basic Setting

We are now ready to design a piece of jewelry. What follows are step–by–step instructions on building the skeleton base for a setting. I concentrate on setting an opal here because opals require a little extra care in design so that they are protected when worn. However, the techniques I employ are applicable to all cabs. In Chapter 28 I will discuss the slight modifications to design that you may wish to incorporate into your base designs for cabs from other materials.

First let me tell you about the way I protect opal in a setting.

SETTING OPAL FOR LASTING BEAUTY

A nice looking lady with a very beautiful faceted blue topaz and diamond ring visited our booth one weekend. "I love opal," she said, "but I can't wear it. It is so fragile I keep breaking the stone. After I broke three opals in this ring I had the jeweler replace it with a topaz." I tried to explain to her that the setting was the problem, not the opal, but she remained unconvinced. She walked away still loving opals but certain they were too fragile for her to wear.

I cannot tell you how many times this story is repeated. Most commercially set opals that you see in jewelry stores are set improperly. The setting does not protect the opal. Frequently the stones in such settings break and are lost, giving opal an undeserved bad name. The problem is that these opals are set in four prong findings designed for faceted stones like diamonds. Opals are not diamonds. They have a different character and toughness and must be treated differently. The purpose of this chapter is to show you how to set an opal so that it is protected. Properly set, opals will last a lifetime under normal wear. I am not going to claim that an opal will never break if set properly, but after I developed the setting technique I am going to explain, I have never had a piece returned because the stone broke. And that includes a number of men's rings set with solid opals.

Let me tell you a true story (I swear). A young lady named Sue purchased one of my opal rings. About a week later her mother, obviously upset, called us for help. Sue had slammed a car door on her new opal ring but was too distraught to call herself. We asked what happened to Sue's finger—which was fine—and to the opal. "Oh, the opal is fine," her mother said, "but the ring is crushed!" She sent us the ring which we straightened and re-polished *without* removing the opal. The last time I saw Sue she was still wearing the ring every day and has been for years. Opal is much tougher than people give it credit for being. Properly set, opals will last a lifetime.

Why Opals Crack in Settings. The bumps and bangs of normal wear put stress on the opal as they do any jewelry. This stress could cause an opal to crack. There are two reasons why opals crack when set in prong settings. The first reason is that the prong itself is trying to break the opal and sometimes it succeeds. The second is that the thin bottom edge of the opal is broken when hit with a sharp object.

Opal does not have a crystal structure like amethyst, agate, or diamond. Instead it is a solidified silica gel (a lot of little balls closely packed together) which produce a conchoidal fracture when enough pressure is put on the opal. Simply, it is a lot like glass. If you place a piece of glass between a pair of tile nippers and squeeze, the glass will fracture in one neat line all the way across in the direction the tile nippers are pointing. An opal will do the very same thing. In fact, miners use *tile nippers* to break away unwanted potch and dirt from the precious opal they find. Now visualize a single prong in a four-prong faceted stone setting (see Figure 27-1,A). In setting a stone the upper part of the prong is cut away and a seat made in the lower part of the prong for the stone to sit on. When the top of the prong is brought down on the stone, it acts just like those tile nippers. A facet setting holds the opal in mid air with four sets of tile nippers. If the opal does not crack in the setting process—and it often does as any jewelry bench worker will tell you—it is ripe for breaking later.

In effect the tile nippers have been applied but with not quite enough pressure to break the stone. All that is needed is a slight additional pressure in the right spot and the opal cracks.

Correct and Incorrect Opal Settings

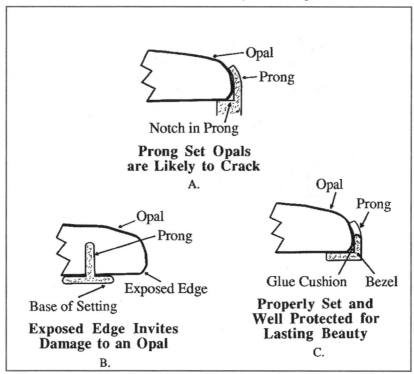

Figure 27-1

The same sort of pressure causes the thin edge of the opal to chip or crack. A bump on that exposed edge with a sharp object may produce one of these conchoidal fractures. Many commercial settings have the opal laying on a ring of gold and held down by prongs. While this is an improvement over the four prong setting, the edge of the opal is still exposed and subject to chipping. In Figure 27-1,B, the edge of the opal extends beyond the gold. This unprotected edge is inviting trouble. One good whack and it's gone.

The system I have developed to set opals takes into consideration the nature of the stone. To protect your opal it must be set so that the entire edge is cushioned in gold or silver. This does two things. The metal prevents a sharp blow to the thin bottom edge of the opal. It also provides a broad even seat so that any pressure put on the opal is spread through the entire edge of the stone rather than localized at one point as would be the case with a prong setting.

THE BASIC SETTING: PENDANT

The basics of building a wax model for a cabochon setting are simple. To illustrate them, let's make a simple pendant. This basic pendant will form the skeleton for the design elements you will apply later. This will be an opal pendant but the technique transfers perfectly to setting any other gem cabochon.

STEP ONE: Supporting the Opal. Select an uncut bezel wax. This wax is "L" shaped. The shorter part of the "L" is the base for the setting. The "L" should be large enough to cover the side of the opal, at least half the thickness of the stone with three-quarters being better. I find that Freeman's 8–gauge uncut bezel is the best size for most opals. The uncut bezel has a thick upright. This thickness prevents the wax from melting rapidly as heat is applied. Regular bezel wax tapers to a thin upper edge which would make it easier to bend over a stone. This edge, however, disappears rapidly the instant any heat is near, leaving a large, ugly gap that no amount of repair work can make right. I use only the uncut bezel wax and throw the regular bezel wax away. In my

setting technique the bezel is not turned over the stone anyway, so the uncut bezel is not too thick.

Wrap the bezel around the opal. Mold it so that the opal sits on the short part of the "L" all the way around the opal. This provides the support the opal needs. Do not force it to

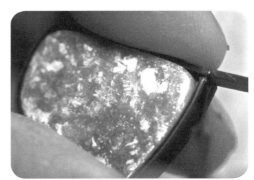

Fitting Bezel

the shape of the stone, as excess pressure will change the shape of the "L", bending it over the stone. When cast, a bent bezel makes it very difficult to set the opal. The bent bezel is smaller on the top than the widest part of the stone. When the stone is removed from the wax bezel the sides of the "L" are forced open, but they spring back somewhat after the stone is removed. When cast, the opening of the now metal bezel is smaller than the stone. Either the metal must be ground away to make the opening bigger or the stone must be cut smaller to fit. Save yourself a lot of hassle. Keep the top of the bezel straight.

Cut the wax so that the two ends fit butt to butt without a gap or bulge in the wax bezel. The bezel should conform to the shape of the stone but not be really tight. The opal should be easy to remove from the wax. This is because the setting will shrink slightly during casting so a little space is needed for proper fit. Some designers put a layer of scotch tape around the edge of the stone before fitting the bezel to adjust for this shrinkage.

To cut the wax for proper fit, overlap the two sides. Heat a knife with your alcohol lamp just enough to slightly melt the wax and cut both parts of the bezel where they overlap. The seam should be placed at the top of the stone where the bail will be placed. Now, using some of the red designer wax and the curved probe, solder the two butts together.

> **The bezel should conform to the shape of the stone but not be really tight.**

The first time you try to solder two pieces of wax together can be very interesting. Expect to melt the bezel away. It takes practice to get the heat just right. You want to have the bezel wax melt *slightly* and to have the red wax flow into the gap between the wax pieces to fill it.

The curved probe works well because it is fairly easy to control the heat. Here is the secret. Heat the curved portion of the probe, not the tip, in the alcohol lamp. Get it hot, but not red hot. Now place the tip into the red wax. The wax will melt and a drop will be picked up the tool. This drop will stay near the point because the probe is hotter at the bend than at the tip. The wax flows to the cooler portion of the tool...the tip. If the wax smokes or burns, you have the tip too hot.

Place the tip with the drop of red wax on the butt joint while holding the butts together. Keep your fingers clear as the wax is hot and will burn. Leave the opal in the bezel. The heat will not damage the stone. The tip of the tool will melt the blue wax slightly just at the gap and the red wax will flow into the gap. Well, if you do it right it will. Now move the tip slightly to blend the red wax into the gap. If the drop of wax is not enough to fill the gap completely, repeat the process with another drop of red wax. Try to get the red wax to be even and just slightly above the surface of the bezel wax. Fill both the base and side of the "L".

If the red wax does not flow, the tool is not quite hot enough. If the blue wax melts away, increasing the size of the gap, the tool is too hot. It takes some practice to get everything just right. The beauty of this system is that the wax is cheap. If you make a mistake, just ball it up and cut a new piece of wax.

Be sure to hold the bezel wax together with your fingers until the wax has cooled. If the wax is still molten the seam will separate.

To solder with the electric pen, set the temperature setting at the middle of the range and allow it to heat. Pick up some red designer wax with the V–tip and apply it to the joint. The blue wax will melt a little and the red wax will flow into the joint, soldering the two ends together. Remove the waxer point and continue to hold the two sides of the bezel wax until the wax cools; about a minute. The waxer controls the temperature so it is always just right. No more melted bezels! Adjust the temperature to get the best result. Cold days may require a higher temperature setting. With the wax pen, the job is done in half the time and, with practice, will be done right the first time. However, the wax pen tip is fairly thick, thus it will produce a large weld area. If you do not want this in your design, use the probe.

At this point the opal should be surrounded by a blue wax bezel. The bottom edge of the stone should be resting on the bottom of the "L" everywhere. The opal should be easy to remove from the bezel but not loose in it. Frequently the wax will have melted onto the surface of the opal at the solder point. Remove the opal carefully so you do not bend the wax. Remove any wax from the opal. Touch up the solder joint if the wax is damaged. Then replace the opal and remold the bottom for proper fit if needed.

STEP TWO: The Bail. Select a rectangle of wax that is not too big or too small. I use 8-gauge most of the time. Ten-gauge bends in metal unless some support is added in the design. Six-gauge looks thick and wastes metal, except in very large designs. This will be a simple one piece bail, not a rabbit ear bail. Leave the wax long.

Bend the wax to form the bail (see Figure 27-1, A). I use the smooth round shaft part of the larger compactor dental tool as a frame to bend the wax on. Smooth metal or wooden dowels can also be used. The frame is needed as the wax will not bend smoothly if bent by itself.

Figure 27-1, A

Forming Bail

Develop a nice, smooth 180 degree bend. The inside of the bend should be large enough to easily accommodate the largest chain one would likely use and to allow the smaller end of the clasp mechanism to pass through the opening. Move the frame tool away from the bend slightly and bend the loose end so it touches the shank of the bail (see arrow in Figure 27-1, A). Cut the loose end of the wax on an angle with a warm knife so the end sits flat on the shank. Solder the pieces together with red wax. Round the inside and outside as shown and solder the sides. Be careful not to use too much heat and do not touch the sides of the bail wax as they will

Adjusting Length of Bail

melt. Repairing a hole takes a lot of time. Here again the electric waxer works wonderfully. Pick up some red designer wax and touch it to the bail joint. Move the point slightly and the job is done. I use the curved probe to do the inside rounding. Allow the bail to cool.

The length of the bail must now be adjusted. To do this, place the bail at the top of the stone oriented the way it will be when attached. The long shank of the bail will be over the top of the opal. Move the bail up and down until the proportions between the opal and bail appear correct. Cut the length of the bail at the bezel wax with a hot knife.

Solder the bail onto the bezel at the joint you produce to hold the bezel together. This should be at the top of the opal. The base of the bail should be approximately in the middle of the bezel front to back (see Figure 27-1, B). Solder the two pieces to-

Attaching Bail

gether from the back with the opal laying on its face on your glass work area. I use a bit of Fun Tac™ on my glass that I press the top of the stone on to prevent it from moving when I solder the bail. Create a round seam on the back. Allow the wax to cool while holding the bail in place. Now solder the sides, leaving a small round wax buildup as on the back (see arrows in Figures 27-1, B and 27-1, C).

Figure 27-1, B

The round edges to these solder joints are essential. When metal flows into a mold, it tries to go straight ahead. Forcing it to make a 90 degree turn is difficult. The metal may form tiny bubbles as it turns, called porosity, causing weakness and pits in the finished piece. Porosity must be avoided. Leaving a rounded, concave edge to your solders allows the metal to flow smoothly around the corner, resulting in no porosity and no problems. At this point the front edge of the bail to bezel joint has not been soldered. This will be done as we add a prong.

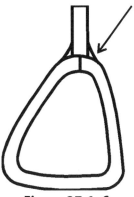

Figure 27-1, C

STEP THREE: Attach Prongs. Although it can be done, I do not like to turn the bezel onto an opal. There is too much danger of breaking the stone. Furthermore, the opal is almost impossible to remove from a setting with a turned bezel if metal repairs or sizing are needed. Instead, I set the opal with a combination of glue and one or more prongs. Actually if correctly done, the glue is sufficient. Prongs add security and design elements but the glue holds the stone in the setting. Opals set using this technique and glue will survive in situations where "properly set" opals might break.

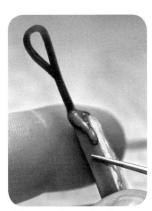

Placing Grove for Prong

Select a piece of round wax wire, 18- or 20-gauge, for the prong. The prong will be placed on the bezel and soldered in place.

To do this, first form a groove for the prong to be placed in. The grove can be formed with a heated needle which is slightly larger in diameter than the prong wax. Heat the needle slightly, just enough to barely melt the blue wax. Lay the needle on the bezel with the point toward the bail at an angle so that a groove is melted in the bezel. Note that the prong will generally fit

239

into your design if it is set at an angle as shown, rather than straight up and down. The groove should be almost through the bezel wax at the front and angled so that it is just barely below the surface at the bail. Allow the point to penetrate the bail slightly to form a small hole.

Before the wax cools, place the prong wax in the groove and force it *slightly* into the small hole. Hold it until the wax hardens somewhat—30 seconds or so. Cut off the prong to leave it about half again as long as you plan to have the finished prong. This allows room to

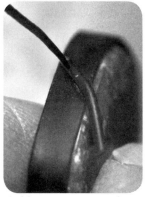

work the prong when setting. It also allows for possible miscasting of the prong which sometimes comes out shorter in metal than the wax model.

Solder in the sides and end of the prong with red designer wax. Use the sharp point of the curved dental probe, heated just enough for a drop of red wax to flow into the joint between the sides of the prong and the bezel. Do not melt the top of the prong.

Soldering Prong in Place

In addition to, or instead of, placing a prong on the side of the bezel, a prong can be placed at the junction of the bezel and the bail. To do this heat a needle just enough to melt the wax. Place it at an angle as shown in Figure 27-1, D and melt a bit of the bezel while at the same time allow the needle point to penetrate the bail slightly. While the wax is still soft, insert a wax wire into the hole and along the groove. Solder it in with red wax to create a smooth transition.

Additionally prongs can be added around the bezel if desired. Number and placement will be a function of your design.

STEP FOUR: Smooth The Wax. The basic setting is now complete. Before adding design elements, smooth the wax. First, check each weld

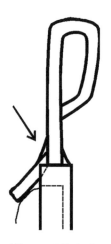

Figure 27-1, D

to make sure they are complete, well rounded, and even, reworking as needed. Then polish the wax. This is done with panty hose. I knew you wondered why they were on the tool list. Wrap a single layer of hose around your index finger. Using a rapid motion, rub the wax surface. The hose will smooth and polish the wax. Actually this step is not absolutely necessary. The wax will cast fine without smoothing. However, sanding the metal to a smooth surface will take longer and may take off some of your design. It is a lot easier to smooth in the wax. Do not work too hard at this. Do just enough to produce a smooth satin finish, not a shiny one.

At this point the basic pendant wax is done, ready to add design elements as you see fit (see Chapter 29). I start every opal pendant design...and most agate pendant designs...by building this basic framework.

THE BASIC SETTING: RING

There is only one thing that differentiates a basic ring setting from a basic pendant wax. Instead of a bail, a ring shank must be fitted.

STEP ONE: Supporting The Opal. Like a pendant, a ring setting starts with a wax bezel. The bezel should be the same thickness as you would make it for a pendant. The joint should be placed at a point where you plan to place a prong, usually where the ring shank joins to the bezel.

STEP TWO: The Shank. Select a rectangle for the shank. The size depends upon the size of the ring and your design intentions. A thin shank saves metal but is prone to bending during wear. A thick shank wastes metal and may cause the setting to look heavy. Most women prefer a lighter look to a ring while most men prefer heavier. I use an 8-gauge rectangle for most women's rings and 4-gauge for most men's rings.

Determine the size of the ring. When in doubt make a women's ring a size 7. The rule of thumb is that the average woman wears a size 6. I believe this is no longer true. I sell four size 7 rings for every size 6. Men's sizes are far more variable with no size that is most popular.

I make men's rings size 10 because that size will fit one or another finger for most men. It also fits me, so worst case, if the ring doesn't sell, I can wear it.

Bend the shank rectangle evenly over a ring mandrel. Ring mandrels with stands are available specifically set up for wax designers. They are made of wood or aluminum. Some have steps at each even size which allows for an even rather than angled size. I prefer these to the tapered mandrels. There are also mandrels with separate tubes for each size, even and odd. These are the easiest to work with but are more expensive (see Photo 26-2).

I shape the wax to the size I wish in the ring. Realize that the metal will shrink somewhat relative to the wax. If you need a true 7 rather than a 6¾, make the shank fit loosely on the size 7 mandrel to compensate for the shrinkage.

To start forming the shank, use the section of the mandrel, one or two sizes smaller than the ring size you wish. Bend the shank wax evenly over the mandrel. Overlap a little. When the wax is removed it will spring out to the desired bend.

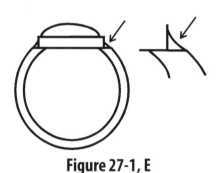

Figure 27-1, E

Cut one end at an angle with a hot knife as shown in Figure 27-1, E. Place the opal and wax bezel on top of the mandrel. Place the angle-cut end of the shank under one side of the bezel wax where you wish the shank to be attached. Holding the shank and opal in place, solder the shank to the bezel. Hold until the wax cools. Here is another case where the electric waxer is far superior. The gap between the shank and bezel can be quite large. The waxer can pick up enough red designer wax to fill it easily and will retain its heat so that the red and blue wax will melt together forming a better solder.

Holding the opal and shank in place, wrap the shank around the mandrel at the desired size. The shank should be long enough to overlap the bezel on the un-soldered side. Carefully cut the shank at an angle and to a length that just fits between the bezel and the mandrel as you did on the first side (see Fig-

Soldering Ring Shank to Bezel

ure 27-1, E). Tuck this cut end under the bezel and solder as you did the first end. Try to keep the shank even and round with the opal centered on the mandrel. A straight line can be marked on the mandrel by turning it as a felt tip pen is held on one spot. This line can then be used to check the straightness of the shank. Make sure you have placed the shank so that the opal is aligned at the angle you intend for your design. Allow this second solder to cool. Add red wax as needed to create an even rounded seam between the shank and bezel on the top and both sides (see Figure 27-1, E). Allow to cool.

Remove the ring from the mandrel carefully. Complete the soldering of the shank where the two pieces meet on the sides and inside the bezel. Be careful not to use too much red wax on the inside of the ring. Excess wax will not allow the ring to fit back on the mandrel and should be removed now as it changes the size. Keep the solders smooth and in the flow of the shank. Round the solder joints to the sides and top for better metal flow.

STEP THREE: Attach Prongs. I typically use two prongs to protect and hold the opal. As with the pendant, select a round wax wire of 18- or 20-gauge. Melt a groove in the bezel with a hot needle as you did for the pendant. The groove should be almost through the bezel at the top and just barely creasing it at the

Prongs Set in Ring Bezel and Shank

shank. Solder each prong, being careful to round and smooth each into the ring. See the photo showing a prong in place. Note the bend of the prong and its extra length.

The number and placement of prongs is a matter of choice. Two prongs are enough to hold the stone which will also be glued into the bezel. These prongs need not be exactly across from one another as your design will fill in as needed.

STEP FOUR: Smooth The Wax Be careful to smooth the inside as well as the outside of the shank. The area at the bottom of the bezel where the shank is attached may be a bit irregular as this will not show when the ring is worn. However, the neater the solder areas, the more professional will be the look of the finished piece. Finally, polish the wax with panty hose, being careful not to change the shape of the shank or bezel.

We have now produced a skeleton pendant and ring with no design. Before we turn to the design process, let's talk about how this basic skeleton might be modified if you are setting an agate or other cab…rather Than opal.

Chapter 28

Setting Other Cabochons

All cabs can be set using the basics I have outlined in Chapter 27. However, while you can use the uncut bezel wire to frame the stone, it is not necessary for protection. That is, assuming the stone is fairly tough…like agate, chrysoprase or jade. For softer stones like turquoise it is probably best to use the bezel. Still, if you do not use the bezel you will need at least three prongs to secure the stone. The common number of prongs is four, but let your design determine how many you need.

To set a cab without a bezel, use square wax wire. Working on the bottom of the stone, carefully shape the wax so that it follows the outline just at the edge. Make sure that this base does not stick out beyond the edge because then it will interfere with your design. Weld the joint together producing as smooth a joint as possible. I use Fun Tac to hold the stone in place as I fit and weld the wax.

Base for Chrysoprase Cab

Now this seat can be attached to a bail for a pendant or shank for a ring, just as we did for the opals in the previous chapter. Prongs are attached to this seat and rise above the cab. Leave them long enough to bend over the stone when setting it. Note, however, that the prongs need not be perpendicular to this seat. Their placement and angle is purely dependent upon your design as is the number of prongs. I find that an odd number of prongs seems to suite my designs better, but this is all predicated upon the shape and size of your stone. You do need to pay additional attention to how the prongs secure the stone. The stone will not be held in place by a bezel so the prongs must do this job. You need at least three prongs, more or less evenly placed, around the stone.

There you have it. The basics of a wax setting for a pendant or ring. All that is needed now is to add some design.

Chapter 29

Dribble Design Technique

I do not consider myself an artist. I cannot draw. I have no training in jewelry design. I never sketch out a jewelry design ahead of actual wax work. I just pick up a cut opal…or other gemstone…examine it from all angles, and let it tell me what it wants to be and how it wants to be set. Then I just do it. Alright, when I was starting out a lot of my designs ended up as wax balls in the trash. Just do it…learn as you go!

The design technique I have developed over many years I call the *dribble technique*. I heat wax until it flows easily and then dribble this wax onto the basic pendant or ring prepared as in Chapter 27 or 28. The dribbles are in balls or longer strings. They are controlled as to shape and size and are intentionally placed.

The dribble technique is easy to do and great entertainment. Start with the basics I offer here and develop your own style. Don't feel wed to anything I say. Take it as a jumping off place. Experiment. Have fun. If you attempt something and it doesn't work, no problem. It's only wax. Ball it up and start again!

DESIGN PRINCIPLES

I took one art class in college…Creative Design. I got the only B in class, all the rest got an A; so much for my talent! I learned two things in that class which have served me well in jewelry design: *balance* and *negative space*. I took several engineering courses. In those classes I learned another element needed in jewelry design: *structural strength*. I don't know where I learned the fourth element needed in lost wax design: *flow*, both visual and metal. The last element is *texture*.

Balance. Think of a jewelry design as a balance beam. The two sides should be of equal visual weight, i.e., artistic balance. Or in dictionary terms "the harmonious integration of components in an artistic work."

When working on a design, I try to maintain balance at all times. If something is added to one side, something must be added to the other side to retain balance. If the piece appears top or bottom heavy, add something to the opposite end to retain balance; or remove something from the heavy side.

Remember, this is visual balance, not weight of metal. Balance does not require identical items on each side. It is achieved by considering the overall appearance of the piece. Your sense of balance—we all have it—will tell you that something is needed in a particular area to reestablish balance.

Consider a freeform opal placed in a basic pendant wax. You will have oriented the opal so that the fire and beauty of the stone will show best when worn (see discussion of orientation presented in Chapter 7). The result often is a very unbalanced look to the basic pendant. By adding design elements, balance can be established. When this is done, the opal and setting become a harmonious whole.

Negative Space. Visual effect can be created by the presence of something or by its absence. The absence of something is called negative space. The presence of something is positive space. Balance can be established by a combination of positive and negative space. The negative can offset and balance the positive.

In jewelry design, negative space is the open areas in the design where there is no metal. For an open area to work as negative space it must be enclosed. Otherwise it bleeds out into the rest of the world and doesn't count visually in the design.

By the judicious use of negative space openings a design can be made light and airy. Balance can be obtained without visual weight. If a design you are working on looks balanced but heavy or "clunky" (a highly technical term for ugly), try removing some of the wax to create open space. Balance can be retained while the piece is lightened both physically and visually.

Dribble Design Technique

Structural Strength. Jewelry is practical art. A piece of jewelry must be strong enough to hold and protect the opal or other gem, yet be worn without bending or breaking. Structural strength can be obtained by increasing the thickness of the wax in the design. For example, a thicker bail is stronger, but it also adds weight and visual heaviness. Is there another way to gain structural strength? Yes. Strength can be gained by triangulation. Recall the structure of a trestle bridge. It is made up of many short, straight beams that form triangular shapes. This triangulation stiffens the structure.

> **Triangulation stiffens the structure.**

This same principle can be used in jewelry design. Suppose that a basic pendant wax has been made with a long, thin bail. The bail bends and moves easily, suggesting that it might not be strong enough in metal. It can be strengthened easily. Add a length of 18-gauge wax wire to the bail. Start about one-quarter of the way down from the top of the bail. Tack it in with red wax. Now tack the bottom of the wax wire into the side of the bezel. Do the same with the other side.

Note what has happened. One, the bail no longer bends easily. Two, the two wires, if properly placed, create a balance to the piece. Three, the open triangular areas create negative space which adds to the design. The net result is a stronger, lighter and better creation.

By the way, these triangular pieces need not be straight. Try a curved wire. It, too, will add strength and negative space.

Flow. There are two elements to flow: visual and mechanical. They are related. Let's look at visual flow first.

When you look at a piece of jewelry your eye follows the design toward its focal point. This focal point is its visual center. The process of moving your eye to that focal point is the visual flow of the piece.

In my designs I want to draw attention to the opal or other central gemstone. It should be the focal point of the design. To do this I use dribbles or wires (often prongs) to direct the eye toward the stone.

Dribbles flow down from the bail to the stone. Prongs move the eye to the best color and away from the lesser beauty in some parts of the stone. A prong on the bottom pointing in toward the stone moves the eye up to the gemstone. Visual flow need not be by straight lines. A tightening swirl of lines can draw the eye in to the center. I find that in most cases, rounded lines are more effective at creating the flow I desire. Straight lines are more harsh. The eye does not move as easily. Experiment and you will find what works for you.

Mechanical flow has to do with how the molten metal flows into the mold when cast. Recall that the metal tries to go straight. Sharp bends are difficult and can cause porosity. The smaller the cross-section of the wax, the more difficulty the metal has in flowing. So, smaller diameter waxes should flow smoothly into one another and be attached to something with a larger diameter at the source of the metal. Round the joints at each end. Do not expect metal to move at sharp angles or you may get a casting that is missing some of its parts.

Each design must have a sprue placed on it so the setting can be cast. The sprue is attached to the wax design after it is completed. Since the sprue is the only path the metal can take to get into the design, all flow considerations start from where the sprue is attached to the wax. The metal will fill the design and then the sprue. The sprue is removed when the metal casting is finished. If you have someone cast your design it is best to let them decide where to place the sprue as it depends on how they set up the casting process.

Pendants usually have a sprue at the top of the bail. This means that metal will flow from the top and reach the bottom last. Design the flow of the piece to facilitate this flow. Rings usually have a sprue at the bottom of the shank. This means that the metal reaches the bezel and prongs last. Make the flow to these last places as easy as possible, flowing naturally from the shank.

Fortunately, visual flow and mechanical flow typically work together. A visual flow which draws the eye to the opal will also encourage the flow of metal when casting. Sometimes I add wax wires to connect areas where flow may be a problem to main flow areas. The wires are internal sprues and are removed in metal finishing or can be left if they add strength and do not interfere with design.

Texture. Texture is generated by the degree of roughness of the surface; coarse, rough, fine. By its finish; smooth, bright, mat. And by its roundness; sharp, angular, round, soft. Together these features generate the overall texture of a piece of jewelry. We talk of a design as being light and airy, heavy, or feminine/masculine. All these and more are texture.

There you have my five design principles: balance, negative space, strength, flow and texture. Some experimentation will teach you more than I can by writing another book's worth. Remember, these principles are general guidelines. Feel free to bend them to meet your perception of what the opal or agate is telling you it wants to be.

DRIBBLE TEXTURES

I have developed four types of dribbles which I use separately or in combination. These are candle, stick, ball and nugget dribbles. Together with flat areas and different metal finishes, they form the texture of the piece. Let's see how to do each dribble texture.

Candle Dribbles. Remember when candles dripped? The wax would build up in a depression around the wick. Finally the side would melt and wax would flow down the side of the candle. As it flowed, it cooled and slowed. The top of the drip would be thin and fairly flat. Toward the bottom the wax would ball up. Later another dribble of wax would flow over the first. Then another. The result was that fantastic pattern on the Chianti bottle at the Italian restaurant. The candle dribble technique takes its inspiration from this restaurant candle.

Candle Dribbles

A candle dribble can be made with the curved point dental probe or the electric wax pen. Heat the bend of the probe and pick up a ball of red wax on the point. Holding the basic design vertically, start at the top where you want the dribble to begin. Allow the point of the probe to touch the blue wax and melt it slightly. Now move the point down the piece, touching the blue wax the whole way. Some of the red wax will blend with the blue at the top. The rest will flow down to where the point of the probe is. When you get to the point where you wish the dribble to end, stop the point. Allow it to stay there for a moment, then lift it from the surface. Allow the red wax to cool a bit without moving the basic wax. There you have it, a candle dribble.

The electric wax pen makes the candle dribble easy, but the result is often a bit thicker than when using a point. Set the heat at about half. Pick up a fair amount of red designer wax in the V–point. Touch the point to the blue wax and draw it down. Some of the red wax will flow out of the V. Stop the point and more wax will puddle, forming a perfect dribble. Increase the heat to have a flatter dribble. Reduce the heat to get a higher relief. The dribble can also be made broader by moving the point in a circle at the bottom of the dribble.

A design can utilize one candle dribble or it can have numerous dribbles, built one upon another. To build up several dribbles, start with the lowest one first. Make this a larger dribble by heating the pick more and picking up more wax. If the dribble is still not large enough, heat the pick and apply more wax, allowing the point to re-melt the red wax you previously applied.

The direction and flow of a candle dribble can be controlled. Simply move the point on the blue wax in the direction you wish the dribble to go. You may also angle the basic wax to get gravity to help create the flow you wish. Try a curve or slight hook at the lower end of the dribble to add interest.

Allow the first dribble to cool. Now add more dribbles, each starting a little above and to one side or the other of the first dribble. In this way you can make the candle dribble as elaborate as you wish. The longer you let each dribble cool before applying the next dribble, the more definition you will get. Also, a cooler tool or waxer makes a dribble with higher relief.

Stick Dribbles. The idea of the stick dribble is to make the area

Dribble Design Technique

Stick Dribbles

look like a branch with a main stem and off-shooting sticks. I don't mean to make actual branches with bark and knotholes, just achieve the general impression.

To make a stick dribble, heat the curved probe but not as hot as for the candle dribble. Pick up the red wax. Just slightly touch the blue wax with the point, not allowing the blue to melt much. Draw the point rapidly in the direction you want. Barely touch the blue wax. A long, thin, high, roundish line of red wax should be left where the point moved. To get more depth, heat the tool and add more wax after the first wax has cooled some. Repeating as often as necessary, a high relief can be achieved. The electric waxer can be used to make stick dribbles. Back off on the heat and use less red wax. Now just barely touch the blue wax. It works, but for fine detail the probe works better.

To get side branches for the stick dribble, simply start another line at the main stick and shoot it off in the direction you wish. Stick dribbles can be as simple or elaborate as you wish. To add side sticks I often use bits of fine wax wire. Solder these to the main stem then place the stick dribble on top of them.

Ball Dribbles. Balls of wax the shape, dimensions and height you wish are easy to make. Balls add texture and sparkle to a setting. They can be an accent or the entire design. Frequently I will use balls in places where side stones might be used. They have the same visual effect.

Ball Dribbles

Using the curved probe, pick up some red wax. Allow the wax to flow to a ball at the point by heating the bend. Touch the point to the blue wax. Do not move the point. Now lift it from the surface slowly.

Some of the drop of red wax will flow onto the blue wax. When the point is removed while the wax is still molten, a drop of red wax will be left which will ball up. You have now created a ball dribble.

Making a Ball Dribble

Ball dribbles can be controlled in size and shape. If you want a large, flattish ball with dome, heat the tool more. Then, when you touch the point to the blue wax, move it in a circle as big as you wish the ball to be. Remove the point while it is still hot. The red wax will flatten into a more dome–like ball.

Small, high balls can be produced as well. Use less heat and pick up less wax. Touch the point to the blue wax only sightly and briefly so almost none of the blue wax melts. Lift the point above the blue wax and hold it until the red wax starts to cool but is still soft. Remove the point. A high, round ball of red wax will be left with its largest diameter above the blue wax. To get really fine balls use a very fine needle. Put tape on the other end so that the hot needle will not burn your fingers.

Balls can be placed next to one another, even touching. Care must be taken to use only as much heat as is needed to form the ball. Excess heat will melt adjacent balls, the wax will flow together, and you get a lump instead of two balls. No matter. Clean the wax from the tool, heat it and lift most of the red wax from the blue wax surface. Smooth the area by melting it slightly with a clean point. Allow the surface to cool and try it again.

Larger balls can be made too. Put more red wax on the point of the tool. If the ball is still not big and high enough, add more wax to the point. Allow the point to penetrate the red wax of the ball you wish to make larger. Move the point around until the top and sides of the ball melt and blend with the new wax on the point. The base of the ball should remain slightly solid or the ball will spread out. Now lift the point and allow the red wax to cool some before removing the point. A larger, higher ball should be produced.

Dribble Design Technique

The use of many small balls on the surface is traditional and is called granulation in jewelry design. In the middle ages European designers used granulation to produce regular patterns of crosses and other shapes on flat plates of gold. Whether you make regular patterns or a random collection, ball dribbles will prove useful in your designs.

Nugget Dribbles. Gold nuggets are very attractive roundish blobs. We find them so attractive that we design jewelry with small nuggets soldered to the gold. A wax nugget dribble can be made to give the general texture of gold nuggets attached to a ring. This nugget look is popular, especially in men's rings.

Nugget dribbles are simply irregularly shaped blobs of wax. They are made in the same way balls are made except the base is expanded and made irregular in shape.

Heat a curved dental tool and pick up some red wax. Allow the point to penetrate into the blue wax and melt it. Move the point around to melt a large irregular area. The red wax will spread out over the melted area. Lift the point. You should be left with a low irregular dome of red wax. Allow it to cool some—30 seconds or so. Now heat

Nugget Dribbles

the tool and apply more wax to some of this dome leaving other parts solid. Repeat as desired to produce a nugget texture.

The electric waxer is excellent for making nugget dribbles. Move the V–point around to get the shape desired and allow more or less of the red wax to flow onto the design. Quick dabbing creates a very rough texture, while slow movement creates a smoother nugget effect.

A nugget texture can be as flat or as irregular and deep as you wish. Add more layers in some areas and use a cooler tool to get more depth. A hot tool will flatten the texture. Try Perfect Purple wax for a smooth nugget texture.

Usually nugget dribbles are used over all or most of the surface of a piece. However, that need not be the case. Nugget dribbles can be used in small areas of a piece and in conjunction with other textures.

That is probably more than you ever thought you needed to know about design. Don't worry. In the Chapter 31 I will show you how to put it all together into a step–by–step jewelry piece.

Before you try to apply these techniques to a design, I suggest you practice, practice, practice! Take some pieces of blue wax and try to apply the various types of dribbles with red wax. Make a closely spaced line of balls, an elaborate candle Mama Mia would be proud of, and the world record nugget hanging on a stick dribble tree! Have fun and play with the wax. Getting comfortable with textures before applying them to a design will make your success much easier.

Or you can do what Harry Leadthumb would do. Heat up the wax tool, apply it to the basic design and melt the entire thing!

Chapter 30

Design to Complement Your Gemstone

Each stone you cut will have its own character. This is the combination of its shape, color and pattern. Your task is to develop your design to complement this uniqueness.

For example, suppose you have cut an agate into an oval. The agate has a long, bending shape to its bands of color. These *"U"* shapes open at one end of the long axis of the oval. Setting the stone in a pendant you could leave the *"U"* shape with the open end up or down. If the opening is down, there is a natural downward flow to the stone. Adding stick dribbles to the bail which are complementary to the shape of the color bands can form an integrated downward flowing design. If the *"U"* is up, there is a completely different flow to the piece.

Other stones have different patterns. A lace agate has many rounded and irregular bands of color. A multi–angled design with lots of open negative space may work best.

Shape also affects the flow of the design. Suppose you have cut a chrysoprase into a fairly long narrow triangle–like stone. Here there is no pattern to help with the design, just luscious, translucent green color. When you move the stone around so that each point in succession is at the top of a potential pendant, one orientation will stand out as best. The stone will have a flow to it. Setting it with another point up will never be as satisfactory.

The pattern of the stone can be complemented in the pattern and texture of the setting. Rutilated quartz has showy straight lines of rutile sometimes exploding from one spot. Straight lines in your design will enhance the stone.

Now consider texture. Opals come in many patterns. Typically these range from large flashfire to fine flash or pinfire. A small pattern, particularly a pinfire pattern, lends itself well to a small ball texture. A large pattern suggests a big, broad, shallow dribble pattern. An intermediate fire pattern lends itself to a candle dribble texture. Let your imagination soar!

Agates and other gems also have a texture. A fine lace agate will require small design elements while an agate with sweeping bands requires a broad sweeping design.

The design projects which follow will further explain how I make this all fit together.

Chapter 31

Design Projects

Enough theory, let's make some jewelry. In the next two chapters I am going to take you through several design projects using stones we cut earlier in the book. Each will be designed and ultimately set to produce a finished piece of jewelry. The process will be explained and illustrated with color as well as black and white photos.

A SIMPLE SETTING

The first setting could not be simpler. You don't even need to make a frame for the stone. All you need is a bail and a couple of prongs.

Remember that piece of lace agate with ET eyes that we started to cut as an oval...then adjusted to an irregular shape? Let's make the simplest possible setting for it. Start with a piece of rectangular wax. Make a good size bail on one end. Now set the wax on the back of the stone and cut the length to about two-thirds of the height of the stone (see CP-61, 62, 63, and 64 to follow these steps).

Next place a prong at the top front of the stone and adjust its length. Solder a piece of wax wire onto the bottom of the bail wax. Turn the ends over the stone and cut them to the length desired. Finally, add some ball dribbles to the bail and at the tip of each prong to accentuate the eye pattern of the lace agate and we are finished. Well, except for the back. Smooth the wax joints with a ball compactor and make sure there is a smooth, rounded transition into the lower prongs so that they will cast. Now you are done. I told you it was simple!

MOSS AGATE

That nice moss agate freeform we cut lends itself to a fairly clean design. A lot of metal would take away from that great pattern in the stone. Because the stone is so translucent, any metal behind the stone would show from the front. Consequently, I have decided to set the stone with a bezel (see CP 65, 66, 67 and 68).

Surrounding the stone with a bezel and adding a bail gives us a basic design. Keeping with the simplicity idea, I add a few candle and ball dribbles around the prong at the bail completing the design. I check the balance of the piece by hanging it from a needle. If it does not hang in the orientation you want, it may be a simple matter of bending the bail wire to the right or left.

OPAL TRIPLET

The beautiful opal triplet we cut will look great as a pendant. There is one thing that we have to pay attention to. The sides of the cab are a bit thick since they include a black back, an opal layer and the bottom of the clear cap. The finished jewelry will look best if this thick side is covered by a bezel. Consequently, I choose a deeper bezel wax wire than I would ordinarily use for this size stone.

The design itself is fairly straight forward (see CP-71). I employ candle dribbles that move the eye down to the stone. I thought about adding some dribbles to the left side or on the bottom, but decided that these would make the piece look too heavy.

AGATE TRIANGLE

The simple lines of the brown agate triangle we cut lend themselves to a clear, simple design. After framing the stone with a bezel, I adjusted the bail length. A little experimentation showed that the bail should be quite short. A longer bail took away from the beautiful shape of the stone.

A small prong at the point of the triangle allows the design to flow into the stone. If I placed prongs anywhere else, including the other two points, they took away the clean line of the stone. A few candle dribbles down the bail help bring the eye to the stone.

Because the sides of the triangle are long, I have placed a wax wire across the back about half way down the sides. This wire will stabilize the wax so it will retain its shape while being case and will help the flow of metal. The finished setting is shown in CP-72.

260

BOULDER OPAL

The boulder opal we cut has a couple of interesting challenges for setting. The best orientation is for the sharpest point to be pointing to the lower left. This leaves the brown inclusion on the lower right and the right side a bit unbalanced with the left.

Having placed bezel wax around the outside, I then formed and attached a bail. The length of bail I choose was sufficient to allow the buildup of the sides as it neared the stone so that the whole form would create a general triangle shape. I added a prong at the top to break up the roundness of this corner of the stone.

Blend this prong into the bezel using candle dribbles. Start at the base of the bezel. Form a dribble that covers the bail joint. The dribbles will hide the seam making it invisible once the piece is finished. This is an important point. Use the texture system to cover and hide seams and joints. Finishing and perfectly smoothing a joint or seam so that it becomes invisible takes a lot of time and work. It is far faster and just as effective to cover it with a dribble or two. Now add dribbles up the bail. These can overlap if you wish. Be sparing at first. I find it more effective to do a little bit of dribble at a time, then come back later as I feel more is needed. The more you do in one area, the more you must add elsewhere to keep the piece in balance.

> **Use the texture system to cover and hide seams and joints.**

To distract from the brown inclusion I placed a prong at an angle that visually brings the eye from the lower right back to the center of the stone (see Figure 31-1). To blend this prong into the design and to help establish right/left balance, I add dribbles to the base of the prong, flowing to the lower right to counterbalance the opal point on the lower left (see Figure 31-2).

Figure 31-1

Figure 31-2

Add dribbles to each side, again working from the bottom up. As you do this, work the dribbles into the prong. Get the flow of the set of dribbles to move the eye down the bail, spreading out to the stone on each side. Bring some of the dribbles up onto the base of the prong so that it blends into the design. Having done all that I still had a problem. The lower right was shorter than the lower left, leaving an unbalanced look to the piece. To add some visual weight to the lower right, I added some nugget dribbles to that corner. Just a little does the trick. A lot of nugget would make the piece look heavy. The final result is shown in CP-73.

DOUBLET RING

Long narrow ring stones are traditionally set with the long axis parallel to the finger and the ring shank at right angles to this long axis. But you don't have to follow tradition.

Let's use the long narrow freeform doublet we cut to make a ring. After placing bezel wax around the stone, I play with it on the ring mandrel trying different angles. I settled at an angle of about 30 degrees off the long axis. Why this angle? I don't know; it just felt right.

After attaching a ring shank, I had a piece with a stone that sat well above the ring mandrel at its points. To fill in these gaps and, at the same time broaden and stabilize the ring's base, I added wax wire to the shank. To do this I bent the wax over a thick dowel. I then fit it to the shank shape with the point of the wire under the bezel wax at the point of the stone. The wire then bends smoothly onto the side of the shank. I did that on both sides of the ring, filling in to both ends of the stone. The results can be seen in Photos 31-1. Photo 31-2 shows how this looks from the inside of the ring. At this point I make sure that the wax wire flows into the shank and the bezel so that it will cast properly.

The ring is now ready for the addition of design detail. At this point the ring shank

Photo 31-1

joins the stone bezel at an abrupt angle. To smooth this transition and to add an upward flow of the ring shank into the stone, I add stick dribbles that flow like fingers up the shank into the bezel. I use the same dribbles on the wax wires I have used to broaden the base of the ring. The final result is a set of nubby branches that reach up toward the stone.

Photo 31-2

The final design can be seen from both sides in CP-69 and 70.

In the next chapter I will develop additional designs that are a bit more complex.

Chapter 32

More Design Projects

That was fun! Let's do some more. These designs are a bit more complex.

A CHRYSOPRASE MAN'S RING

A while ago Bobbi and I visited the **Candala Chrysoprase Mine** (see Source Directory) owned by our friends Richard and Mary Lou Osmond. While there Bobbi found a small chunk of gem chrysoprase rough sitting on the ground which we were allowed to keep. I subsequently cut the stone. It turned out beautifully but there was a problem. The stone was too big for Bobbi to wear as a ring and it did not lend itself to being a pendant because the dome was too high. This gem was telling me it wanted to be a ring. There was no option. I confiscated it! The stone was destined to be my new ring. (The story of our trip to the mine can be found in *Rock & Gem Magazine*, November 2007.)

Photo 32-1

I start by building a wire base for the stone to sit on. The stone has beautiful translucent color throughout so I do not want to cover any of it unnecessarily. Thus, I do not want to use a bezel wire. In addition the stone has a very high dome and thick shoulder area, so the bezel wire would have to be very thick, interfering with the design I have in mind. To complete the base for the design I attach a ring shank and add four curved wax wires to broaden the base (see Photo 32-1).

Photo 32-2

The basic design concept I have in mind is to have the stone cradled in a set of tree branches. The stick dribble method is ideal for this. I start with long, thin wax wires that I attach well down the shank. I curve each wire to give it more flow. Each wire is placed so that it wraps up over the stone. Some shorter wires are attached to the longer wires to make a branching effect (see Photo 32-2). Each branch must be connected to the shank and two or three other places to add strength and flow. I add connections from the stone's base wax to the longer prongs. I do this from the inside of the setting, again to add strength. .

To blend the wires into a design I use stick dribbles to cross from the shank onto the wire, then up the wire to its branch with other wires. I cross some wires to give the design a more tree branch like look. Attaching these crossing branches to one another also triangulates the wires and gives strength to the whole design. Using stick dribbles, I blend the whole design, including connections to the stone's base. The end result is seen in from both sides Photos 32-3 A and B.

Photo 32-3, A

Photo 32-3, B

More Design Projects

OPAL PENDANT

Remember that lovely vertical seam opal from Coober Pedy that we cut in Chapter 21. Let's do a pendant using that stone.

The first thing we have to do is decide on the orientation of the stone. This stone has a split personality. It really looks best with the long point of the stone at the lower left corner as the stone would hang as a pendant. While the color is best from this angle, the design problem this creates is almost insurmountable. The stone just has no balance from that orientation.

Fortunately, as I play with the stone, I see that the color is almost as good with the point straight up. There are still balance problems for the design, but they are not overwhelming. It's time to experiment.

I make a basic pendant setting with a bezel wire to hold the stone and a bail adjusted to a length that allows a design that would blend into the stone. Having done this, I hang the pendant from a needle and assess its balance (see Photo 32-4).

Photo 32-4

Photo 32-5

The pendant hangs correctly with the best color for this orientation showing when the piece is viewed from straight ahead.

When viewed from straight ahead one thing is glaringly evident. The left side has a nice sweeping round profile while the right side is as straight as a board. These two profiles clash. The right side needs to be softened.

To do this I add a curved angle prong to the right side starting about half way down and sweeping into the opal (see Photo 32-5).

I now have created an unbalanced look to the piece. The left side looks barren. To regain balance I put a smaller angle prong on the left

267

Photo 32-6

side to generate a visual flow that brings the eye to the stone from both sides (see Photo 32-6).

We still have a bit of a problem with the right side. It remains a little straight. To solve this I can add another short angle prong to the upper right. But I have another concern. What am I going to do to the bail to get it to blend into the rest of the pendant?

We can solve both problems at one time. A wire that starts at the top of the bail, swings right in a nice curve then swings left, then right again would break up the straight lines of the bail. Having it bend over the point of the opal's bezel and smoothly into a short angle prong solves both problems with an integrated approach (see Photo 32-7).

To finish off the design I employ the judicious placement of dribbles. To anchor the squiggle wire to the top of the bail I employ one ball dribble. As the squiggle wire bends across the flat bail wire it leaves two straight edges on the bail that distract. I soften these with two small candle dribbles, one on each side in the curve of the wire.

Photo 32-7

To integrate the angle prongs into the bail and bezel I employ stick dribbles. I start these up on the bail wire, building them up a bit to widen the setting at the connection between the bail and the bezel. I then flow them onto each angle prong so that the whole stick dribble system flows. As I do this I add a short stick dribble on the left bezel but not onto the stone. This gives the viewer a continuity of two swings of gold coming down each side (see Photo 32-8). Neatening up the back and making sure the whole back flows is the last task. The piece is finished and ready for casting.

Photo 32-8

More Design Projects

CHRYSOPRASE PENDANT

I love the shape of the large chrysoprase freeform cab cut in Chapter 5. The teardrop shape with the re-curve on the left creates a very attractive look. Setting this gem in a way that preserves, or even enhances, this shape was proving to be a challenge. I thought about it for many days. One morning it came to me. I needed to make other smaller shapes with this same outline. These shapes would fall down the bail, getting larger as they approached the stone.

Photo 32-9

I started experimenting. First I tried making the shapes with perfect purple wax. That didn't work. I was not happy with the shape but, more important, the clumps of wax looked heavy and distracted from the chrysoprase. I needed the shape without the weight. The solution was wax wire bent to an outline similar to that of the chrysoprase cab.

Photo 32-10

I fit a large shape on the left and in reverse outline to the cab. I then placed a smaller one on the right side in the same profile as the cab (see Photo 32-9). A close-up of these two shapes can be seen in Photo 32-10.

At this point I have made progress, but the piece looks a little like a lopsided bow tie. I need at least one more teardrop. I place this on the bail and just touching the left wire teardrop (see Photo 32-11). I then do a squiggle down the bail flowing into the teardrop wires. To finish off the deesign I form five carefully shaped and sized candle dribbles down the bail. The stone is held by the bezel and one short prong over the point at the top. I do not use any texture on the wire shapes or on the lower bezel. It seems that the smooth, rounded shape of the cab requires no texture in the complimentary elements of the design. This

Photo 32-11

269

progression of shapes leads the eye down to the beautiful chrysoprase gemstone.

Not quite finished. When I take the stone out of the bezel to check all the joints and finish off the back, I find that it looses its shape easily. I also worry that the long bezel will not fully cast (fill with metal). The solution to both these problems is a series of wax wires across the back of the stone. These stiffen the piece and, at the same time, provide additional paths for the metal to flow, thus filling the whole bezel. While these triangle forms can be removed after casting, I decided I liked the look and will keep them in the finished piece. The final design is shown in Photo 32-12.

In the last two chapters we have completed several designs that now are aready to cast and finish before setting the stone. But before we move on to setting, I want to talk a bit more about design.

Photo 32-12

Chapter 33

Design Tricks

Over the years I have developed various tricks which help make jewelry designs successful. Let me share them with you.

PRONGS

It is sometimes difficult to get prongs to cast completely. To solve this problem I do three things. I attempt to integrate the prong into the design so that the metal will flow naturally into it. This requires a broader rounded base for the prongs. I keep the prong wax longer so that if the metal does not complete fill, it will still be long enough to be usable. I also add a ball to the end of each prong. This ball acts as a reservoir for the molten metal, increasing the chances the prong will cast completely.

PERFECT PURPLE

Perfect purple is a wax that is ideal for nugget texture dribbles. This wax smooths out to a lower relief with more even undulations. It is great for character designs as well. Careful dribbling can create a dragon or a fish without any carving of the wax like my Puff design.

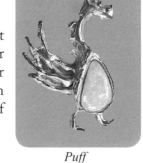

Puff

FLEXIBLE WAX

Flexible Wax Prongs

This wax bends and returns to its original shape once released. If you want a design with many small prongs, each of which just barely covers a part of the gemstone, this is the wax to use. Be careful, the wax does stick to the stone. Use a sharp knife to lift off these prongs, then repair any damage to them with additional flexible wax. The previous photo shows a ring setting that employs several small prongs made with flexible wax.

SIDE STONES

I generally do not like to use side stones in my designs. There are, however, occasions where they are called for. Some people even believe that an opal pendant is not complete without diamond side stones.

If you insist, the easiest way to put baskets for faceted side stones into your designs is in the wax. Several manufacturers produce small four prong wax or plastic settings for 1– to 10–point or more diamonds or other round faceted stones. Using a tweezers to hold the side stone setting in place, tack it in with red wax. Blend the base into the design all around so that the metal will flow into those tiny prongs.

Set the side stones in the completed polished casting before you set the opal. Some people have left diamonds in these wax side stone prongs and cast them. The burnout process leaves the diamonds unharmed, or so they claim. I have never tried it, but it seems to me that the presence of diamonds would complicate cleanup and polishing of the metal. Definitely do not put in other side stones. They can be damaged by the high heat of the casting.

HIDING IMPERFECTIONS

Not every stone you cut is perfect. The stone may have a pit, dull area, gray inclusion, or other "beauty mark." Careful design can hide these imperfections.

The imperfection need not be covered. All that is needed is something which will take the eye away from the problem and toward something of merit.

A prong placed near a pit makes it almost invisible. The prong distracts the eye from the problem. Whatever you do, don't point the design or a prong right at the problem. Over it is fine. Away from it works too. But not right at it. This will make the imperfection stand out rather than blend in. Distraction is the best way to hide imperfections.

Design Tricks

LEAVES

The stick dribble texture lends itself to leaves. There are some wax leaves available. I find them too big for most designs, so I make my own.

Use a flat, thin sheet of wax. The most common thin sheet wax is pink. Trace out a leaf outline on it with a sharp needle point. Now carefully use the point of your slightly heated knife to cut out the outline. Smooth and round the edges with your fingers and a panty hose, keeping the leaf shape. The leaf can be curved at this point to look more like a natural leaf rather than a flat approximation of a leaf. Using red wax, create a higher central stem in the leaf. The stem should be thicker at the base of the leaf and thin out to nothing about 2/3 of the way up the center. This represents the central stem of the leaf which provides circulation. In large leaves side channels can be added. Study natural leaves to get the general idea of structure. Do this very carefully as the thin pink wax melts at the hint of heat, leaving a gap in the leaf.

The leaf can now be attached to the design, usually to a wax wire branch in a stick dribble design. Make sure the stem is smooth and natural looking. Add leaves as you desire. Put a bit of extra wax on the back of the leaf at the attachment to the stick to give a bigger opening for metal to flow into the leaf.

Once all the leaves are in place, turn the piece over. Tack the leaves together and/or to the base of the design from the back in as many places as you can. The leaves are thin and metal may not flow into them easily. Connecting them from the back reduces this problem. Thicker leaves cast better but look heavy. Being mindful of metal flow on the back can solve the casting problem without this excess thickness.

LEAF PRONG

A sneaky way to produce a prong to hold a stone is to use the point of a leaf. The leaf must be thin enough to bend easily in metal and not too long. Long leaves that cover a large portion of the stone make it hard to set the stone.

Okay, there is a way to hide an imperfection that is fairly far into your stone. *If* the stone is going to be set as a pendant, make a wax wire twig that bends over onto the stone toward the imperfection. Place a leaf or several leaves on the twig. Design it so the whole twig can be bent out of the way to remove the stone, then re-bent over the stone once the wax has been cast into metal. It is amazing what can be done using this technique. But don't use it on rings. The point of the leaf will catch on everything!

GRAPEVINE

A combination of leaves, wire and ball dribbles can make a grape vine design. Grape vines have squiggly tendrils that grab onto the trellis to support the vine. Some are loose, creating interesting shapes. These shapes can be simulated by wax. Take a 20–gauge wax wire and wind it tightly around a small diameter round object, like a needle. Make several turns. Slip the wire off the needle carefully to keep all the coils in place. Gently pull both ends of the wire to loosen the coils into the desired squiggles.

Prepare and place grape shaped leaves. Mix a couple of tendrils with them. Then build a grape cluster with ball dribbles. You will be amazed how realistic such a design can be. Do not make it too big as it will distract from your stone.

CIRCLES

The circle is a common element in design. To make small wax circles, wind an 18– or 20–gauge wire tightly around a small round needle. Make sure the wax is even and touching the surface at all points or the circles will be lopsided. Heat a knife slightly and cut the wax wire along the axis of the needle. Slip the wax off the pointed end of the needle. It will fall into numerous open circles. To close each circle, hold the two ends together and tack them carefully with the rounded pick and a little red wax. Heat control is essential here as too much will melt the blue wire wax and alter the circle shape. Lots of red wax leaves a ball at the joint.

These circles can now be used in designs. For example, they can be carefully placed to suggest a flower using several to make its petals. The circles can even be shaped by squeezing one area to produce a part that is narrow for the inside of the petal. You will find all sorts of uses for circles!

BRACING

Sometimes it is helpful to provide some bracing to keep a wax pattern's design and shape while casting or to provide better metal flow. Such bracing can be added, usually to the back of the design, as I did for the chrysoprase pendant in Chapter 32, then removed in the metal before setting or left in place if they do not interfere with the design. .

One place where bracing is a really good idea is in a large pendant. The bezel wire can be easily and inadvertently bent as the mold is made and/or the metal is finished. Also, a long bezel that is not connected to the bail in any other way may not fully cast because the metal has a long way to travel. To prevent these problems, add a couple of pieces of 18–gauge wax wire to the inside of the bezel. One should go from the bail area to the bottom. The other should cross it and be attached to the inside sides of the bezel. Make all joints round to promote metal flow. This cross brace will insure better metal flow and prevent the shape of the bezel from being distorted. The thin wire is easy to remove in metal finishing and can be recycled into another casting.

TEXTURE AND POLISH

When the metal is polished after casting, small amounts are removed. In some cases it is necessary to plan for this loss of metal at the wax stage. If you desire a very high relief texture, make it even higher than you want. The top surface will be removed in metal finishing so that the relief will be brought down to the level you desire.

Ball dribbles are sometimes a problem for metal finishing. The tops of the balls may be worn down, leaving a flat topped ball. I know of no way to prevent this in the wax. Care must be taken in finishing.

Texture can be changed depending on how the metal is polished. Polishing only the higher part of a design, while leaving the lower parts in the matte finish produced by casting, can add to the depth of the texture. Polishing all the little indentations in the design to a high gloss will flatten the texture.

Various textures can be produced in wax. A fine needle point can be used to scratch patterns into a surface. Textured materials can be used in the design so long as they will vaporize in the casting process. However, all such textures are prone to flattening during metal finishing.

Textures can be added to the metal during finishing as well. One of my favorites is produced with an electric engraver. Using a tight circular motion, an area can be filled with tightly packed overlapping swirls. The effect is quite attractive.

Here is another texture secret. Suppose an area of your design miscasts, leaving one or more small pits on the surface. (It happens fairly frequently.) The pits can be filled with metal solder and finished off. That is a lot of work. Instead, consider using the electric engraver to texture the area. The texture may hide the pits. Texture leaf designs with this technique to make the leaves stand out from the branches.

Experiment with metal texture. It can add another element to your designs.

Chapter 34

Sources of Design Ideas

Now that you know how to design and produce a piece of jewelry, you are probably wondering where you might find ideas for designs. In a very real sense the answer is "everywhere." Inspiration can come from a wind bent tree, the pattern in a dress, other jewelry and even the gem itself. If you are seeking jewelry design ideas you will find them in amazing and unexpected places. An open mind and an observant eye will serve you well.

Not very helpful? Okay, how about some specifics.

JEWELRY DESIGNS OF OTHERS

One of the best places to get ideas for your designs is from the jewelry of others. They have solved the design problem more or less successfully. Observing what others have done will help you to learn what works and what will not. Look at all sorts of designs. You hate this particular one. Fine, try to figure out why. It distracts from the stone. It's too heavy. It's unbalanced. It's poorly finished. It's too harsh and angular. You love this one. Good, but why?

Critical examination of jewelry will allow you to develop a clear idea of what you like and don't like. Which elements, textures, etc. may work for you and which clearly will not. In this way you will develop a sense of your personal style in jewelry design. That is exactly what you want, your own style. There is no point in doing your own designs otherwise.

There are lots of good places to find jewelry designs. Articles and ads in jewelry magazines are great sources. Jewelry setting catalogs such as those by TRIPPS are others. *Jewelry Artist* magazine is full of unique designs in every issue. Many catalogs are offered in the jewelry magazines. Send for them and study them. Pieces you see others wear are another great source. Sometimes jewelry looks much different when worn that it does in a catalog. Jewelry stores and art galleries, especially ones that feature one or more custom designers, are never to be missed. They are in the business of selling so they will carry designs that appeal to a large segment of the population.

Custom jewelry designers are another great source. Some display their pieces in jewelry stores or art galleries. Others sell at shows. Gem shows often have several custom jewelers as well as the more standard designs. Arts and craft shows can have unique designers as well. Some are far out, others are common and unimaginative. You can learn from all of them. Even a far out piece you wouldn't be caught dead wearing may have an element in its design you can use to advantage.

Respect For Designers. A word of warning about custom designers. They are in business and some fear that others will copy their designs. If this happens, they may loose the uniqueness that is their stock in trade. Treat designers with the respect you would ask others to give to you. Photograph a designer's jewelry only with permission. If you need to, make a quick sketch of a piece to remind yourself of a design idea; preferably after you have left the designer's booth. Do not linger over a display for a long period. These people are trying to make a living. When you stand in front of their display, you block potential customers.

> **Photograph a designer's jewelry ONLY with permission!**

Some custom designers are happy to talk to you about their work and share their ideas with you. Others are not. Start by explaining that you are learning design and would like to explore some ideas with them. Then accept their willingness, or lack thereof, graciously. Do not pass yourself off as a potential customer. There is nothing more frustrating for a designer than to spend a lot of time with someone who appears to be a potential customer only to find out that the person was just pumping them for ideas. It has happened to me many times and it leaves a bad taste in the mouth. *Always* quit talking and move out of the way to let a designer give his/her full attention to prospective customers. *Never* show your designs to people in front of a designer's display or anywhere else at a show. These people have paid to show their work and it is unfair to compete with them. If you want to sell at a show, rent a booth!

Finding Designers To Learn From. There are custom jewelry designers in most towns. There are even associations of designers who have meetings. Too, many designers are members of the local lapidary club. These people are great sources of new ideas. Frequently these people are incredibly generous with their time and ideas. Nancy Ayotte, a fellow club member, invited me to her home, showed me how she did things and shared her ideas when I was just starting. Her generosity can not be fully repaid. With a little effort you will find such helpful people.

Remember, the idea in looking at jewelry and talking to designers is to get ideas for your own designs. Take away the ideas, mold them to your own taste, and produce your own unique designs. Do not copy someone else's design. Technically, each piece of jewelry has an implied artist's copyright so it is illegal to copy a design. But even so, it is poor form. You want to produce something that is uniquely yours, not a copy of someone else's ideas.

DESIGNS FROM NATURE

Nature is a great source for ideas. Clearly my stick dribble technique was inspired by the branches of trees and bushes. My nugget dribbles draw from gold nuggets. But these are not the only useful forms in nature.

One of the most fascinating forms in nature is the flow of water in a small stream. The water flows over rocks, swirls around boulders, and splashes down waterfalls. The patterns created are very attractive. Observe them and think about

how they might be used in jewelry. Perhaps wax could be heated and allowed to flow and solidify in these patterns.

Bark is another wonderful natural texture. The more irregular shaped patches of bark on cottonwood trees are a great source of design shapes. Pine trees have various different bark textures and patterns.

A willow tree is a wonderful flowing thing. Dogwood flowers make a good jewelry pattern. Aspen leaves have been used successfully in many designs.

Rocks, mountains, rivers, wind blown grass, birds, feathers, and lots more provide shapes and textures. I am sure you get the idea.

YOUR ENVIRONMENT

Cloth patterns, shadows on a wall, even a pile of spaghetti on a plate can be useful.

DOODLES

Still stuck for ideas? Try doodling on a piece of paper. Do not try to draw anything, just let your pen move as you feel like it. Set that paper aside and do it again. Get a collection and look at them. Somewhere in them will be design shapes that would be great.

THE GEMSTONE ITSELF

In most cases I find that the gemstone itself helps me decide on a design. The pattern suggests texture and flow. The shape suggests balance and jewelry shape.

I try to keep an open mind. I find that if I approach a gemstone with the idea that I will make it into a particular design it will almost always not work. Instead, I have in the back of my mind all those different neat ideas I have stored. As I study the stone, an idea will start to crystallize. I will then begin the design. As the design develops I will frequently alter my original concept. If something doesn't work, I change it. Many of my best designs end up looking nothing like what I had in mind when I started. Let your creative juices flow!

At the end of the last color plate section you can see the results of our design examples finished and ready to wear. I also include a number of other designs I have done over the years. They are reproduced to give you an idea of the variety of design that is possible. I do not claim to be a great jewelry designer, so if you hate these designs, that's okay. Look at each and determine what it is that you like…or don't like… and use the good elements in your designs.

There you have my secrets to finding design ideas. Have fun.

Chapter 35

Setting Your Gemstone in Your Design

You already know the basics of setting a cab (see Chapter 26). Setting a cab in your own design is basically the same process.

However, there are some differences when setting a stone in your custom design. The seat for the stone must be checked to make sure it has not accidentally been bent in the casting and finishing process. Prongs must be prepared before pushing them down on the stone and their length must be adjusted afterwards.

In what follows, I explain how to set a gem into your design. While the explanation is specifically for opal, it is applicable for all gems. Additional instructions are offered for settings that do not employ a bezel.

Opals take a little special care. I admit it, setting the opal into the finished metal is no real fun. The opal may break, ruining it and all that design work. Careful preparation makes damaging the opal unlikely. Still, just when I start bragging to myself that I have not broken one, there one goes. The glue and prong setting technique I have developed will protect the stone. In my opinion it is the best way to set an opal so it will not break in the setting process, or in wearing. I use the same techniques for all gemstones…not just opal.

SETTING STEP–BY–STEP

STEP ONE: Preparing the Setting. The wax model has been cast successfully. The metal has been finished to a complete fine polish. Do not save final polishing for later. The metal will be re-polished, as needed, after setting the stone, but the heat of properly polishing the metal could prove a danger to the stone…especially opal…so polish first.

Lift any prongs with a pliers so the stone will be clear to be set in the bezel or open base (see Figure 35–1). Adjust any bent prongs so

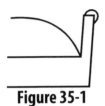

Figure 35-1

they angle in the direction you intended. Check to make sure the bezel or open base has not bent in casting and adjust with pliers as needed. (The pliers should be jewelry pliers with a broad, smooth surface on the two faces that come together–the jaws.)

STEP TWO: Fitting Your Stone. The metal will have shrunk about 5% in casting. Consequently your stone will not fit into the bezel or it may not fully clear the base of the prongs to allow it to sit evenly on its base. For bezel set opals, to get the opal to fit, use a barrel bur in a flexible shaft to cut some metal out of the inside of the bezel. The bur that works best has a slow cutting rate. It has a large diameter, the same diameter top to bottom of the cutting surface, and no point cutting ability. Slow cutting makes it easier to get a smooth, even seat for the opal. The large diameter helps prevent the bur from digging into the metal at any one point. The lack of point cutting prevents digging into the seat (bottom of the "L") as the bezel is opened up.

Use the bur to gently and evenly cut away a small amount of the metal inside the bezel on the upright part of the "L". Do not cut the seat down. Start at one point and work all the way around the inside. Move the bur back and forth with light pressure to prevent cutting deeply into one area. Keep the side of the bezel straight up and down. A bur lubricant will help keep the cut smooth and prevent excess heat buildup. Just take a little metal off the inside.

Once a complete cut around the inside has been made, check to see if the opal fits. It probably won't. Most opals have highly polished sides. Indeed, I am notorious in my cutting classes for requiring the sides be polished. Now I am going to tell you to unpolish them. A slight roughness to the sides of the opal will help the glue hold the opal in the setting.

> **WARNING: If the gemstone you are setting belongs to someone else, get permission before sanding the sides or do all fitting by working the metal.**

Setting Your Gemstone in Your Design

Using the medium sanding wheel (600-grit on a Pixie) lightly work the edge of the opal all around. This can be done holding the stone in your fingers. Keep the edge perpendicular to the base. Make sure this sanded portion of the edge does not rise above the spot on the stone where it is covered by the top of the bezel and that it does not alter the outline of the stone. The result should be a slight straight edge with a bevel remaining on the bottom and the rounded still polished dome on the top. Do not take off much material, just enough to roughen the side. You do not want the opal to be too small for the bezel. If for some reason the bevel is removed from the bottom edge in this process, redo it on the medium wheel *before* attempting to fit the opal into the bezel. A sharp bottom edge can catch on the bezel and chip.

If it looks like the opal is still too big for the opening all over, make another circuit of the bezel with the bur. Repeat as necessary. At some point the opal will start to look like it will fit and may even slide into the bezel at some parts. Carefully work the areas of the bezel that are not quite open enough, but not the areas that already fit. Cut a little and check again. Work the metal until the opal fits into it easily but with only slight pressure. Do not force the opal into the bezel. If the opal fits too tightly in the bezel, the stone may break in setting or wear. If it is too loose, there will be an ugly gap between the opal and the metal. It should be a slight interference fit…just enough to require a bit of pressure to push the opal in place.

The end result should be a bezel the inside of which is relatively smooth. It will have some roughness from the teeth of the bur. It also may have *slight* undulations. The opal should fit in with very slight pressure and no obvious gaps. The sides of the opal above the bezel will remain polished. If not, repolish the exposed areas. The advantage of the slightly rough interior for the bezel is that it provides more purchase for the glue used in the setting procedures.

STEP THREE: Preparing the Prongs. In the process of fitting the opal, the prongs have been bent away from the bezel so the opal could be slipped into it. Now the prongs must be prepared for setting.

The ideal prong is one that lies flat against the opal with no gap at the point. A gap, even a tiny one, can catch fibers on even the finest silk blouse. The results can be ugly. Ruined blouse, lifted prong, unhappy wearer.

To get the prong to lie flat, the rounded bottom of the prong…the part that will lay on the stone…must be flattened. Assess the spot on the prong where it will lie on the opal. Using the same bur used to open the bezel, flatten the inside of the prong. Cut away about 20% to 30% of its thickness. In this way the prong will still appear round from above. Keep this flat area aligned so that all of it will lie flat onto the opal (see Photo 35-1). It will take some practice to get the angle right and the surface even. At the base of the prong where it is attached to the bezel cut into the prong a bit more. This will produce a slight gap later as the prong is bent over the opal (see Figure 35-2). The gap helps prevent the prong from pinching the opal at its most vulnerable edge. The extra cut depth also forces the prong to bend at the base first. This will make it easier to bend the prong

Photo 35-1

flatly and evenly over the opal. **WARNING:** Do not bend the prongs a lot. Move them only as far as necessary to clear the opal. Frequent bending of the prongs in metal can cause them to crack. A crack can be repaired only by soldering the metal and cleanup can prove to be a real problem.

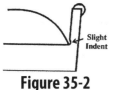

Slight Indent

Figure 35-2

For a setting without a bezel, you may find that shrinkage has made the base of the prongs slightly smaller than the size of the stone, thus preventing it from laying flat on the base. If this happens, use the barrel burr to carefully remove a bit of the inside of the prong. Do not recut or sand the edge of the stone, as this change in shape and finish will be visible after the stone is set. Now prepare each prong as instructed above for an opal in a bezel setting.

The setting instructions below, while oriented toward opal, are applicable to all stones.

Setting Your Gemstone in Your Design

> **Frequent bending of the prongs in metal can cause them to crack.**

STEP FOUR: Setting the Opal. The opal is now ready to set. Make sure the opal is clean. Also clean the inside of the bezel and prongs. This can be done easily with a wooden toothpick and a bit of paper towel. Don't use a Qtip. Save the metal filings, they can quickly add up to serious value when recycled.

Using a wooden toothpick, mix a small batch of clear Epoxy 330. Do not use 5–Minute Epoxy as it sets up too fast to complete the setting job. Using the toothpick, apply a layer of epoxy on the inside of the bezel and the inside of the prongs. Use just enough epoxy to cover the side and bottom of the bezel. Excess glue is messy to clean off the opal and setting. Avoid that problem by being careful not to use too much. The glue helps hold the opal and protect it from shocks in wearing. It also serves as a lubricant as the prongs are rolled onto the opal.

Place the opal down into the bezel. A slight amount of glue will be squeezed out of the bezel. This will be cleaned up in a moment.

Now the tricky part; placing the prongs. Use a prong pusher to carefully bend the prong down over the opal (see Photo 35-2). The metal should bend fairly easily. If not, the prong is too thick. If you have this problem remove the opal, clean the glue from the opal and the setting, and rework the prong with the bur. Do not attempt to overpower the prong to make it bend. The chances of breaking the opal are really good if you do. The extra pressure makes it far more likely that the prong pusher will slip off the prong and onto the opal. Gashes, cracks and very bad language are likely to follow!

Photo 35-2

> **Do not attempt to overpower the prong to make it bend.**

First, using side pressure, bend the lower part of the prong onto the shoulder of the opal. Usually the best place to put pressure on the prong at this point is about half way up the prong, above the slight notch you placed at its base. Move the prong pusher up almost to the point of the prong and apply pressure. This should roll the prong down over the shoulder of the opal

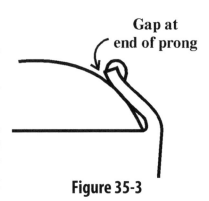

Gap at end of prong

Figure 35-3

so that the flat part of the prong touches the stone everywhere except that little gap at the base. When the pressure is released, the tip of the prong will spring up some. We will fix this in a bit (see Figure 35-3).

The amount of pressure to use is always a source of concern. Too much pressure can cause the prong pusher to slip off the prong, possibly hitting and damaging the opal. Use just enough pressure to bend the prong. More pressure will not force the prong to lie any flatter. Once the prong lies flat on the stone, no amount of additional pressure will make it fit any better.

Recall that the prongs were left a little long and a ball was placed on the end to aid in casting. The ball is still there and the extra length has allowed the prong to lie flat on the shoulder of the opal for the full length that we wanted in the design. All we have to do is get rid of the extra length and the prong point will lay flat and smooth on the opal.

> **Use just enough pressure to bend the prong, no more.**

Clean the excess epoxy off the opal and setting. Use a paper towel to wipe the surface of the opal around the prongs. Wipe toward the bezel. Turn the towel frequently so you do not put glue you just wiped off back onto the opal. Avoid getting epoxy on your fingers as it will spread to the opal and setting. Get as little glue as possible on the setting. There will be a slight bead of epoxy where the bezel meets the opal and under the prongs. A little epoxy here is acceptable, but only a little. Clean off the excess epoxy that has squeezed out of the bottom of the bezel. A very slight haze will probably be left on the surface of the opal at some spots. This will be removed after the epoxy has set.

Allow the setting to lay someplace where it will not be disturbed until the glue sets. The glue will still flow so place the piece so the glue flows down into the bezel. For a ring use aluminum foil to make a ring holder to keep the opal upright.

STEP FIVE: Finishing the Prongs. After the glue has set, use jewelry cutting pliers to cut off the extra prong length. The choice of pliers is very important. They must be made of good steel with thick points. If not, the steel will bend and an even cut will be impossible. The edges of the jaws should mesh completely at the point and should be flat or almost flat on one side. The points of the two jaws should be slightly rounded so that the sharp cutting tips do not touch the opal, but not too rounded or they will not cut the lower part of the prong where it touches the opal. You may find it necessary to sand the tips of the pliers so that they meet this criteria.

Place the pliers over the prong at a length just slightly longer than you want the finished prong. The flat side of the pliers should be toward the base of the prong. The tips of the jaws should be touching the opal but with no pressure on it. Now cut the prong by squeezing the handles together without moving the pliers in any way. Moving the pliers while cutting can cause the prong to lift. Pushing it back down will never make the point lie flat, it will spring back some. To get a smooth flat point in this situation the prong will have to be made shorter. It is best to avoid this problem (see Figure 35-4).

The prong tips will be rough from the pliers cut. Smooth and round them. The best implement for this is a round rubber pumice wheel on a mandrel in a flex shaft.

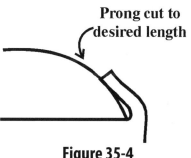

Prong cut to desired length

Figure 35-4

The pumice will cut the metal and leave a slightly satin polish without affecting the surface of the opal. To be sure it doesn't scratch the opal, test the wheel on a scrap piece of polished opal before you use it on your beautifully set opal (see Photo 35-3).

Flatten the end of the wheel so that the top edge will fit down onto the surface of the prong just where the point touches the opal. This can

Photo 35-3

be done by running it against the sharp edge of a broken stone. Work back slightly into the prong to create a flat, even end to the prong (see Figure 35-5). Now round the prong from the sides to create a continuous arc to the tip. Round up from the opal surface as well. The finished

**Blowup of
rounded end
of prong**

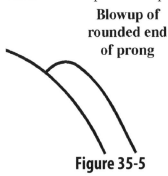

Figure 35-5

prong tip should look like half a ball from the top and a quarter of a ball from the side and sit flat on the opal. This carefully rounded prong tip will not snag fibers. The jewelry is much nicer to wear when this is done right. This shape also gives the prong, and thus the jewelry, a professionally finished look.

STEP SIX: Polishing the Jewelry. At this point there may be a bit of a haze on some of the opal surface and perhaps some areas where the epoxy is still adhering to the opal or metal. The quickest way to remove the slight haze is to polish the opal on a clean rough cotton material. I use the leg of my blue jeans, it works great. Next use a cloth to penetrate around prongs and near the bezel where rubbing on your pant leg does not reach.

There still may be little bits of epoxy stuck on the opal, especially near the prongs and bezel. Remove these with a very dull knife blade. I use the blade-like end of a dental tool. A sharp blade could damage the metal or scratch the opal. With a dull blade the epoxy can be easily scrapped off without any damage. Work with the edge of the blade pointing away from the nearest metal. Do not attempt to cut into that little bead of epoxy around the bezel and under the prongs. It will flake off leaving visible marks.

Now that the opal has been cleaned off, turn to the metal. Again rub the metal on your blue jeans or cotton cloth. The residual epoxy will be removed and a fairly good polish will return to the metal. Switch to a jewelry polishing cloth—the kind with polish impregnated in one cloth and a second cleaning cloth that removes the residual polish and oxidation. This should bring the metal back to the high polish it had before you started to set the opal. Another alternative is to use rubber metal polishing wheels. The result is a faster polish, but care must be taken to avoid heat buildup and check first to make sure the wheel does not scratch the opal. A third alternative is to use a muslin buff on a flexible shaft. charge the buff with jeweler's rouge or other polishing compound. Be careful not to heat up the metal.

At this point the metal must be marked: SS for sterling silver, 14K or 18K for gold. This is a legal requirement if the piece is to be sold. Stamps are available to do this or an electric engraver can be used to do it by hand. Also the piece should be signed. Your initials will do if you are a low volume producer. A registered hallmark may be required if you get into large volume manufacturing.

Finally, use Ivory liquid hand soap and a soft toothbrush (free of old toothpaste and other abrasives) to scrub the entire piece. This will remove any residual jewelry polish or loose dirt. **DO NOT** use jewelry cleaners that are not safe for opal; read the label. Dry the piece with a clean towel.

You're done. A beautiful, shining piece with a well set and protected opal lays before you. Something to be proud of for years.

Chapter 36

The Best is Yet to Come

In my world, ends are really new beginnings. So it is with this book. As you complete it and look back, you are probably amazed at how much you have learned. You feel proud of your accomplishments and you should be! Take a moment to reflect. But only a moment for the best is yet to come.

Working with opals and other gemstones is a lifetime of learning. I have spent over 40 years at it and still learn more every day. There is never an end. Each gemstone presents its own unique challenge. New material, new sources, new design ideas. That's what keeps this wonderful pursuit alluring.

Jewelry design is equally fascinating. There is inspiration everywhere. The techniques I use and have explained here are not the only ones. After I developed my fabrication approach, I took a course on wax carving from GIA. It opened up a whole new range of design options, ones I have not had the time to explore...yet!

So there you have it. You are now better prepared to meet the challenges of opal and gemstone cutting and jewelry design. Enjoy!

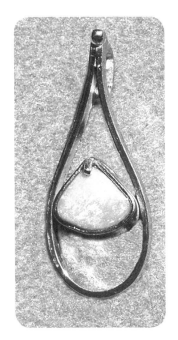

Source Directory

The following represents companies and dealers that I personally know and trust. This is by no means a complete listing of dealers and/or companies. Many will come and go throughout the years. It will be up to you to assess each company you decide to deal with.

EQUIPMENT & SETTINGS

ALPHA SUPPLY
P O Box 2133
Bremerton, WA 98310
(360) 373-3302
www.alpha-supply.com

AMERITOOL LAPIDARY EQUIPMENT
915 Merchant Street, Suite 3
Redding, CA 96002
(530) 223-2031
www.ameritool-inc.com

CRYSTALITE® CORPORATION
P O Box 545
Lewis Center, OH 43035
(740) 548-4100
www.crystalite.com

DIAMOND PACIFIC TOOL CORPORATION
P O Box 1180
Barstow, CA 92312
(800) 253-2954
www.diamondpacific.com

EBERSOLE LAPIDARY SUPPLY, INC.
5830 W. Hendryx
Wichita, KS 67209
(877) 232-7765
www.ebersolelapidary.com

FOREDOM ELECTRIC COMPANY
16 Stony Hill Road
Bethel, CT 06801
(203) 792-8622
www.foredom.com

KENT'S TOOLS
133 E. Grant Road
Tucson, AZ 85705
(520) 624-8098
www.kentstools.com

KINGSLEY NORTH, INC.
P O Box 216
Norway, MI 49870
(906) 563-9228
www.kingsleynorth.com

LAPCRAFT, INC.®
195 W. Olentangy Street
Powell, OH 43065
(800) 432-4748
www.lapcraft.com

RIO GRANDE
7500 Bluewater Road NW
Albuquerque, NM 87121-1962
(800) 545-6566
www.riogrande.com

TRIPPS MANUFACTURING
P O Box 1369
Socorro, NM 87801
(800-256-1574
www.tripps.com

Wax Wires: **PROGRESS TOOL**
(800) 841-8665
onlinesales@progresstool.com
www.progresstool.com

MISCELLANEOUS

American Federation
  of Mineralogical Societies
P.O. Box 302
Glyndon, MD 21071-0302
(410) 833-7926
www.amfed.org

Associated Jewelry, Inc.
(Casting & Finishing)
36 NE First Street
Miami, FL 33132
(305)379-6921

Burnie's Rock Shop Inc.
901 E. Johnson Street
Madison, WI 53703-1621
(608) 251-2601
www.burniesrockshop.com

Candala Pty Ltd
(Candala Chrysoprase)
PO Box 768
Drummoyne, NSW 1470
Australia
+61 (0)42752 9953
www.candalachrysoprase.com

Lapidary Journal, Jewelry Artist
300 Chesterfield Parkway, #100
Malvern, PA 19355 USA
(610) 232-5700
www.lapidaryjournal.com

*LOST WAX CASTING: Old, New,
and Inexpensive Methods*
by Fred R. Sias, Jr.
Woodsmere Press
P.O. Box 726
Pendleton, SC 29670-0726
Phone: (864) 654-6833
www.woodsmerepress.com

Rock & Gem Magazine
Miller Magazines, Inc
290 Maple Court, Suite 232
Ventura, CA 93003
(805) 644-3824
www.rockngem.com

William Holland School
  of Lapidary Arts
P.O. Box 980
Young Harris, GA 30582
(706) 379-2126

OPAL DEALERS

I have attempted to give you a source for each of the locations mentioned, but the dealers listed represent only a small percentage of the companies selling rough.

Talk to members of your club, friends, or investigate yourself, to obtain recommendations and make your own decisions.

Australian Opal Mines (Australia)
Murray Willis
Po Box 345 Magill
South Australia 5072
+61 8 8332 4049
www.austopalmines.net.au

Kingsley North, Inc. (Australian)
P O Box 216
Norway, MI 49870
(800) 338-9280
www.kingsleynorth.com

Manning International (Gilson)
140 Sherman Street, 5th Floor
Fairfield CT, 06824
(800) 223-2555
www.manninginternational.com

Okanagan Opals (Canada)
7879 Hwy 97
Vernon BC V1B 3R9
(250) 542-1103
www.opalscanada.com

Orca Gems (Ethiopian & others)
P O Box 212
Littleton, CO 80160
Cell 720.373.9657
www.orcagems.com

Outback Gems (Koroit & Yowah)
www.outbackgems.com and
www.parchedearthopals.com

Poor Boys Opals (Lightning Ridge)
P O Box 390
Lightning Ridge, NSW 2834
Australia
(386) 985-5376 (U.S.)

Rainbow Ridge Opal Mine (NV)
P O Box 97
Denio, Nevada 89404
(775) 941-0270 Apr thru Oct
(541) 548-4810 Nov thru Mar
www.nevadaopal.com

Royal Peacock Opal Mine (NV)
9535 Hwy.95 N.
Winnemucca, NV 89445
(775) 272-3201
www.royalpeacock.com

Spencer Opal Mines (ID)
27 Opal Ave.
Spencer, Idaho 83446
(208) 374-5476
www.spenceropalmines.com

Sunning Holdings Ltd. (Synthetic)
Room 801, Decca Industrial Centre,
12 Kut Shing Street, Chaiwan,
Hong Kong
(852) 2898 1178
www.sunning.com.hk

Teton Gems (ID)
P O Box 1264
Riggins, Id.   83549-1264
208)-628-4002
www.tetongems.com

The Village Smithy (Australia)
P.O. Box 21704
Billings Montana 59104-1704
(406) 651-4947
www.villagesmithyopals.com

Tony Dabdoub (Honduras)
Email: TropicalGems@cox.net

Other Publications by Majestic Press, Inc.

Opal Cutting Made Easy DVD
FEATURING PAUL DOWNING $29.95
Look over Paul's shoulder as he takes an opal from rough to finished gem.
(Also available in VHS format.)

Handbook of Western Fly Fishing
BY PAUL DOWNING $19.95

Follow along with Paul as he unselfishly shares observations, insights and knowledge of his favorite fishing spots in the Western U.S.

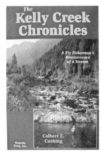

The Kelly Creek Chronicles
BY COLBERT E. CUSHING $15.95
Join Cush and his friends as they spend 18 years watching river otters cavort in a crystal green pool while tempting finicky Westslope cutthroat trout in Idaho.

The Uthgar Journals: Rebel Beginnings
BY J. K. RAGLAND $8.95
First in a trilogy. Christian-based, youth oriented science fiction story about a young family and their return to the way of the Lord.

299

Opal & Traditional Birthstones

January	Red/Orange Opal	Garnet
Alternate	Honey Matrix Opal	
February	Red/Blue Opal	Amethyst
Alternate	Banded Opal	
March	Blue/Green Opal	Aquamarine
Alternate	Doublet Opal	
April	Crystal Opal	Diamond
Alternate	Idaho Star Triplet Opal	
May	Green Crystal Opal	Emerald
Alternate	Idaho Catseye Triplet Opal	
June	Boulder Opal	Pearl
Alternate	Boulder Doublet Opal	
July	Red Opal	Ruby
Alternate	Triplet Opal	
August	Black Opal	Peridot
Alternate	Treated Matrix Opal	
September	Green/Orange Opal	Sapphire
Alternate	Precious Honey Opal	
October	Any Opal	Opal
Alternate	Any Other Opal	
November	Mexican Opal	Citrine
Alternate	Mexican Matrix Opal	
December	Blue Crystal Opal	Blue Topaz
Alternate	Blue Jelly Opal	

Unknown origin.
Given to me by an opal dealer in Sydney

300

Index

About the Author

Paul's love affair with the world of rocks and gems began way back in 2nd Grade. He collected trilobites and belemnite fossils from the piles of crushed limestone being spread on the school parking lot.

In college he discovered **Burnie's Rock Shop** in the basement of his dorm. Burnie hooked him on the fascinating hobby of cutting and setting agate, jade and other gemstones.

His love of opals began in 1963 while in graduate school and over the past 45 years he has addicted many others as dyed-in-the-wool "opalholics."

He started cutting opal to provide a break from his studies; sitting for hours in front of the television set watching the Green Bay Packers play while he polished his stones by hand. During this time in graduate school he spent as much time as possible working for—and learning from—Burnie Frankie.

He became an opal dealer in 1981. In 1984, following numerous requests for assistance in cutting, *Opal Cutting Made Easy* was born, followed in 1986 by a companion video tape (now updated to DVD) to help beginning lapidary enthusiasts get started in the field of opal cutting. Met by outstanding reviews, his readers cried for more.

Numerous trips to Australia and around the world buying opal led to *Opal Adventures* in 1990, an armchair trip to various opal fields, riding in his coat pocket. But still there was one more area that his customers needed help—identifying and placing an accurate value on the stones they cut.

The monumental task of researching and authenticating opal values began in earnest. After years of interviews and trips to various opal locations, *Opal Identification and Value* made its way to the market-place in 1992. Not only was it highly received in the United States, it received rave reviews in Australia. It became the bible for identification and valuing of opal worldwide. In addition to these three books, Paul has written numerous articles for "Lapidary Journal" (now "Jewelry Artist") and "Rock & Gem Magazine," as well as several professional gemstone newsletters. In 1992 and 1993 he received three highly coveted AGTA Cutting Edge awards.

Along the way, more and more people associated *Opal* and *Paul Downing* in the same breath. He gave lectures on the opal fields; taught opal cutting classes to lapidary societies as well as to individuals; presented AGTA Conference talks at Tucson to "standing room only" crowds of the world's top gemstone professionals. He also presented opal identification classes with hands-on stones for class work to professional appraisers. At times students were examining hundreds of thousands of dollars worth of cut and polished opals …an opportunity not many would have had in a lifetime. Such was Paul's desire to educate and assist those who wanted to know about his favorite stone.

After a lifetime of exploration and 18 years of involvement with the opal business, he decided that he would retire July 1, 1998 to pursue other endeavors (such as fly fishing and writing about his adventures on the streams). His final evaluation class was held in London, England, March 1999.

Still, one more opal book had to be written. *Opal Advanced Cutting & Setting* was Paul's effort to condense everything he didn't get to tell you about opal in the other books into one final(?) opal book. Books are like that; they sit inside his head developing and when the time is right they just have to come out. This one boiled in his brain for several years. Being elected to the Rockhound and Lapidary Hall of Fame in 1999 was the catalyst which moved it from ideas to the printed word. That book is the foundation of the Section Three of this book.

Subsequently *Opal Identification and Value* became dated and in need of work. Instead of a light redo, Paul decided to start almost from scratch. By now he had learned how to photograph opal. This, and his extensive collection of classroom examples, allowed him to explain with words *and* pictures exactly what he was discussing in text. The final book was changed to *Opal Identification* **&** *Value* in order for the marketplace to know it was about the same thing; but a totally different book!

It's been a wonderful trip; one he loved to share with all who would listen. But, most importantly, he was given the privilege of getting to know and love...OPAL

When both *Opal Cutting Made Easy* and *Opal Advanced Cutting & Setting* reached out–of–print status...at virtually the same time... folks began clambering to find copies; paying upwards of $75 per copy on eBay. Researching titles available on cutting gemstones; jade, chrysoprase, agate, etc., it became apparent that many, many years had passed since John Sinkankas published his wonderful book. (Smaller and less detailed books on the market today are all over 20 years old.) So much has changed in the lapidary industry...both with cutting techniques and cutting equipment...that it became obvious that a new title was warranted. This book addresses that need with up–to–date equipment, time–honored techniques, and resources for all your needs.

In a sense, Paul has gone back to his roots for this book. It starts where he started...cutting agate and jade. It progresses to cutting opal, then, as he did, explores advanced techniques for cutting opal and other gemstones. Finally it explores his latest endeavor, designing and setting jewelry using the lost wax technique.

This book represents a history of Paul's journey into the world of gemstones. Hope you enjoy the ride!